CHRONICLES
—— *to* ——
NEHEMIAH

Text copyright © Michael Tunnicliffe 1999

The author asserts the moral right
to be identified as the author of this work

Published by
The Bible Reading Fellowship
Peter's Way, Sandy Lane West
Oxford OX4 5HG
ISBN 1 84101 070 7

First published 1999
10 9 8 7 6 5 4 3 2 1 0

Acknowledgments
Unless otherwise stated, scripture quotations are taken from The
New Revised Standard Version of the Bible, Anglicized Edition,
copyright © 1989, 1995 by the Division of Christian Education
of the National Council of the Churches of Christ in the USA,
and are used by permission. All rights reserved.
Scripture quotations taken from the *Holy Bible, New International
Version*, copyright © 1973, 1978, 1984 by International Bible
Society. Used by permission of Hodder & Stoughton Limited.
All rights reserved. 'NIV' is a registered trademark of
International Bible Society. UK trademark number 1448790.
Scriptures quoted from the Good News Bible published by
The Bible Societies/HarperCollins Publishers Ltd, UK ©
American Bible Society 1966, 1971, 1976, 1992, used by
permission.
Extracts from the Authorized Version of the Bible (The King
James Bible), the rights in which are vested in the Crown, are
reproduced by permission of the Crown's Patentee, Cambridge
University Press.

A catalogue record for this book is available
from the British Library

Printed and bound in Great Britain
by Caledonian Book Manufacturing International, Glasgow

CHRONICLES
to
NEHEMIAH

THE PEOPLE'S
BIBLE COMMENTARY

MICHAEL
TUNNICLIFFE

A BIBLE COMMENTARY FOR EVERY DAY

The Bible Reading Fellowship
OPENING THE BIBLE

INTRODUCING THE PEOPLE'S BIBLE COMMENTARY SERIES

Congratulations! You are embarking on a voyage of discovery—or rediscovery. You may feel you know the Bible very well; you may never have turned its pages before. You may be looking for a fresh way of approaching daily Bible study; you may be searching for useful insights to share in a study group or from a pulpit.

The People's Bible Commentary (PBC) series is designed for all those who want to study the scriptures in a way that will warm the heart as well as instructing the mind. To help you, the series distils the best of scholarly insights into the straightforward language and devotional emphasis of Bible reading notes. Explanation of background material, and discussion of the original Greek and Hebrew, will always aim to be brief.

- If you have never really studied the Bible before, the series offers a serious yet accessible way in.

- If you help to lead a church study group, or are otherwise involved in regular preaching and teaching, you can find invaluable 'snapshots' of a Bible passage through the PBC approach.

- If you are a church worker or minister, burned out on the Bible, this series could help you recover the wonder of scripture.

Using a People's Bible Commentary

The series is designed for use alongside any version of the Bible. You may have your own favourite translation, but you might like to consider trying a different one in order to gain fresh perspectives on familiar passages.

Many Bible translations come in a range of editions, including study and reference editions that have concordances, various kinds of special index, maps and marginal notes. These can all prove helpful in studying the relevant passage. The Notes section at the back of each PBC volume provides space for you to write personal reflections, points to follow up, questions and comments.

Each People's Bible Commentary can be used on a daily basis, instead of Bible reading notes. Alternatively, it can be read straight through, or used as a resource book for insight into particular verses of the biblical book.

If you have enjoyed using this commentary and would like to progress further in Bible study, you will find details of other volumes in the series listed at the back, together with information about a special offer from BRF.

While it is important to deepen understanding of a given passage, this series always aims to engage both heart and mind in the study of the Bible. The scriptures point to our Lord himself and our task is to use them to build our relationship with him. When we read, let us do so prayerfully, slowly, reverently, expecting him to speak to our hearts.

CONTENTS

PBC CHRONICLES TO NEHEMIAH:
INTRODUCTION

Anyone who sits down to read, let alone write a commentary on, 1 and 2 Chronicles, Ezra and Nehemiah is faced with a daunting task. The scope of the material in these books is indeed great. They provide a survey of history which begins with Adam in the first verse of 1 Chronicles, and goes on until the very end of the Old Testament period of history at the close of the book of Nehemiah. So there is a grand panorama of biblical history presented in these books.

In some respects, the pictures presented, at least in Chronicles, are rather like the 'time-lapse' sequences you sometimes see in nature programmes on television. Everything is speeded up so that you see, in the space of a few minutes, the way in which a flower opens and closes and grows over a period of time. Much of the information in Chronicles has been presented once before in earlier books of the Bible. Therefore, the author of Chronicles—who is usually simply called by the title 'the Chronicler'—has to be very selective in his choice of material. For example, the first nine chapters of 1 Chronicles cover the whole of the biblical story from Adam to King Saul, by means of detailed family lists. The Chronicler will present a distinctive slant on the material—he does not merely retell it. Otherwise there would be little point including such repetition in the Bible. In particular, the Chronicler will make clear to his readers who are the heroes and who are the villains in the story. He works with a clear idea of what is right and wrong, acceptable and unacceptable behaviour, especially among kings.

For those who get rather giddy watching fast-moving time-lapse photography, the books of Ezra and Nehemiah will come as a relief. The frantic pace of the flow of history slows down. We are able to concentrate on the specific work of two very influential characters who were near contemporaries around the middle of the fifth century BC. These books provide a fascinating window that sheds light on an otherwise dark corner of biblical history.

These books also cover a wide geographical area. Most of the attention is focused in and around Jerusalem. Nevertheless, the Holy Land was a crossroads where many civilizations trod and left their mark. In the course of the story we shall meet Egyptian pharaohs, rulers of

Damascus, warrior kings from the Mesopotamian civilizations of Assyria and Babylon, Arab tribes, horses from what is now Turkey, and archives from the Persian court. Perhaps these neglected books of the Bible will prove to be rather more interesting than we might have supposed!

Reading strategies, or 'How to survive this commentary'

The commentary is divided into 119 sections, most of which cover about one chapter of the Bible. In order to make sense of both the historical and geographical information in the book, I have supplied a couple of pages of time-charts and two maps, one of the Holy Land and one of the wider world of the ancient Near East. Most of the basic information should be provided by the charts and maps, but anybody wanting more information may find a Bible atlas useful.

One problem for readers and commentators is to decide what to do about those sections which comprise long family lists of names. This is particularly the case for the whole of 1 Chronicles 1—9. You may well be tempted to skip over reading these sections altogether in your Bible. If you do, don't feel guilty about it! Nevertheless, I have tried to provide enough guidelines to help you make sense of the mass of names. There is not enough space in a book of this size to go into great detail. For that, you will have to consult a more specialized commentary. I hope that I have done enough to separate the wood from the trees and so enable you to find your way through this particular forest.

My hope is that, through this book, readers of this series will be able to explore some of the more out-of-the-way paths of the scriptures. Sometimes the content may seem a million miles away from our present-day world in the twenty-first century. However, I have been constantly surprised at the way stories from these books have 'rung bells' for me. In the notes, and particularly in the concluding sections of prayer and meditation, I have tried to make connections between the world of the Old Testament text and our contemporary situation. I hope you will not find these points of contact forced or artificial.

When quoting directly from the Bible, I have used the New Revised Standard Version, unless stated otherwise. Where other translations differ, I have sometimes made reference to this. However, I hope that this commentary will be user-friendly with any translation.

I would like to express my gratitude to BRF for inviting me to write this commentary and in encouraging me along the way. It has made me wrestle with a set of texts with which I was not very familiar. Now I feel that I, at least, understand them better! Finally I would like to dedicate this book to my wife Kate, without whose belief, practical support and love this book would never have seen the light of day.

TIME CHART

Date BC	Major characters	Other events affecting the land and people
2000–1500	Possible dates for Abraham, Isaac, Jacob and Joseph (Genesis).	
1300–1200	Possible date for story of Moses as told in Exodus.	
1200–1000	Israelite tribes settle in the land of Canaan (Joshua and Judges).	
1000	Death of King Saul.	
About 970	Death of David.	
970–960	Solomon begins building the temple.	
932	Death of Solomon.	
932–916	Rehoboam. Division of the kingdom into North (Israel) and South (Judah).	Invasion by Pharaoh Shishak in 928.
916–914	Abijah.	
914–874	Asa.	Invasion by Zerah the Cushite.
874–850	Jehoshaphat. Political alliance of Israel and Judah, sealed by marriage between the two royal houses.	Aram (Syria) powerful. Moabites, Ammonites and Meunites invade.
850–843	Jehoram.	
843–842	Ahaziah.	
842–836	Athaliah.	
836–797	Joash.	
797–769	Amaziah.	War against Edom.
769–741	Uzziah.	
741–734	Jotham.	The Assyrian empire begins to grow.
734–715	Ahaz.	War with Syria and Ephraim (Israel).
722	Fall of the northern kingdom. Prophecies of Isaiah.	
715–697	Hezekiah. Time of religious reformation.	Assyrian invasion by Sennacherib. Jerusalem is saved 701.

Date	Judah / Israel	World events
697–642	Manasseh.	Last days of Assyrian greatness.
642–640	Amon.	
640–609	Josiah. Discovery of law code in the temple—more reforms. Prophecies of Jeremiah begin.	Assyrian empire crumbles. Babylon now the dominant power, having defeated Egypt in 605.
609	Jehoahaz.	
609–598	Jehoiakim.	Nebuchadnezzar invades. First deportation to Babylon.
598	Jehoiachin.	
598–587	Zedekiah. Destruction of temple. Prophecy of Ezekiel.	Many prominent leaders and people taken into exile.
571	Jehoiachin released from prison in Babylon. Jerusalem and temple in ruins. Prophecies in Isaiah 40—66.	Cyrus becomes king of Persia in 556. Cyrus captures Babylon in 539.
537	First group of exiles return under Sheshbazzar.	Cyrus' edict allows exiles to go home, 538.
520–515	Prophecies of Haggai and Zechariah.	Darius king of Persia.
515	Second temple is completed. Zerubbabel as governor, Joshua as high priest.	
500–450	Various unnamed governors.	Xerxes king of Persia. Persians at war with Greeks.
458	Ezra arrives in Jerusalem.	
445–432	Nehemiah is governor in Jerusalem.	
400–300	Possible date for editing of Chronicles, Ezra, Nehemiah.	Alexander the Great conquers Persian empire in 331.

The LAND & TRIBES *of* ISRAEL

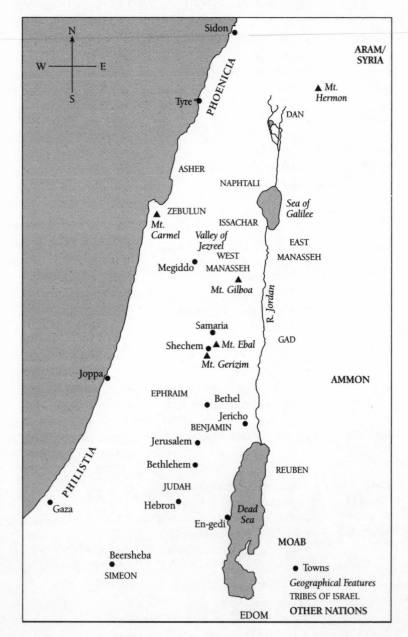

The WORLD *of* CHRONICLES, EZRA & NEHEMIAH

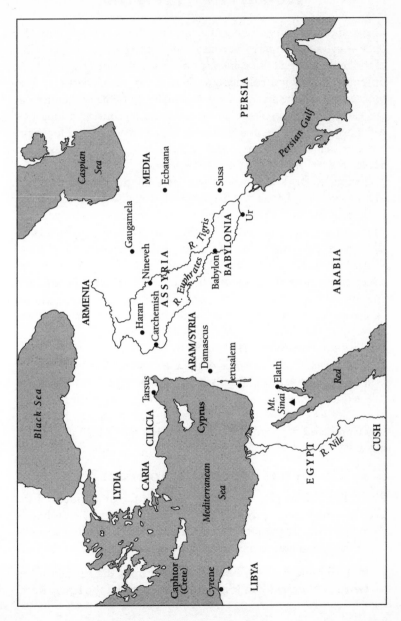

1   1 & 2 CHRONICLES

REWRITING HISTORY

In the minds of some readers of scripture, Chronicles is worthy of a prize—an award for the most consistently boring section in the whole of the Bible. After all, it begins with no less than nine chapters made up entirely of names belonging to bewildering family trees. It then proceeds to tell the stories of events which have already been told in the earlier history books. Chronicles seems to consist of long lists we're not interested in and bits we've already read. Hence, for Western Christian readers, they tend to be among the most neglected books in what we call the Old Testament.

Chronicles plays a rather different role in the Hebrew tradition. The order of the books is different in the Hebrew Bible, which was preserved by the rabbis in the synagogue, compared with the Christian tradition, preserved by the Church. The Church placed Chronicles, Ezra and Nehemiah, along with Esther, towards the end of the 'history section' of the Bible, and before the 'poetry section' which begins with the book of Job. The Hebrew Bible is ordered differently, with three distinct sections: first Law, then Prophets and finally Writings. Ezra, Nehemiah and Chronicles are the last three books of the section of the Writings—in that order. So Chronicles is the very last book of the Hebrew Bible. Its title in the Hebrew Bible is *divere hayamin* or 'the words of the days', so the name Chronicles is not a bad translation of the Hebrew. In Greek and Latin Bibles, the title is quite a mouthful—*Paralipomenon*, which means 'the things left over'. Not a very flattering description, but one which points to the way Chronicles supplements our information rather than just repeating it.

What were the sources?

By the time Chronicles was written, many of the other books of the Old Testament were probably already in existence. The author of Chronicles was therefore able to use a variety of written material which he edited and re-presented.

1. In 1 Chronicles 1—9, he uses material from the genealogies in Genesis, Numbers and Joshua in order to create the family trees.

2. From 1 Chronicles 10 to the end of 2 Chronicles, his main source is the material in Samuel and Kings, which had probably been edited around 550BC.

3. In both the family trees and in the narratives, however, there is additional material which may have come from sources now lost to us. Perhaps this was material preserved among the archives in Jerusalem.

4. Finally, the author will have added his own comments, perhaps based on oral information available to him, but also demonstrating his own viewpoint.

What is special about Chronicles?

The author did not simply copy word for word the material he had in front of him in Samuel and Kings. Sometimes he left things out. For instance, he omits information about all of the kings of the northern kingdom who ruled from Samaria. He concentrates instead on the story of the southern kings of Judah who ruled from Jerusalem. Sometimes he put things in. For instance, he gives information about David, Solomon and later kings that doesn't appear in the earlier history work.

We should therefore appreciate Chronicles as a work in its own right, not just a pale imitation of Samuel-Kings. It has its own distinctive outlook and theology. The author is telling an old, familiar story, but in a new way and with a new slant. He is 'rewriting history', in that he is presenting the history of Israel for a new generation of readers. He is also a teacher, seeking to instruct the reader in the lessons of history.

It is to the questions of when, where and who that we must now turn. Why did the author of Chronicles feel the time had come to publish a new 'history of Israel' from creation to the return from exile in Babylon?

PRAYER

Pray for those of our own time who seek to interpret history and to help us to learn from its lessons. May we take seriously the wise words of warning: 'Those who do not learn from history are destined to repeat it.'

WHO, WHEN & WHERE?

Where?

We will tackle the easiest question first. There seems little doubt that Chronicles was composed in or near Jerusalem. The holy city is extremely important in these books. For the author, the stories of David bringing the ark of the covenant to Jerusalem and Solomon building the temple are vitally important. Jerusalem is the true place where God's presence abides and where God is to be worshipped. The northern tribes commit a great sin by breaking away from the Jerusalem temple and the house of David. King Abijah's speech in 2 Chronicles 13 makes this point very clearly. Rulers such as Hezekiah or Josiah, who reform temple worship and seek to bring the northern tribes back, are highly praised. The author loved Jerusalem and almost certainly lived there.

When?

There are some clues to the dating of Chronicles in the book itself, but they are general rather than specific. 2 Chronicles ends with the edict of Cyrus in the year 538BC, so Chronicles must be later than this. It is probably considerably later, however, as the long list of David's descendants in 1 Chronicles 3 shows. This list includes the name of Zerubbabel, whose story is told in Ezra 3—5 and who appears in the prophecies of Haggai and Zechariah. Zerubbabel was active in Jerusalem around 520BC and the list of descendants covers at least six generations following Zerubbabel, which would bring the date down to around 400BC.

This takes us well down into the Persian period of ancient Near Eastern history. The Persians gained control of the Holy Land following Cyrus' victory over the Babylonians in 539. The Persian empire lasted until its army was defeated by Alexander the Great at the battles of Issus in 333 and Gaugamela in 331. There does not appear to be any reference in Chronicles to the period of Greek domination that followed. This may not be significant, since the author is telling the story of a much earlier period of Jewish history. Nevertheless, a date in the late Persian period, perhaps around 350BC, seems most likely. It is only approximate, however. Some biblical scholars would prefer a date a couple of generations later in the early Greek period, around 300. Unfortunately, the biblical history books do not cover this period of the fourth and third centuries, so our knowledge of it is quite limited.

Who?

The traditional Jewish answer to this question is to assert that Ezra the scribe wrote Chronicles, as well as the books of Ezra and Nehemiah. Later Jewish rabbis certainly regarded Ezra as an extremely important figure. Furthermore, there are links between the end of Chronicles and the beginning of the book of Ezra that might suggest a common author. However, a date around 350 is one hundred years later than the probable time of Ezra's mission to Jerusalem. Therefore, modern scholars have tended to see the author of Chronicles as the editor of Ezra-Nehemiah—the opposite way round to the Jewish tradition.

Given the difficulty in fixing an exact date for Chronicles, it is best to admit that we do not really know who wrote it. However, like modern-day detectives, we can perhaps build up a 'photo-fit' impression of what he was like. We can do this based upon what he puts in and leaves out of his account.

He gives a great deal of emphasis to the temple and its priesthood. Therefore, he may have been a priest himself. On the other hand, he is also sympathetic to the position of the various orders of Levites who assisted the priests in the temple duties. On balance, it is perhaps more likely that he is to be found among the Levites. He quotes from the book of Psalms and clearly relished joy in worship, even if some of that worship might seem rather formal to us.

Since he had read so many of the biblical books, he must have been well educated for his day. Perhaps he might be classed as an early example of the scribes whom we meet in the New Testament. These were the people who knew and interpreted the scriptures for their own day. Since we cannot give him a name, the best we can do is to give him a title, and simply call him 'the Chronicler'.

MEDITATION

Reflect quietly on the places, times and people that have made a difference to you in your own spiritual journey.

The CHRONICLER & EZRA-NEHEMIAH

Similarities

We have seen that the ancient rabbis connected the work of Chronicles and Ezra-Nehemiah by assuming that Ezra was the common author. The end of 2 Chronicles and the start of Ezra are virtually the same account of the edict of King Cyrus of Persia. Furthermore, the list of those who returned from exile given in 1 Chronicles 9 is reproduced very closely in Nehemiah 11. There is much common vocabulary among all these books and they seem to share a very similar outlook and theology.

Perhaps it was the intention of the Chronicler to produce a history covering not only the time of the kings but also beyond into the period after the return from exile. He may have wanted not just to rewrite the earlier history work of Samuel-Kings, but to extend it too. If this is the case, he did it by incorporating the 'memoirs' of Ezra and Nehemiah into his work.

Some support for this view can be found in one of the books of the Apocrypha called 1 Esdras. The Apocrypha is a collection of books dating from about 200BC to AD100, most of which were originally written in Hebrew. They have been preserved mostly in Greek and Latin translations by the Roman Catholic and Orthodox churches, who regard them as scripture. However, they are not accepted as part of the Bible by Protestants or Jews. The book called 1 Esdras contains the final two chapters of 2 Chronicles and the book of Ezra, plus some additions. So here, part of the Chronicler's work is associated with the book of Ezra. Did they originally belong together, only to be separated in the Hebrew Bible? Or is 1 Esdras a later combination of books that were originally separate?

There are certainly similarities of vocabulary, theme and outlook in Chronicles, Ezra and Nehemiah. However, this may simply indicate that they come from roughly the same time and place, rather than that they were written by the same person.

Differences

In fact there are some differences of emphasis between the books.

One difference which may well be significant is the outlook towards the northern tribes. These were the ten tribes which split away from the rule of David's grandson, Rehoboam, to form their own separate kingdom. There is no doubt that all the books of Chronicles, Ezra and Nehemiah reflect the outlook of Jerusalem and of its religious establishment. In Ezra and Nehemiah, however, the element of southern nationalism is much stronger. All attempts by those living in the north of the country to assist in the rebuilding programme are rejected. We see here, perhaps, the early stages of the divide between Jews and Samaritans. By the time of Jesus, this hostility was centuries old and had become permanent and ingrained. To a Jewish audience, the notion of a 'good' Samaritan was quite incredible. In the books of Chronicles there is certainly a negative attitude towards the northern kingdom and its capital, Samaria. However, the Chronicler seems to look forward in hope to a time when the northerners will return. The concept of 'all Israel' seems to mean a great deal to him.

The same, but different

A possible solution to this dilemma of 'same but different' is to see Chronicles, Ezra and Nehemiah as related but distinct works. They come from roughly the same period and the same circles of thought. Chronicles may be slightly later than the books of Ezra and Nehemiah and have a slightly different emphasis and purpose. It certainly makes sense to study all these books together.

These books provide an insight into the events and outlook of the period after the exile. It is sometimes called the 'second temple period', following the consecration of the new temple in 515BC. In many ways it is quite an obscure period and our information on it is scanty. Nevertheless, it was a formative time in Jewish history, leading on to the era of the New Testament at the very end of the second temple period. The books contain more than just historical interest, however, for they show how different authors responded to the challenge of difficult times and sometimes of dark days. They continue to speak a message to God's people today.

REFLECTION

Think of your local church and the denomination to which you belong. How 'open' or 'closed' is it to those who think differently?

FAMILY HISTORY

Like many people, I have a keen interest in family history. Personally, I started to trace my family tree after the death of my mother, because I felt I wanted to discover more about my own history. After much searching, I have traced many of my family lines back three hundred years. On the face of it, family trees may appear very boring—especially if they are not your own! Yet when I meet or correspond with a distant relation who shares one of my lines, we get really absorbed and interested.

Modern-day family historians have all sorts of archive material to help them. There are civil registers of births, marriages and deaths going back to the reign of Henry VIII. For more recent information, there are local newspapers, not forgetting the importance of the oral tradition of older family members. Sometimes it gets frustrating when vital bits of information are missing and you have to make 'educated guesses'. It takes time and effort to gather the information, but these days there are computer programs and CD-ROMs to help.

Family trees in the Bible

What is true of my personal interest in family trees is also true of the individuals and the nation that was ancient Israel. Genealogies can be found in many places in the Old Testament, and both Matthew and Luke are keen to portray the family line of Jesus. 1 Chronicles 1—9 is the longest sustained genealogical list in the whole Bible.

The material in these chapters systematically covers the period from Adam to King Saul. In this grand sweep of history, the Chronicler is trying to do a number of things. Firstly, he establishes a link with the distant past. The people of Israel have a long and proud history. In the humble and difficult circumstances under Persian domination in the fourth century, they needed to be reminded of that. Secondly, he establishes a sense of national identity over against the other nations round about. Again, that was vital in the period after the exile. There is no doubt that the experience of exile was a deeply traumatic one for the nation. My personal search for identity began when my mother died, as part of the process of grieving. Likewise, these family trees are a way for the nation of Israel collectively to come to terms with the disaster of exile.

There are several long genealogies in the books of Ezra and Nehemiah too. These serve an additional purpose. They are more 'up-to-date' lists of those who resettled back in the Holy Land after the exile. In order to return and claim land, it was necessary to prove your ancestry, and some of those who returned found it difficult to do so. Personal identity and land are bound up together. After all, the names of the twelve sons of Jacob represent not just twelve individuals but also the twelve tribes and the land that they occupied. So in the lists of the sons of Jacob that fill chapters 2—8, it is worth noting that often the personal names are also place names. For example, we find in 1 Chronicles 2:51 'Salma father of Bethlehem'. These lists are about geography and tribal towns and villages as well as about history. That is why, as tribal boundaries sometimes shifted, genealogies could be changed; a name found in one list can sometimes be transferred to another. So we shouldn't expect the biblical genealogies always to agree.

Searching the archives

The Chronicler had no CD-ROM to help him but he may well have had access to a variety of resources. There were the genealogical lists in the other books of the Bible, especially in Genesis, Numbers and Joshua. The list from Adam to Jacob in 1 Chronicles 1 is taken straight from Genesis. Other material may have been available, such as:

- census and conscription lists, for example in 1 Chronicles 12.
- military lists and details of battles fought, for example in 1 Chronicles 5.
- lists from the temple relating to the ancestry of ceremonial officials, for example in 1 Chronicles 6.

The Chronicler would have used his own research and oral tradition too, though no doubt there remained gaps in some of the family lists— that is the nature of family history!

I do not think my family history is boring. Neither did the authors of our books consider their genealogies dull. For the Chronicler, chapters 1—9 are his way of doing theology. It may not be our way, but it is his and we should respect it.

REFLECTION

Why does finding one's 'roots' matter so much to some individuals or communities?

5   1 CHRONICLES 1—9 (II)

The WOOD & *the* TREES

It is not possible in a commentary of this size to go into detail in the study of the genealogies—one of the larger commentaries must be consulted for that. In this section, I will simply point out some significant features of chapters 1—9. You may find it useful to refer to the map of the Holy Land on page 16, which shows the areas occupied by the twelve tribes.

From Adam to Jacob

The lists of names in chapter 1 are based on similar lists in Genesis chapters 5, 10, 11, 25 and 36. The Chronicler concentrates on the names of the descendants of Noah and of Abraham. In dealing with their descendants, he lists the children in reverse order (1:5–27). So the list of the sons of Noah—Japheth (Indo-European peoples), Ham (African peoples) and Shem (Semitic peoples)—gives pride of place to Shem, the ancestor of Abraham.

In the case of Abraham, he deals first with Ishmael, born of the slave girl Hagar (1:28–31); then with the children of Abraham's concubine, Keturah (1:32–33); and finally with Isaac, the son of Abraham's wife Sarah. Isaac and Rebecca had two sons, Jacob (Israel) and Esau (Edom). The chapter ends with some detailed lists of Edomite tribes. Jacob's brother Esau occupied the area called Seir or Edom, across the River Jordan from the land of Israel.

The twelve tribes of Israel

The names of the twelve sons of Jacob (also known as Israel) appear in 1 Chronicles 2:1–2. Each tribe was allocated land, except for Levi. As the priestly tribe, they did not own property but lived scattered in 'levitical cities' among the other tribes. To maintain the number twelve, the important tribe of Joseph was divided between his two sons, Ephraim and Manasseh (see Genesis 48). So in Bible atlases the names of Levi and Joseph will not be found. Ephraim and Manasseh take their places. Furthermore, the tribe of Manasseh occupied land on both sides of the Jordan, so could be described as West Manasseh and East Manasseh.

The order of the tribes followed in chapters 2—8 is not based on the order of the birth of the sons. The Chronicler concedes as much in his comments at 5:1–2. The order followed is a geographical one instead. It begins with the southernmost tribes of Judah and Simeon (chs. 2—4). This is followed by the tribes across the Jordan, moving from south to north: Reuben, Gad and East Manasseh (ch. 5). Then comes the tribe of Levi, which has no land but dwells 'in the midst of the tribes' (ch. 6). In chapter 7 we have the tribes of the north and centre of the land: Issachar, Naphtali, West Manasseh, Ephraim and Asher. Finally, with the tribe of Benjamin in chapter 8, we come full circle to the borders of Jerusalem.

Astute readers who compare this with the list of tribes in 2:1–2 will notice that two are missing, namely Dan and Zebulun. The tribe of Naphtali also only manages one verse. Some commentators think that there has been some disruption or loss of material in chapter 7, which is where we would expect to find reference to the northern tribes of Dan and Zebulun. In 7:6–12, there is a short genealogy of Benjamin, which seems out of place since the Chronicler will deal fully with this tribe in chapter 8. Some people think these verses should belong to Zebulun, or that they have been put here to replace lost material on Zebulun.

The end of 7:12 is also odd. It refers to Ir, Hushim and Aher. Genesis 46:23 gives Hushim as the only son of Dan. Perhaps this verse in Chronicles originally contained the genealogy of Dan. What should Bible translators do at this point? Should they render what is there in the text, even if it seems to be wrong or inaccurate? Or should they offer an interpretation of what may have been the original text? Most versions opt for the former policy with regard to 7:12. However, both the New English Bible and the Good News Bible adopt the conjectured reading and make Hushim the son of Dan, thus bringing the tribe of Dan back into the lists. It reminds us that keeping accurate family lists is never easy. Vital material may sometimes be lost, destroyed or misread by copyists. This is true for ancient family trees as much as for modern ones.

PRAYER

Pray for those who preserve and administer public records today.

6   1 CHRONICLES 1—9 (III)

SOME FAMOUS LINES

The genealogies of the individual tribes often concentrate on the famous characters within the tribal history. Thus, the Judah family history includes the ancestry of King David (2:9–15), his immediate family (3:1–9) and the kings of David's line from his son Solomon to the last king, Zedekiah (3:10–16). There then follows the list of the descendants of the last but one king, Jehoiachin, who was taken into exile in Babylon. Although it was in exile in a strange land, the royal family did not die out. Eventually Jehoiachin was released from prison and treated kindly, according to 2 Kings 25:27–30. His line, passing through his descendant Zerubbabel, is traced through many generations into the post-exilic period (3:17–24). This section is often used to try to work out when Chronicles was written. Some commentators assume that the sons of Elioenai mentioned in verse 24 were alive at the time of the Chronicler. This would still only give a rough and ready estimate of the date. Working out how long to allow for each 'generation' can be a hazardous business.

Usually, the Chronicler follows his sources faithfully, but sometimes he makes small but significant changes. In 2:14, David is given as the youngest of seven sons of Jesse, whereas in the story in 1 Samuel 16 he is the eighth son. In many traditions, of course, it is the seventh son who is favoured or special.

Chapter 6 includes the list of the high priests in Solomon's temple who were descended from Eleazar (6:4–15). It is also interested in the role of the Levites and the temple musicians and describes them as being organized by King David himself (6:31). Each of the lines of the three sons of Levi produced a famous musician who became the head of his guild and is mentioned in some of the Psalm headings:

- Kohath was the ancestor of Heman (see Psalm 88).

- Gershom was the ancestor of Asaph (see Psalms 73—83).

- Merari was the ancestor of Ethan (see Psalm 89).

Chapter 8, which is about the tribe of Benjamin, focuses particularly on the family of Saul, the first king of Israel (8:33–40).

Those who returned

Chapter 9 brings the story down closer to the time of the Chronicler, and focuses on the groups who returned. The tribes of Levi, Judah and Benjamin form the core of the returners, and these are the tribes that interest the Chronicler most throughout chapters 2—8. However, he also mentions the tribes of Joseph's sons, Manasseh and Ephraim, showing that he was not opposed to the northerners. Much attention is given to the priests and Levites (9:10–16), and there is a whole section on the lesser temple servants (9:17–32).

Finally the section of genealogies ends with a repetition of King Saul's family tree, which leads into the account of his tragic death in the next chapter. The Chronicler clearly knew a great deal more about Saul and his family than he tells us here. He focuses exclusively on the line of David, and therefore passes over the early 'experiment' in kingship under Saul. Saul's line did not continue to rule over the people. The baton of kingship was given to David and his family. According to the biblical writers, this was a direct result of the disobedience of Saul, and of the special election of David by God himself. Nevertheless, the family line of Saul, through his son Jonathan, continues for many generations, perhaps down as far as the time of the deportation to Babylon.

REFLECTION

Ponder the sense of continuity that these lists represent.
Remember that each of us is part of a larger, older, unfolding story.

1 CHRONICLES 10

The DEATH of SAUL

The first book of Samuel tells the story of the birth of the prophet Samuel, the reign of the first king, Saul, from its bright beginnings to eventual disintegration, and the early years of David. David rises from shepherd boy to military warrior and son-in-law to King Saul, only to fall foul of the king's jealousy. The Chronicler tells none of these stories. He probably assumes that his readers will know them. The only story that he relates is from the final chapter (1 Samuel 31), on the death of Saul.

A day of disaster

Our author is not really interested in Saul's life, but does describe the circumstances of his death (vv. 1–12). This took place around the year 1000BC at the fateful battle on Mount Gilboa. The Israelites were routed by their enemies, the Philistines, who were pushing into the heartland of Israel from their territory along the coast.

He describes the deaths of Saul's three eldest sons—Jonathan, Abinadab and Malchishua—and then those of Saul himself and his armour bearer (vv. 2–5). He sums up in verse 6, 'Thus Saul died; he and his three sons and all his house died together.' Now this is not literally true, as the Chronicler knows full well. For he himself has recorded the descendants of Saul through his eldest son Jonathan in 1 Chronicles 8:34–39. There was also a fourth son of Saul, Eshbaal (8:33), who did not die on Mount Gilboa. He reigned for seven years in the north, while David ruled from Hebron over his native tribe of Judah. Eventually, Eshbaal was assassinated and David took control over the whole country. The Chronicler, however, does not mention Eshbaal's reign but presents David ruling from day one over the whole of a united country. He does not wish it to appear that David is a usurper of the throne in any sense.

In some ways, the Chronicler softens the description of the ill treatment and mutilation of Saul's body. The practice of displaying the head of the defeated warrior was gruesome but common in the ancient world. In just such a way, David had cut off and paraded the head of the Philistine champion, Goliath (1 Samuel 17:54). Now the Philistines exact their revenge on the first king of Israel. The ancient

Israelites considered the desecration of bodies to be a dreadful thing, and it was a solemn duty to bury corpses properly. In the story in 1 Samuel 31, Saul's body is hung on the walls of Beth-shan, eventually to be rescued by the men of Jabesh-gilead. In Chronicles, it reads as though the men of Jabesh found the headless corpse on the battle-field. Either way, they act with bravery and honour to rescue the bodies of the dead king and princes.

The reasons why

Verses 13 and 14 are the Chronicler's own summary of the reign of Saul. He spells out bluntly the reasons why Saul lost both the king-ship and his life. These brief verses allude to incidents in the life of Saul described in detail in 1 Samuel. Here in Chronicles they provide a brief theological reflection on the reign of Israel's first king.

1 Samuel presents Saul as a complex and often tragic figure. He begins so well, but eventually he descends into jealousy and mad-ness, which leads to family feuding and a sense of being abandoned even by God. This vivid portrait is lacking in Chronicles, which is not really interested in the details of Saul's life.

The Chronicler works with a simple belief in divine retribution—good kings prosper and bad ones come to a sticky end. It is a theol-ogy designed for the education of his readers. Saul was disobedient and he lost the kingdom, just as later kings turned from God and the disaster of exile followed. As God restored the nation once under the faithful David, so he can restore it again. The Chronicler insists that there are theological lessons to be learned from the contrast between Saul and David.

While there is truth in the Chronicler's presentation, it is not the whole story. Prosperity is not always the result of faithfulness—despite what some slick TV evangelists might say. Nor is disaster a sign that people are being punished. Jesus recognized this when he was asked about the collective disaster following the collapse of the Tower of Siloam (Luke 13:4), and the individual disaster of the man born blind (John 9:2–3). So we must beware of applying the Chronicler's scheme in a crude way to our own circumstances.

REFLECTION

What makes Saul's story into a 'tragedy'?

LONG LIVE KING DAVID!

In his idealized portrait of the reign of David, the Chronicler has rather telescoped the events of David's early years as king. The unity of all Israel and the prominence of the city of Jerusalem are the main theological features.

All Israel

There is no mention of the seven-year reign of Saul's surviving son, Eshbaal, in competition to David's rule in Hebron. Rather, David is presented as king of 'all Israel' from the very beginning (vv. 1–3). The transition from Saul to David is complete, and the representatives of all the tribes gather to affirm it. They acknowledge that even when Saul was king, it was really David who commanded the army of Israel (v. 2).

David, the one-time shepherd boy, is now portrayed as the shepherd of the people of Israel. 'Shepherd' was a common title for a ruler in the ancient world. It emphasized the care and protection that a good sovereign should offer to his people. Perhaps it is not surprising, then, that the most famous psalm of David should begin, 'The Lord is my shepherd'. The Chronicler is also keen to emphasize that David's ascent to the throne is no coincidence. Even though he has not told the story of Samuel, he reminds his readers that the prophet Samuel had spoken the word of the Lord affirming that David would be king. Prophecy and kingship will exist side by side throughout Chronicles.

Jerusalem

A Canaanite clan called the Jebusites originally occupied the city of Jerusalem and it remained a Canaanite enclave until the time of David. The capture of the city by David's troops was strategically important (vv. 4–9). Jerusalem was on the border between the tribal lands of Benjamin and Judah. It was therefore 'neutral territory', and David's choice of the city as his capital was an astute political move. It would help to foster a sense of unity among the Israelite tribes.

2 Samuel 5:6–10 describes the capture of the city, but the Chronicler adds some details of his own. In particular, he mentions

the exploits of Joab, first in capturing the city, then in rebuilding it. As a result, Joab became the commander-in-chief of the army. By mentioning his brave deeds here, the Chronicler paves the way for the description of 'The Three' and 'The Thirty' later in the chapter. Since Joab is not mentioned in these lists, his place at the head of the army is explained by his endeavours in securing the capture of Jerusalem.

Two out of three

For the rest of the chapter, there now follow lists of other famous individuals. Two groups in particular are specified: 'The Three' and 'The Thirty'. These titles may be the equivalent of modern military terms such as 'officers' or 'captains'.

The Chronicler's account should be compared with the version in 2 Samuel 23:8–12. Then it will be clear that in the copying of the story (either by the Chronicler himself or by a later scribe), part of the account has been missed out. Chronicles names only two out of the three heroes, Jashobeam and Eleazar (vv. 11–12). The 2 Samuel account supplies the third name, Shammah son of Agee (2 Samuel 23:11). Furthermore, it is Shammah who is credited with the incident in the field, rather than Eleazar, who performed a different deed of valour. Presumably, in the copying, the eye of the scribe has slipped and thus part of the story has been lost. There does not seem to be any reason why Shammah should have been deliberately omitted from the list. Comparisons such as these help us to see what changes, deliberate or accidental, have taken place in the retelling of the story.

By focusing on the exploits of Joab and The Three, and then The Thirty, the Chronicler is making a significant point. In the version in 2 Samuel, these accounts come right at the end of the story of David, almost as an appendix to the David narrative. Here in Chronicles, they stand right at the beginning of David's reign. The Chronicler may be seeking to emphasize that all these 'mighty men' stood behind and alongside David. Thus the unity of Israel is again emphasized and, despite David's being a particular favourite of the Chronicler, the point is made that it was far from being a 'one man show'. When 'all Israel' is united behind their faithful king, then they will be victorious.

PRAYER

Pray that one day Jerusalem may again be a symbol of unity rather than of division.

DARING DEEDS

After the exploits of 'The Three', there follow summaries of other daring deeds (vv. 15–25) and then a long list of famous soldiers (vv. 26–47).

Blood and water

The names of the three heroes involved in the episode in verses 15–19 are not given. Are they meant to be 'The Three' from the previous section, or were their names forgotten? This incident probably took place during the time when David was an outlaw, on the run from King Saul. The cave of Adullam was one of the hideouts of the fugitive David. The Philistines had even occupied Bethlehem in the Judean hill-country, showing how far they had advanced in their campaign. Things had reached a parlous state during the final years of Saul's reign.

We might think that the soldiers would be aggrieved at David's action. After all, they risked their lives for this cup of cold water from the well at Bethlehem. Now, rather than drink the water, David pours it out as a 'drink-offering' to the Lord. His reasoning, however, is clear. The men have procured the water, but could have lost their lives. To drink the water would be tantamount to drinking their blood. Jewish law forbade the consuming of blood, so David is seen to act in a way that is both honourable and scrupulous.

Abishai and Benaiah

The daring deeds of these two men are now described (vv. 20–25). There is some confusion in the Hebrew text here and in 2 Samuel 23 between the terms 'three' and 'thirty'. However, most English transla-tions take the comments in verses 21 and 25 to imply that although they were indeed famous among 'The Thirty', they did not make the ranks of 'The Three'.

Abishai was the brother of Joab, and they were both related to David, being sons of his sister Zeruiah (1 Chronicles 2:16). It is not too surprising, then, that they should rise to positions of prominence under David. The books of Samuel tell many stories about Abishai, including one battle in which he saved the life of King David (2 Samuel 21:15–17). Benaiah's valiant deeds are reminiscent of the more famous exploits of others. Firstly, his killing of a lion is similar to a story told about Samson (Judges 14:5–6). In Old Testament times, lions were still to be found in Israel, especially in the thick undergrowth near the River Jordan. The unusual circumstances of the snowy day and the pit helped to preserve the memory of the story. Secondly, Benaiah's battle with the Egyptian evokes memories of David's encounter with the Philistine champion, Goliath. He too was described as having a spear 'like a weaver's beam' (1 Samuel 17:7). In later times, Benaiah supported Solomon against the rival claims of the king's half-brother, Adonijah, and was responsible for the execution of Adonijah (1 Kings 2:25) and of the old commander Joab (1 Kings 2:28–34). In Solomon's new regime, Benaiah reached the number one spot and became Joab's successor as commander-in-chief (1 Kings 2:35).

The Thirty plus

The list of names from Asahel in verse 26 to Uriah in verse 41 is taken from 2 Samuel 23. Asahel was a younger brother of Joab and Abishai, and so another of David's relatives. 2 Samuel 2:17–23 recounts his untimely and unnecessary death in battle at the hands of Eshbaal's army commander, Abner. It led to a bitter blood feud and the murder of Abner by Joab and Abishai (2 Samuel 3:22–30).

Uriah the Hittite is best known as the husband of Bathsheba. An honest man, he was deceived and betrayed to death by David so that he could marry the pregnant Bathsheba (2 Samuel 11). The Chronicler does not tell this story, which reflects very badly on David, but includes Uriah's name in this list. The list itself may contain the original names of those who made up 'The Thirty'.

The names from Uriah onwards are not found in Samuel. The Chronicler must therefore have had access to some other archive material, perhaps going back to the time of David. The names are otherwise unknown, but often include the place where the men came from. Significantly, all these places are in Transjordan, on the east side of the Jordan. Note, for instance, the reference to the tribe of Reuben in verse 42. Even the Moabite, Ithmah, is included in the list in verse 46. Perhaps this additional list represents a contingent of leading officers from the eastern part of David's kingdom.

PRAYER

Pray for those who have responsibility today for leading the armed forces of the nation.

10 1 CHRONICLES 12:1–22

GATHERING STRENGTH

This section looks back to the last years of King Saul. As his kingdom goes down in flames, so David's star is on the rise. From 1 and 2 Samuel we learn that David's career went through four distinct phases after he fled from the paranoia of Saul.

1. As a fugitive in the Judean wilderness, with a number of hiding places such as the cave of Adullam. For several years he managed to evade Saul in this way (1 Samuel 22—26).

2. As an ally of Achish, king of Gath. This was the 'Philistine phase' of David's career, but many Philistines were still suspicious of him (1 Samuel 27—30).

3. As part-ruler of the kingdom. David became master of the south and ruled from Hebron for seven years (2 Samuel 2).

4. As king of all Israel following the assassination of Eshbaal (2 Samuel 5). The account of the assassination is given in 2 Samuel 4, where Eshbaal's name is spelled Ishbaal or Ishbosheth.

The Chronicler has not recounted the events of phases 1 to 3, but here in this chapter he alludes to them, assuming that his readers will know the story. In verses 1–22, he tells how various groups allied themselves to David and his cause, either during phase one at the stronghold or phase two at Ziklag. Groups representing four of the tribes are described as coming to join forces with David.

Benjamin

This is perhaps the most surprising group of all (vv. 1–7), since Saul was of the tribe of Benjamin. If people of Saul's own tribe have deserted him, then the writing must surely be on the wall for him. The Chronicler stresses this point in verse 2 and emphasizes the skill of these mighty warriors. The Benjamites always had a reputation as fierce fighters. When the kingdom is divided after Solomon's death, the tribe of Benjamin still remains loyal to the house of David. For the Chronicler, the two tribes of Judah and Benjamin constitute the very heart of the restored community in post-exilic times.

Gad

Surprisingly, David wins the allegiance of one of the more distant tribes as well (vv. 8–15). Gad was one of the tribes on the eastern side of the Jordan, along with Reuben and half of Manasseh. David seems to have had family connections in this area. To reach him, they would have to cross over the Jordan. The first month of the Israelite year would be around March, when melting snows in the north would cause the river to become a raging torrent.

Judah

It is less surprising to find that members of David's own tribe form part of his gathering support (vv. 16–18). No names are given in this instance, except for that of Amasai. Suddenly the Chronicler includes a portion of poetry, a snatch of song. For him, Amasai's words are prophetic, inspired by the Holy Spirit. They are words of blessing spoken over David and his enterprise. When the united monarchy dissolves into the northern and southern kingdoms after Solomon's death, the Chronicler will include another piece of song (2 Chronicles 10:16). That song will be modelled on this one, but will annul the words of blessing. Then, instead of unity will come division.

Manasseh

1 Samuel 29 tells the story of David's non-participation in the battle at Mount Gilboa. On the eve of that battle, some members of the tribe of Manasseh desert to David (vv. 19–22). From a military point of view they perhaps see the way the wind is blowing. The Chronicler, however, does not see things from a military point of view. He sees things theologically, and discerns the directing purposes of God here. As Saul decreases, so David increases.

David now has recruits from the south (Benjamin and Judah), from the north (Manasseh) and from the east (Gad). Day by day his numbers grow, until he has an army 'like an army of God'. The Chronicler's theological statement shows his approval of David and his actions. He wants to stress that David is not a rebel, a traitor or a political opportunist. Rather, he is a man of God and things are going his way.

TO CONSIDER

'One man's terrorist is another man's freedom fighter.'
'History is written by the winners.'

CORONATION DAY

This section tells of the gathering of forces loyal to David, and of his eventual coronation. The description of David becoming king in Hebron in 2 Samuel 2:1–4 is a very modest affair. Only the people of Judah are present. David rules there for seven and a half years (2 Samuel 2:11) and there is a rival claimant to the throne. Many in the north of Israel regard the son of Saul as the legitimate king. Only when this rival is assassinated is David finally proclaimed king over all Israel.

The Chronicler's view of things is very different. For him, there is an immediate transfer of kingship to David and this is accepted and approved by all the tribes of Israel. So, in a very idealized presentation, the Chronicler portrays all Israel united under one ruler. This is his interpretation of how things were and, by implication, how things will be in the future. The idealized past is held up as a blueprint for what is to happen in days to come.

Military lists

Verses 23–27 are among the most detailed and comprehensive military lists in the whole Bible, and it is possible that the Chronicler took them from a military census or conscription list. As usual, the order of the tribes is very deliberate and is based on geography. It starts with the southern tribes, then moves to the centre, then the north, and finally to the east across the Jordan. Included among these fighting units, surprisingly for us perhaps, is the tribe of Levi (vv. 26–28). A distinction is made between ordinary Levites (v. 26), and priests of the line of Aaron (v. 27). Furthermore, special mention is made of the young Zadok (v. 28) who will rise to become chief priest under Solomon. This distinction between Levites, priests and Zadokites is important in the Chronicler's theological system.

The number of armed men who gather at Hebron is very large, and the numbers per tribe get bigger as the list progresses. In all, the total number enrolled is 339,600. Some people think that the term 'thousand' should be understood not as a number, but as a military term for a unit of men. This may have been its original meaning, but the Chronicler appears to accept it as a straightforward number. By means of these large numbers, our author emphasizes the unity of all Israel. Having named the famous men who came to David at Hebron in verses 1–22, he now includes all the ordinary soldiers who pledged their loyalty. Their names cannot be recorded, but the huge numbers speak of the unity of purpose. They have all come to make David king, and to do it with an undivided heart (v. 33).

The king's banquet

In portraying scenes such as this (vv. 38–40), the Chronicler always emphasizes the note of joy. His religious outlook, though rather formal, was not sombre. Joy keeps bubbling up to the surface in his storytelling.

It may seem surprising that the Chronicler does not emphasize rather more the religious nature of the coronation day. There is no mention of any ceremonies performed by the priests or Levites, indeed no explicit reference to David's crowning at all. This is probably because, as yet, Jerusalem is not in the possession of David. It is only at Jerusalem, the place specially chosen by God, that proper religious ceremonies can take place. Therefore, in the next chapter the Chronicler will move swiftly to recount the story of the capture of Jerusalem.

Instead, the emphasis is on the festivities at Hebron, and particularly on the eating and drinking. Food is brought, even from faraway tribes, by various beasts of burden (v. 40). We must always bear in mind that meals in the ancient world often had religious significance. A lavish, ceremonial meal often accompanied the making of a covenant. The Chronicler therefore portrays the king, the Lord's anointed, surrounded by the representatives of all the twelve tribes of Israel. It is a royal banquet, a banquet of the anointed one with his people. In later Judaism and in Christianity, the lovely image of a messianic banquet (for Messiah or Christ means 'Anointed One') is a vital part of the future hope. So at the last supper, Christ, the Anointed One of God, sits at table with his twelve apostles, who represent the twelve tribes. In the upper room, he makes a new covenant as they eat and drink together. This stream of imagery and hopes links our Chronicles story with every celebration of holy communion.

PRAYER

Give thanks that you are called to share in Christ's royal banquet.

FINDING *the* ARK

From Hebron, the scene now shifts to Jerusalem, the city of David (v. 13), and to David's wish to bring the sacred ark of the covenant to his new capital. According to the book of Exodus, the ark was built during the period of the wilderness wanderings. It contained the two tablets of the Law, inscribed with the Ten Commandments (1 Kings 8:9). They acted as a permanent reminder of the covenant with God made at Sinai. The ark, with its carved figures of cherubim, was also pictured as the footstool of God (1 Chronicles 28:2). So it represented the very presence of the Lord among his people, 'enthroned on the cherubim' (v. 6). The ark had resided at Shiloh until the time of the old priest, Eli. Then the Philistines captured it, before it was finally returned to the house of Abinadab at Kiriath-jearim (1 Samuel 4—7).

Democracy

The Chronicler introduces the story of the transfer of the ark in his own way in verses 1–4, and is not dependent on the version in 2 Samuel 6. According to the Chronicler, David convenes a large assembly of 'all Israel', including priests and Levites (v. 2). The decision to bring the ark to Jerusalem is therefore not David's alone. It is a collective decision of 'all Israel'. In some respects, therefore, the Chronicler is 'democratic' in outlook, compared to the author of Samuel. In Chronicles, David is no autocrat, no petty despot. He consults with his people and convinces them of the rightness of the action. Writing as he was in the post-exilic age when there was no king, the Chronicler presents a picture of complete harmony and unity of purpose between the monarch and his people.

Dancing

Verse 5 gives the limits of David's territory as from Shihor on the borders of Egypt to the entrance to Hamath. The more usual boundaries of the land of Israel, north to south, are 'from Dan to Beersheba'. Shihor is either the wadi El-Arish, or the Nile itself, and Hamath is a town on the River Orontes in Syria. So these place names designate the boundaries of David's empire in the south-west and north-east.

The concern shown by David for the ark's welfare stands in sharp contrast to its neglect in the days of Saul, when it languished in obscurity. Once again, David is presented as the very opposite of Saul. His personal devotion and commitment to honour the glorious presence of the Lord in Israel are signs that his heart is right with God. So, after twenty years of neglect, the transfer of the ark to Jerusalem is arranged. Festivities are at their height, as the list of musical instruments in verse 8 testifies, when suddenly disaster strikes.

Disaster

Many stories in the Old Testament seek to explain the meaning of the names of people or of places. This story in verses 9–14 explains the name of the place Perez-uzzah. The Hebrew word *perez* means 'breaking out', and the Chronicler uses it a number of times in chapters 13—17. This play on words is typical of Hebrew story-telling.

The concept of holiness in ancient Israel centred on ideas of separateness and distinctiveness. The 'holy' was not to be trifled with or treated lightly. That is why specially designated people, such as priests and Levites, were set apart to minister to holy things. The holy could be dangerous—and the ark was a supremely holy object. The death of Uzzah for lending a steadying hand may seem very harsh. Perhaps we should let it stand as a witness to us that the Holy One of Israel is not to be domesticated! Uzzah's action could be interpreted as an attitude of unfaithfulness. He thought that the ark (and therefore, by implication, God as well) needed his help. Not so—the God of Israel can take care of himself.

Obed-edom is described as a Gittite, that is a native of Gath. So he may have been a near neighbour of Goliath! It seems unlikely that he was a Philistine, but rather an Israelite born in that city. For the Chronicler, it is fitting that anyone entrusted with looking after the ark should be a Levite. He and his family descendants are listed among the Levites in 1 Chronicles 26:4. For the moment, however, David's plans for the ark are 'on hold'.

PRAYER

Remember those times when your own schemes have been postponed and you have had to wait for God's time instead.

13

BUILDING *on* SUCCESS

The Chronicler mentions a three-month stay for the ark at the home of Obed-edom. So in the gap between the end of chapter 13 and the continuation of the ark's transfer in chapter 15, he inserts this chapter with its account of David's fortunes. Clearly we are not meant to think that all these events took place within the three-month period—especially the birth of thirteen children! Nevertheless, the deliberate placing of the chapter here is part of the careful crafting of the story by the Chronicler. Historically, the war with the Philistines probably came first and the arrangements with Hiram last. In three distinct ways this chapter portrays the success of David, which is proof that God is with him and has truly established him as king over God's people.

The royal palace

Hiram was king of Tyre, a city on the coast of Phoenicia (vv. 1–2). This area is to the north of Israel, in modern-day Lebanon. The Phoenicians were a cultured people with a reputation for building. So Hiram sends cedars of Lebanon and skilled workers to build a palace for David, a place fit for a king to live in. Whether this was part of a mutual trade agreement, or whether Hiram was a vassal, subject to King David, is not clear. Hiram appears again later in Chronicles, providing more resources for the building of the temple. David is firmly established on the throne and the grand royal buildings going up in Jerusalem are a testimony to that.

The royal family

For people of ancient times, a large family was considered to be a sign of God's blessing. This is summed up in texts such as Psalm 127:3–5 and 128:3–4. Sons in particular are a blessing, and now, to add to the children born to him in earlier days, thirteen sons are born to David in Jerusalem itself (vv. 3–7). Their names have already been given in the royal genealogy in 1 Chronicles 3. We know nothing about any of these children, with the one important exception of Solomon.

The royal victories

In his outlaw days, David had been a useful ally of the Philistines, especially to Achish, king of Gath. The Philistines had exploited the division between Saul and David, using the age-old principle that 'my enemy's enemy is my friend'. Now that David is king of all Israel, however, the situation is changed (vv. 8–17). The growth in David's power and influence poses a direct threat to the Philistine hopes of expanding their territory. Consequently they mount an attack against their former ally.

The Chronicler portrays David as both a devout servant of the Lord and also an astute military commander. In both battles, David first inquires of God whether he should fight. The contrast between this and Saul's heroic but futile 'go it alone' approach on Mount Gilboa (1 Samuel 31) is stark. Furthermore, David listens carefully to God's directions and follows them to the letter. He thus uses different tactics to win each of these important battles, so pushing back the advance of the Philistine armies.

The victories are complete and the tables are turned. As once the Philistines captured the ark, the symbol of the presence of God (1 Samuel 4), so now their gods are captured by David's forces. The Chronicler makes a small but significant change in his description in verse 12. In 2 Samuel 5:21, David and his men pick up the idols and carry them off as booty. In his account, the Chronicler has David order that the idols be burned. Thus David acts in full conformity with the instruction in Deuteronomy 7:5 to 'burn their idols with fire'.

The Chronicler continues to play on words in this chapter. That word *perez* occurs again, as David exclaims, 'God has burst out against my enemies by my hand, like a bursting flood' (v. 11). So another place name, Baal-perazim, is explained.

All in all, this chapter reinforces the view that David is truly a man of God. The incident with the ark is not a sign of God's disapproval of David, far from it. As God blessed the house of Obed-edom, so he has now abundantly blessed the house of David. It is time to try to move the ark again.

REFLECTION

What are the 'marks of success' today? Compare the answer of modern society against the values of the gospel.

TRYING AGAIN

The building of houses for King David in the holy city again raises the question of an appropriate resting place for the ark of the covenant. The blessings conferred on Obed-edom during the ark's three-month stay at his house, along with the blessings conferred on David, lead to one conclusion. The decision to move the ark was a correct one. It was the way it was done that caused the problem. Careful preparations are therefore necessary if the second stage of the process is to be successful.

David commands that the task of carrying the ark belongs exclusively to the Levites. This is, once again, in fulfilment of the laws of Moses. The book of Deuteronomy states that the tribe of Levi is set apart to carry the ark (10:8) and to minister before the Lord 'for all time' (18:5). David now follows these biblical instructions scrupulously.

The levitical groups

The mention of six levitical groups in verses 4–10 is rather unusual. The more normal number is three, represented by the first three names of Kohath, Merari and Gershom. The other three names are elsewhere given as sons or grandsons of the Kohath line. For example, Exodus 6:18 and 22 give the following family tree:

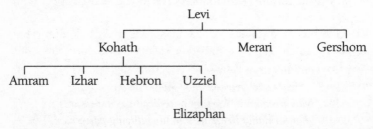

So in this section, three of the secondary branches seem to have been raised to primary status. These differences may represent different traditions, or point to traditions coming from different periods. The Chronicler may well have incorporated material from lists originally deriving from different times. Over time, some family groups would grow in importance and others would diminish. The names of the chiefs of these six levitical groups at the time are then given:

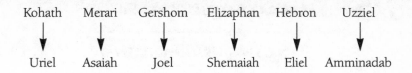

Kohath	Merari	Gershom	Elizaphan	Hebron	Uzziel
Uriel	Asaiah	Joel	Shemaiah	Eliel	Amminadab

The proper way

In contrast to the rather haphazard and undignified way in which the ark was moved at the first attempt, things are much better organized this time (vv. 11–15). All those directly responsible for carrying the ark are Levites. Instead of being perched precariously on an ox-wagon, the ark is carried properly on the shoulders of the Levites, who use poles to support it. In this way, no one will physically touch it as the unfortunate Uzzah did. Again, this conforms to the instructions of Moses in the Law. According to Numbers 7:9, holy things had to be carried on the shoulders. Exodus 25:12–15 describes the procedure for making the poles and their accompanying rings.

Verse 13 employs the word *perez* ('breaking forth') again. David believes that the breaking forth was due solely to the lack of proper care taken in the first attempt. They will take no chances the second time around. Before commencing the task, all the religious personnel must sanctify themselves. This would include appropriate ritual worship and abstinence from sexual relations. Thus, in a ritually pure state, the Levites can approach the holy presence of God and perform the delicate task of bringing the ark to its final resting-place in the city David has rebuilt.

PRAYER

Lord, in our worship teach us to get the balance right.
Help us to treasure both spontaneity and order.
May freedom in worship never lead to carelessness,
nor formality freeze us into unchanging patterns.

SINGING & DANCING

The Chronicler seems to be particularly interested in the role of the Levites, and has depicted them carrying the ark to its final resting-place. How are they to be employed once the ark has reached its final destination and a permanent house is built? The answer is that it was from the ranks of the Levites that the musicians and temple singers were drawn. They will continue to exercise a ministry in the temple, before the ark, now that their carrying days are over.

The singers

The names in verses 16–24 should be compared with those in 1 Chronicles 6. Each of the three heads of the levitical singers traces his ancestry back to the sons of Levi. The partial family tree is as follows:

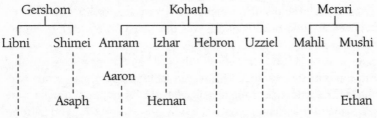

(Levites) (singers) (priests) (singers) (Levites) (Levites) (Levites) (singers)

In each case, the singers are descended from the second son. This probably denotes their 'secondary' or subordinate position over against the other Levites. Nevertheless, the singers are seen as fully integrated into the levitical family tree.

The list of singers is given twice. First we have the list of names in verses 17–18, with a distinction between first and second order. Verses 19–21 repeat the names, and specify each group's responsibilities. The first order had charge of cymbals, while the second order was to play either harps or lyres. Then verse 22 gives us the name of the director of music, Chenaniah. Verse 23 names two gatekeepers, Berechiah and Elkanah, and verse 24 gives the names of seven priests blowing trumpets. According to Numbers 10:8, trumpets were a priestly instrument. Only sons of Aaron, not ordinary Levites, could be responsible for them.

There appears some confusion in the lists regarding the duties of

Obed-edom and Jeiel/Jehiah. In verse 18 and verse 24 they are gate-keepers, while in verse 21 they are musicians of the second order who play the lyre. It is possible that these families started as temple singers but ended up as gatekeepers. In other words they lost influence and were 'demoted'. Nevertheless, even the role of a gatekeeper was a significant one, as the author of Psalm 84 reminds us: 'I would rather be a doorkeeper in the house of my God than live in the tents of wickedness.' It somehow seems appropriate that the gatekeepers of the house of Obed-edom should trace their ancestry back to the man who looked after the ark. It is noteworthy that the heading to Psalm 84 includes the phrase 'according to The Gittith'. Is this an echo of the description of Obed-edom as the Gittite? If so, it is not surprising to find this psalm speaking favourably of doorkeepers.

The subject of psalm titles also has a bearing on verses 20–21. One group of musicians is to play 'according to Alamoth' and another 'according to the Sheminith'. No one knows quite what these terms mean, though one suggestion relates them to soprano and bass. The term *alamoth* also occurs in the heading to Psalm 46 and *sheminith* in the heading to Psalms 6 and 12.

Rejoicing and bitterness

Once more, the note of rejoicing is prominent in Chronicles (vv. 25–29). Sacrifices performed by the priests accompany the procession, and all those taking part are finely dressed in linen. David is portrayed wearing an ephod. This term can mean a priestly garment, but it is not exclusively priestly. It is hardly the intention of the Chronicler to present David in priestly terms. He is a prince of the tribe of Judah. He does not belong to the priestly tribe of Levi.

Brief mention is made of the bitterness between David and his estranged wife Michal. In 2 Samuel 6, the reason for Michal's displeasure is that David had made an exhibition of himself before the servant girls. Here in Chronicles, no reason is given. Perhaps the Chronicler intends us to see Michal's negative attitude as a continuation of the house of Saul's hostility or indifference towards the ark.

PRAYER

Pray for singers, choir leaders, soloists and musicians who enhance worship. Pray also for the equivalent of the 'doorkeepers' who do vital work but never seek the limelight.

The TWO TENTS

This chapter concludes the details of the arrangements David makes for the ark of the covenant. By the end of the chapter, the Chronicler has depicted David as responsible, down to the last detail, for ordering the worship life of ancient Israel. The roles of priests, Levites, singers and gatekeepers are all carefully defined by the actions of the great king of Israel.

The tent at Jerusalem

The ark is now housed in a brand new tent in the city of Jerusalem (vv. 1–6). Appropriate sacrifices of various kinds are offered. These include:

- whole burnt offerings in which all the carcass is burnt on the altar.

- peace offerings in which part of the beast is burnt on the altar while some of the flesh is distributed and eaten. Through them, unity and peace (*shalom*) are established between the people and God and also among all who share in the sacrificial banquet.

Verse 3 emphasizes how 'all Israel' receives from the bounty of King David.

One of the three groups of levitical singers is then appointed to remain at Jerusalem with the ark. It is the group led by Asaph that has this responsibility. There is some indication that in the post-exilic period the Asaph group became predominant. It eventually replaced the Heman group as the leading body of levitical singers. Note that in verse 5 Obed-edom returns to his position as a musician. Again it is stressed that the 'secondary' musicians play harps and lyres, the 'primary' musicians such as Asaph sound the cymbals, while trumpets are for the priests, Benaiah and Jahaziel.

David is portrayed as taking a particular interest in the whole area of religious music. According to the earlier biblical tradition in 1 Samuel 16:18–23, David himself was a skilful player of the harp. His name was also linked with the book of Psalms. Nearly half the psalms contain the note 'of David' in their headings. The Chronicler is therefore building on the tradition of David the lover of music.

The tent at Gibeon

The ark (v. 37) was only one of the ceremonial objects associated with the wilderness wanderings. The book of Exodus also describes the 'tent of meeting' and a host of assorted religious objects associated with it. So far, only the ark has been brought to Jerusalem. There is no altar built at Jerusalem as yet—so the tent of meeting remains at the old sanctuary at Gibeon, which goes back to the time of Joshua.

The confusion over the status of Obed-edom continues in verse 38, where his name appears twice. In the second instance he has been 'demoted' to gatekeeper, unless this verse is evidence that the Chronicler thought in terms of two Obed-edoms. The first, Obed-edom the Gittite, was among the musicians; the second, Obed-edom the son of Jeduthun, was among the gatekeepers. Many of the modern English versions seem to imply that this is what verse 38 means, though the Good News Bible has them the other way round.

While Asaph and a quota of priests, Levites, singers and gate-keepers remain at Jerusalem, the other groups are sent back to Gibeon (vv. 39–43). Since the main altar is there, it is appropriate for Zadok the priest to return to Gibeon. The other two levitical singing groups also return there. We might expect the names of Heman and Ethan to appear as the leaders of the singers. Instead we find Heman and Jeduthun. The simplest explanation is that Ethan/Jeduthun are two names for the same person. The other alternative is that we have another example of one group being replaced, over time, by another. If this is the case, Jeduthun was eventually superseded by Ethan. Verse 42 mentions that the sons of Jeduthun were gatekeepers, which might indicate their eventual change in status. Interestingly, both names appear in psalm headings, Ethan in the heading to Psalm 89, and Jeduthun in the headings to Psalms 39, 62 and 77.

All is now in place for the proper observance of religious practice. Until Solomon builds the temple, there will be two tents or taber-nacles, one for the ark at Jerusalem and one at Gibeon.

REFLECTION

How important is 'status' or 'position' in your church fellowship? Have you ever been demoted in some way? How did it feel?

SING *a* NEW SONG

Having described the meticulous preparations David made for the organization of music at the tent (and, by implication, the later temple), the Chronicler now gives an example of the kind of hymnody used. He does this by producing a typical psalm sung by the levitical choirs. In fact, the quotation that he gives is made up of three psalms that have been joined together. The psalms involved are 105:1–15; 96; and the opening and closing verses of 106. Thus, by the time the author of Chronicles was writing in the fourth century, it would appear that the book of Psalms was virtually complete. The manner in which the Chronicler splices psalms together was by no means unique. Among the fragments from the Dead Sea Scrolls, dating from the time of Jesus, are examples of biblical psalms joined together in an order quite different from that in our Bibles. They produced a new hymn book for their generation.

In many modern hymn books, the editors will make slight changes to some of the older hymns in order to bring them up to date or to make the language easier to understand. Some people complain at this, especially those 'purists' who think that nothing should be changed in the old hymns. Yet this is not just a modern phenomenon. The Chronicler reproduced the psalms almost, but not quite, word for word. He makes some small but significant changes. These are not always easy to spot in English Bibles because some translations harmonize the Chronicles version with that of the Psalms, ironing out the differences. The Chronicler, however, was aware of the need for change, for two reasons. He wanted both to relate the psalm to the historical setting in the time of David, and to make it relevant to his audience in his own time.

Wonderful deeds

Verses 8–22 are based on Psalm 105:1–15. The stress throughout is on the wonderful things God has done for his people. Here is a catalogue of things for which they should never cease to praise and thank him. Psalm 105 is a long psalm that rehearses God's dealings with the people from the time of Abraham until the entry into the promised land. The Chronicler only reproduces the first part of the psalm, covering the time of the patriarchs, Abraham, Isaac and Jacob. The promise of land was given to them even though they were few in number. That theme would have a special meaning for the Chronicler's audience in the post-exilic period, for they occupied only a part of the land promised to their ancestors. The Chronicler introduces one of his subtle changes in verse 13. Whereas Psalm 105:6 has 'offspring of his servant Abraham', the Chronicler writes 'offspring of his servant Israel'. In Chronicles, Abraham plays a fairly small part; the really significant patriarch is Jacob (also known as Israel).

The Lord reigns

Verses 23–33 reproduce the whole of Psalm 96, in which the theme is the incomparable nature of God. God is supreme, above all, and it is his judgments that count. Therefore, all nations are invited to worship the one sovereign Lord of the universe. Such a psalm of praise and thanksgiving was clearly very appropriate for the joyful setting in David's time. However, to avoid one historical anomaly, the Chronicler makes a minor change in verse 29. Instead of 'bring an offering and come into his courts', he has 'bring an offering and come before him'. For in the time of David there was no temple, and therefore no temple courts. The historical setting requires the change to the more general 'before him'.

Save us

The words of verse 34 are found as the opening verse for Psalms 106 and 118. Verses 35–36 are the final verses of Psalm 106. They form the doxology which closes not only that psalm but the whole section of the Psalms known as Book 4 (Psalms 90—106). The prayer to 'gather and rescue us from among the nations' would certainly find an echo among the Chronicler's audience. In the period after the exile, many Jews still lived in distant lands, far away from Jerusalem. The hope for a full and final return lived on in the hearts of the people of Israel.

At the end of this 'new song', made up from pieces of old ones, all the people in David's Jerusalem respond 'amen'. No doubt the Chronicler expected his own audience to add their 'amen' too.

ACTIVITY

Either try singing or learning a new hymn
or try writing your own song of praise.

HOUSE BUILDING

David is now comfortably settled in his new capital city, Jerusalem. He has a royal palace built of cedar wood in which to live. By contrast, God still dwells in a mere tent. Surely the time is right to build a more appropriate 'dwelling-place' for the Lord? After all, the gods of the surrounding nations each had their own temples, often beautifully crafted. The king consults with his advisor, the prophet Nathan, who was the dominant prophetic figure in the reign of David. This is one of many incidents in which prophets play an important role in the book of Chronicles. Acting on his own initiative, Nathan gives his approval, a green light for the building of a house for God.

No

It would seem, however, that God has other ideas. The message that Nathan receives in verses 3–6 would appear to turn the green light into a red. God is quite content with his unpretentious dwelling-place and has no desire to move up-market. Ever since the days of the wilderness wanderings, the occupation of the land of Canaan, and the period of the judges, God has been moving with his people. The tent symbolizes a God who is on the move, a mobile rather than a static deity. The problem with temples, and with church buildings for that matter, is that they speak of stability, even immobility. So along with those traditions in the Old Testament which extol the temple in Jerusalem, there are others which are critical of the whole idea. For example, contrast the love for the temple in Psalms 84 and 48 with the warning voice of Jeremiah 7:4.

Not yet

Even such a pro-temple writer as the Chronicler was aware of the dangers of pride and complacency, of trust in bricks and mortar. Therefore, the emphasis in verses 7–12 is not on what David can do for God. Rather, it is on what God has done for David. It is God who has been building up David and his reputation, not vice versa.

There is a play on words running through this whole section. David has a plan to build a 'house' (that is, a temple) for God. God has a different plan, to build a 'house' (that is, a dynasty) for David. God's plan must take precedence. Only when David's dynasty is secure and Solomon is on the throne will it be the right time to construct the temple. So it is not a red light after all, but rather an amber one. It is not a complete rejection of the idea, merely a postponement.

The Chronicler knew full well that David had not built the temple, that only in Solomon's day was the dream brought to completion. Nevertheless, in the subsequent chapters of 1 Chronicles he is able to show how David made all the necessary preparations for the building work. David was a warrior who had shed blood and therefore could not build the temple. Solomon is a man of peace (his name comes from the word *shalom*, meaning peace). Therefore, in Solomon's day, when the children of Israel are finally at rest, the Lord himself will 'settle down' on Mount Zion. Both time and place will be of God's choosing.

Father and son

Nathan's oracle also contains specific words of promise for Solomon and his descendants (vv. 13–15). God will be in a special covenant relationship with the family of David. This will be so close that it will be like a father-son relationship. 'I will be a father to him and he shall be a son to me.' Many of the psalms highlight the special relationship between the anointed king and God. A typical example is Psalm 2:6–7, which describes the king as the begotten son of God.

In days to come, when there was no king of David's line sitting on the throne in Jerusalem, the psalmist's words were understood in a messianic way. They spoke of the Anointed One of God who was to come. In the New Testament, passages like Psalm 2 and our Chronicles text are quoted with reference to Jesus, as for instance in Hebrews 1:5. For Christians, the life of Jesus exemplifies the special relationship that was meant to exist between God and the king. Here truly the prophecy of Nathan was fulfilled. The Messiah, the Christ, was indeed the 'Son of God'.

PRAYER

Lord, when I pray, help me to take seriously 'no' and 'not yet'
as well as 'yes'.

DAVID'S PRAYER

The way a person prays will tell you a great deal about what a person believes. One of the most important vehicles for the theology of Chronicles is through the medium of spoken prayers. At significant moments in the life of the nation, a king or other representative will speak directly to God in prayer. This is one of those occasions, and it provides a fascinating glimpse into the character and psychology of David as portrayed by the Chronicler.

There is no doubt that David, together with Solomon, is the hero of the book of Chronicles. He scarcely ever puts a foot wrong. There may be times when we feel that the David in the pages of Chronicles is rather too good to be true. Yet he is, above all, a man of faith. Here in this prayer, we are allowed to eavesdrop on a man in conversation with his God. Many of the set-piece prayers in later chapters are spoken in public before the assembly of Israel. It is not so with this prayer, for David is alone with the Lord. In it we hear tones of respect, awe and profound thankfulness.

Acceptance

This prayer comes at a psychologically significant time for David. His great plans for building a house for God have been overturned. Instead God will build a house for him. David, in a gentle but very firm way, has been put in his place. He has received both bad news and good news.

This is reflected in the way he addresses God throughout the prayer. Apart from the beginning of the prayer, he never uses the first person pronoun 'I'. Instead he speaks about himself as 'your servant', though unfortunately the Good News Bible smooths this out! The prayer is full of exclamations and invocations of God, such as 'O Lord God', 'O God', 'O Lord', 'God of Israel'. Through this prayer, David is getting things into perspective. His grandiose plans must give way to the greater plans of the Almighty (vv. 16–19).

Acclaim

To help get things into proper perspective, the middle part of the prayer in verses 20–22 focuses on the nature and character of God and away from David's immediate situation. David rehearses the sacred story of the history of salvation. The events of the Exodus and the conquest of the promised land remind him, and those of us who overhear his prayer, of the 'big picture'. The story of David and Solomon is not to be seen in isolation but as part of a much greater whole.

In those great deeds God had made a name for himself. The name of the God of Israel was spread abroad as a God of liberation. God had chosen the insignificant people of Israel, brought them out of slavery in Egypt and given them a land of their own. In time past, God had chosen one nation among many. Now he has chosen one man from among many to be king. The themes of God's choosing, his election, his covenant love are to the fore here. They are vital themes for the Chronicler and for his audience.

Amen

At the end of the prayer (vv. 23–27), all that David can really say is 'amen', or in English, 'let it be so'. The promise that has been made is almost too good to be true. One almost senses that David is anxious not to appear greedy or grasping in claiming the promise, lest it appears as self-aggrandisement. His closing prayer is that God will indeed establish David's house as he has promised.

No doubt the first readers of Chronicles would have wanted to make this prayer their own too. They lived in a time when other empires, rather than the independent kings of David's line, ruled over them. Perhaps they understood this prayer not just as a prayer from past history but as a pattern for their own praying. It gave them hope that one day another king of David's line would be established according to the covenant promises of God.

PRAYER

Lord, grant to me a will that accepts what you give,
a voice to acclaim your goodness,
a heart that rests content in the everlasting 'Amen'.

DAVID'S WARS

The Chronicler has ordered his material very carefully. Chapters 18—20 are accounts of David's wars, which the Chronicler has brought together from various parts of 2 Samuel 8—21. This material is strategically placed between chapter 17, which tells of David's plan for the temple, and chapter 21, which describes the beginning of the preparatory work for the temple. By providing summaries of David's achievements, the Chronicler is able to paint a picture of the military, political and economic advances that were made.

Victory on all fronts

Brief summaries tell of David's stunning victories over enemy nations all around (vv. 1–6). First he defeats the Philistines in the west. They have not yet been fully subdued, and the loss of the significant city of Gath is a blow to them. Then David turns his attention to the east. The Moabites across the Jordan are incorporated into his empire and have to pay tribute. Subsequently David travels further afield to the north-east. The territory of Hadadezer, king of Zobah, lay somewhere north of the city of Damascus. Despite the intervention of the citizens of Damascus, David succeeds in extending his rule still further.

Tribute

These wars clearly occupied much of David's time and energy. The land of Israel was not yet at rest, nor would it be until the time of Solomon. This is a further reason, in the Chronicler's view, why David cannot build the temple. The consequence of his military career is that he is a 'man of blood' (1 Chronicles 22:8) and therefore it is inappropriate for him to do so.

Nevertheless, there was a way in which even the wars David fought could benefit the temple project (vv. 8–13). According to the rules of so-called 'holy war', spoils taken in battle were not to enrich the king and his army, but had to be dedicated to God. It was, in part, Saul's failure to do this that led to his rejection by the Lord, according to 1 Samuel 15. The actions of David are again contrasted with those of Saul. David does dedicate the gold, silver and bronze to the Lord. These precious metals, taken as plunder or as tribute, provided the resources for the precious objects that would adorn the temple in Solomon's days. So even here David is seen to be preparing the way for his successor.

David uses diplomacy as well as warfare to extend his influence. The city of Hamath was further north than the territory of Zobah. The two were near neighbours and rivals. The king of Hamath therefore forms an alliance with David and sends gifts or tribute to him. King David has extended his influence even as far as the city of Hamath (see the comment on 1 Chronicles 13:5).

Administration

Verses 14–17 mention a particular campaign fought against the Edomites in the south-east. The battle in the Valley of Salt was clearly an important one, fought near the area of the Dead Sea perhaps. However, the name of the commander of the battle varies in different biblical traditions. In 2 Samuel 8:13, it is David himself who wins the victory and gains a reputation. Here in Chronicles, it is Abishai, David's nephew. According to the heading of Psalm 60, it was Abishai's brother Joab. Whichever leader was at the head of the campaign, it all adds to David's growing reputation. The Edomites too are incorporated into David's empire and troops are garrisoned there.

The chapter ends with a short list of officials. David built not just an empire but an efficient empire, and we are given the names of the officials who acted as army commander, recorder, priests and secretary. The term 'Cherethites and Pelethites' (v. 17) seems to refer to a special corps of troops who were David's personal bodyguard (see the Good News Bible translation). Mention is also made of some of David's sons as chief officials. All this reinforces the impression of a well-organized administration. There is no hint of the strife and bickering among the children of David which 2 Samuel depicts. David is portrayed instead as a fine warrior, a just ruler, and a good father.

REFLECTION

Consider how these attributes of victory, tribute and wise administration helped to shape ideas about the coming Messiah or Son of David.

An INSULT LEADS *to* WAR

Reference to the brothers Joab and Abishai at the end of the last chapter leads on to a story involving their joint heroism. Having defeated a variety of enemy nations one by one, the Israelite army now faces a dangerous coalition involving the Ammonites and their allies, the Syrians or Arameans.

Ambassadors and embarrassment

The Ammonites (vv. 1–5) were one of the groups of Semitic peoples who occupied the land on the other side of the Jordan, close neighbours of the Moabites and Edomites. Even today, the modern capital of the Kingdom of Jordan is Amman, which reminds us of the name of the people of Ammon. It would appear that up to this point David had been on friendly terms with Nahash, the old king of Ammon. Upon his death, the new, inexperienced king listens to the advice of his counsellors. A similar story of a new ruler, bad advice and a disastrous policy move is told of Rehoboam, the son of Solomon, in 2 Chronicles 10. New leaders seeking to impress can often make stupid mistakes.

The treatment of the ambassadors is outrageous and provocative. In the Middle East, both in the past and today, the concept of honour and shame is very strong. So the humiliation meted out to David's ambassadors cannot be ignored. Furthermore, King Hanun has broken the rules of proper hospitality towards guests—another fundamental breach of etiquette. This is not the way to conduct diplomacy, to win friends or to influence people!

Bought men and battle lines

The Ammonites immediately begin to make preparations for war (vv. 6–9). Since they are not particularly strong militarily, they need reinforcements. They hire mercenaries from the Aramean cities of the land of Syria. These various Aramean city states occupied the area up to Mesopotamia (modern Iraq) and were well equipped with infantry and chariots. Ammon and Aram together therefore pose a formidable threat to David.

The battle lines are drawn, with the Ammonites situated at the entrance to their city and the Aramean mercenaries in the open country. The Israelite army positioned between will therefore have to fight on two fronts.

Tactics and trust

As the armies prepare to fight, the two sons of Zeruiah plan their strategy (vv. 10–15). Joab will concentrate on the Arameans in the open country, and Abishai on the Ammonite forces. However, if either of them is in need of reinforcement the other will provide it. The tactics are carefully worked out, but the Chronicler is at pains to show that strategy alone will not win the day. Ultimately, as verse 13 makes plain, the outcome of the battle is in the hands of God.

When the battle is won, Joab returns to Jerusalem. He has won one battle, but not the war. He returns to Jerusalem either to consult about the conduct of the campaign or to gain further reinforcements. For all kinds of reasons, the war against the alliance is one of the most significant of David's campaigns.

PRAYER

O Lord! thou knowest how busy I must be this day:
if I forget thee, do not thou forget me.

A prayer of Sir Jacob Astley (1579–1652), composed before the battle of Edgehill, during the English Civil War

SETTLING SCORES

The next three brief sections relate the outcome of the final battles in David's wars against Arameans, Ammonites and Philistines.

Arameans

Having been drawn in as hired mercenary troops, the Arameans now find themselves part of a much wider conflict (vv. 16–19). They send for reinforcements from the Aramean tribes beyond the River Euphrates. David takes charge of the operations and finds himself pitted once more against Hadadezer, the king of Zobah, who is at the head of the coalition. Again the Arameans are defeated and sue for peace. The alliance with their former partners, the Ammonites, is at an end, and David is free to turn his attention to the upstart young king. There are still scores to be settled on account of the humiliation of the ambassadors.

Ammonites

The Chronicler takes his information in 20:1–3 about the siege of the Ammonite capital, Rabbah, from the first verse of 2 Samuel 11 and the last two verses of 2 Samuel 12. The rest of 2 Samuel 11—12 he omits entirely. This is the story of David's adultery with Bathsheba and the disgraceful plot to organize the death of her husband, Uriah the Hittite. It is during the battle at the walls of Rabbah that Uriah is betrayed and slain. This 'human interest' story, which so fascinates modern readers, does not feature at all in the work of the Chronicler. Not only is he concerned to downplay David's faults, but he is also concerned primarily with the public, not the private, face of David. It is David the king, the warrior, the organizer, who interests the Chronicler. The sordid details of David's domestic life do not concern him. Therefore, as well as missing out most of 2 Samuel 11—12, he omits all the material on the convulsions that rocked David's family, which are presented in 2 Samuel 13:1—23:7.

Under Joab's direction, the Ammonites are defeated, their city falls and the people are put to forced labour. David takes the crown, weighing a 'talent of gold', from the image of the Ammonite deity, Milcom (a name which means 'their king'). Now it is the turn of the

Ammonites to be humiliated as forced labourers, while their god Milcom also suffers the indignity of losing his precious crown.

Philistines

A brief report (vv. 4–8) recounts more conflict with the Philistines. It is another tale of daring deeds by some of David's fighters, similar to the material in 1 Chronicles 11. Attention is focused on the defeat of three particular Philistine champions. They are described as 'descendants of the Rephaim' or 'giants'. Deuteronomy 2:20–21 and 3:10–11 mention these Rephaim or giants who inhabited the land of Canaan. They were of great height and strength, and the six fingers and toes of the unnamed giant made him a formidable enemy.

It is worth comparing the note about Elhanan in verse 5 with the corresponding account in 2 Samuel 21:19. In the Samuel text, Elhanan, who is from Bethlehem, slays Goliath himself. In the Chronicles version, Elhanan slays Lahmi, the brother of Goliath. Did the Chronicler make the small changes in Hebrew that make Elhanan slay the brother of Goliath, because he knew the familiar story of David slaying the giant? Or did he preserve the original reading of the Samuel text, which has since been miscopied by a careless scribe? Some scholars are convinced that the Chronicler always made changes like this to suit his purpose, but others think that he sometimes preserves better readings of the text of Samuel. The Dead Sea Scroll fragments of the book of Samuel sometimes agree with the text of Chronicles over against that of Samuel. So perhaps the Chronicler was a more careful historian than we sometimes give him credit for.

REFLECTION

Do you think the Chronicler was right to miss out the sordid details of David's private life? Was he simply being 'economical with the truth', or is there a deeper theological reason for his choice of material?

CALLED *to* ACCOUNT

This chapter is a very significant one. It involves the one sinful act that King David commits in the book of Chronicles. The Chronicler has taken the story from 2 Samuel 24, but has made a number of modifications to it. He heightens its significance by linking it very explicitly with the purchase of the temple site in Jerusalem.

Counting the people

The first change in the story occurs right at the beginning of the chapter. In 2 Samuel 24, it is God who incites David to take the census, and then, rather perversely, punishes him for doing so. In the Chronicler's account, it is not God but Satan who is responsible.

Although the figure of Satan is a familiar one in the New Testament, there are only three references to the title 'the Satan' in the whole of the Old Testament. The term 'satan' means 'accuser'. In legal terms he is the prosecuting counsel, the one trying to get a conviction. This role is the exact opposite of the New Testament term for the Holy Spirit. In John's Gospel, the Spirit is called the 'paraclete' or 'comforter', the one who stands by us as our defending counsel in the heavenly court. While Satan works to get us convicted, the Spirit strives to get us acquitted.

The role of Satan as 'the accuser' is seen very clearly in the first two Old Testament texts. In Zechariah 3, the Satan seeks to bring a charge against the high priest, Joshua. In Job 1 and 2, the Satan accuses Job of self-interest and is permitted to put him to the test. Note, however, that in the Hebrew of these two texts the phrase used is *the* Satan. Here in Chronicles there is no definite article. It is not 'the Satan' but just 'Satan'. Some Bible commentators suggest that this means that instead of a title (the Satan) we now have a name (Satan), and that this shows how ideas about evil were developing in the post-exilic period. Certainly there were some developments in thinking between the Old Testament period and the New. Religious ideas do not stand still, even though a core of beliefs remains central. On the other hand, another suggestion is that without the definite article this is not a reference to a supernatural Satan at all. Rather it refers to 'a satan', that is, a human accuser or adversary.

Whichever suggestion is correct, the change is important theologically. Compared with the Samuel text, God is no longer the instigator of the sinful action. God is not the accuser, tempter or provoker. In the New Testament we find the saying, 'No one, when tempted, should say, "I am being tempted by God"; for God cannot be tempted by evil and he himself tempts no one' (James 1:13).

Joab is instructed to count all Israel 'from Beersheba to Dan' (vv. 2–6). This is the most common designation for the limits of Israel's territory. We are not told why Joab opposes the census, but he clearly considers it wrong. The census may have been taken for taxation purposes, or for military reasons, since verse 5 refers to arms-bearing soldiers. Perhaps by undertaking such military preparations David is ceasing to trust in the strength which God supplies. Perhaps it indicates a reliance on human effort rather than divine help.

Counting the cost

David had been warned not to take the census but failed to listen. For the Chronicler, the punishment that inevitably follows is justified by the wilful disobedience of those who, like David, fail to heed good advice.

We are now introduced to a new prophetic figure, the seer Gad (vv. 7–14). As punishment for taking the census, he gives David three unenviable choices—famine, sword or pestilence. The differing time scales of three years, three months or three days indicate the intensity of the punishment. It may be a prolonged difficult period, or it may be short and very intense. Similar imagery is used by the author of the book of Revelation. In Revelation 6:8, the last of the four horsemen of the Apocalypse is called Death, and he has authority to kill 'with sword, famine and pestilence'.

In the end, David chooses what he thinks will be the least worst option. He chooses neither natural disaster nor human agents of destruction, but opts for the sword of the angel of God. Nevertheless, the price to be paid is a high one. When the plague falls upon Israel, then 70,000 people die. When powerful kings sin, it is often the common people who pay the price. This is confirmed not only by the Bible witness, but both also by ancient and modern history.

REFLECTION

The punishment does seem out of proportion to the sin here.
Do you agree with the sentiments of the last paragraph above?

PAYING *the* PRICE

The cost in human misery of David's action in counting the people has been very great. Now David will be portrayed as truly penitent and ready to pay well over the odds to secure a piece of land, a site for the future temple in Jerusalem.

The threshing floor

This destroying angel in verses 15–21 is reminiscent of the 'Angel of Death' who appears in the story of the plagues in Exodus 12. In fact our present story contains many deliberate echoes of other biblical stories, especially those concerned with holy places and altars. Notice, for instance, the following 'connections':

* Abraham's purchase of the cave at Machpelah near Hebron as a burial plot in Genesis 23.

* Joshua and the angel with the drawn sword in Joshua 5:13–15.

* Gideon's meeting with the angel of the Lord at the wine press at Ophrah in Judges 6.

* Elijah and the fire sent down on the altar on Mount Carmel in 1 Kings 18.

In the equivalent story to this in 2 Samuel 24, the owner of the threshing floor is called Araunah. Here in Chronicles he is called Ornan. (Some translations smooth over the spelling difference and call him Araunah in Chronicles too.) He is a Jebusite, one of the native Canaanite population around the city of Jerusalem. The original Canaanite city of Jebus, which David captured, occupied a spur of land overlooking the Kidron valley. The threshing floor was some way farther north, and gradually the city expanded northwards. In present-day Jerusalem, the Dome of the Rock occupies the site of the threshing floor and is in the south-eastern corner of the walled Old City of Jerusalem. However, paradoxically, Jerusalem/Jebus, the original city of David, is now *outside* the city walls built by the Ottoman Sultan Suleiman in the sixteenth century.

The full amount

In 2 Samuel 24, David pays fifty shekels of silver for the plot of land. Here in Chronicles (vv. 22–27), it is six hundred shekels of gold. Since this is twelve times the amount, and a more precious metal, it is often linked with the theme of the twelve tribes of Israel. This is to be a place for all Israel, all twelve tribes, to worship. Ornan, no doubt aware of David's power, offers to give him the site. David refuses this and, like Abraham negotiating for the cave at Machpelah, he insists on paying the full price. He does not want to get this plot as a gift from its owner. Rather he insists, 'I will not offer to the Lord that which has cost me nothing.' There is a profound truth here. Genuine religion is not to be had 'on the cheap'. In the 1930s, the German theologian Dietrich Bonhoeffer deplored the fashion for preaching what he called 'cheap grace', that is, a religious life that really costs us nothing. Later, Bonhoeffer himself was to pay the ultimate price, executed by the Nazis in 1945.

A new site

With the purchase of the threshing floor, a major step has been taken in establishing the priority of Jerusalem (vv. 28–30; 22:1). The story of the angel hovering between heaven and earth helps to establish Jerusalem as the spot which God himself has chosen. The book of Chronicles is quite open propaganda for the Jerusalem temple and its clergy.

The Chronicler is convinced that there can be only one place in Israel to offer legitimate sacrifices. Although the ark is in Jerusalem, the tent of meeting and the altar for burnt offerings are still in Gibeon. By the sign granted at the threshing floor, it is clear that Gibeon's days as the central sanctuary for all Israel are numbered. Sacrifices will still be offered there for the time being, and Solomon will consult with God there in 2 Chronicles 1. Once the temple at Jerusalem is built, however, all the religious ceremonies will transfer to the new sanctuary. The sacred city of Gibeon will slide into obscurity, lost in the shadow of the new Jerusalem.

MEDITATION

Cheap grace is the preaching of forgiveness without requiring repentance, baptism without church discipline, communion without confession, absolution without personal confession. Cheap grace is grace without discipleship, grace without the cross.

The Cost of Discipleship, Dietrich Bonhoeffer (1905–1945)

BUILDING PLANS

For much of the story of David so far, the Chronicler has used and adapted material from 2 Samuel. For the rest of the story of David, from this chapter to the end of 1 Chronicles, there is no comparable material in 2 Samuel. This section is part of the distinctive portrait painted by the Chronicler. The next few chapters present David and Solomon working closely in harmony. The building of the temple becomes, in effect, a joint enterprise. David does the bulk of the preparatory work; Solomon is responsible for the actual execution of the building plans.

In many respects, Solomon stands in relation to David as Joshua did to Moses. In David's words to Solomon in verses 7–13, there are striking similarities with Deuteronomy 31. There Moses gives parting instructions to his lieutenant Joshua, as he hands over responsibility to the younger man. Again we can expect the Chronicler's readers to be alert to these similarities.

Preparations

Much of the preparatory work which the Chronicler attributes to David is credited to Solomon by the author of 1 Kings (ch. 5). The Chronicler, however, is eager to show the continuity between the reigns of David and Solomon. The policy of the one was also the policy of the other. In verse 2, there is mention of David gathering together the 'aliens', that is, non-Israelites who were resident in the land of Israel. The need for a cheap labour force perhaps partly explains the reason for organizing the fateful census of the previous chapter. Verse 4 mentions once again the Phoenician towns of Tyre and Sidon and their contribution of cedar wood for the temple structure. Solomon is portrayed as young and inexperienced and in need of wisdom and understanding. In his opening prayer in 2 Chronicles 1, these are the qualities the young king will pray for.

The charge to Solomon

In verse 8, the Chronicler spells out clearly the theological reason why David, great king though he was, could not build the temple. Like Saul, his reign was a turbulent one with many wars against the enemies of

Israel. The shedding of blood was thought to pollute the land, so that it was impossible for David as a man of war to build a sanctuary to God.

In Deuteronomy 12:10–11, God promises that when he has given the people rest from their enemies, then will be the time for the choice of a dwelling-place for his name. The reigns of Saul and David were not a time of rest, but that of Solomon will be. This is reflected by a play on words in verse 9: 'His name shall be Solomon, and I will give peace (*shalom*) and quiet to Israel in his days.' King Solomon ('Shlomo' in Hebrew) will be the king of *shalom*.

The father-son relationship between God and the king is now promised to Solomon in verse 10. Nevertheless, Solomon is not being promised a blank cheque. If he has privileges as the Lord's anointed, he also has responsibilities. He must carefully observe the Law of Moses and all the statutes and ordinances (v. 13). David may have provided a huge amount of raw material—gold, silver, bronze, iron, wood and stone—but Solomon must also add his own contribution (v. 14).

The charge to the people

It is made clear to the assembly that Solomon is the chosen successor to King David (vv. 17–19). The transition from David to Solomon will be a smooth one in Chronicles, unlike the messy affair in 1 Kings 1. In that earlier account, Solomon and his supporters vie for the throne against his half-brother Adonijah and his followers. Of this power struggle there is no hint at all in Chronicles. In 1 Kings, David's last years are blighted by feebleness and the infirmities of age. Here in Chronicles, David remains resolutely in charge in mind and body right to the very end.

By calling together the leaders, David is able to share his vision for the temple with them. This building project will not be the harebrained scheme of one man but will be a genuine community enterprise. Too many monarchs in past history, and too many dictators in recent times, have gone ahead with ruinous, expensive and extravagant building projects in order to enhance their own reputations. When the temple is built, it must be for the honour of the name of the Lord, and all the people must give their backing and support.

REFLECTION

How do you discern whether a new project in your church is truly 'of God' rather than someone's 'pet' project?

The LEVITES

Chapters 23—27 describe the way in which David organized the religious and secular institutions of the kingdom. They deal in turn with the ordinary Levites (ch. 23), the priests (ch. 24), the singers (ch. 25), the gatekeepers (ch. 26) and the secular officials (ch. 27).

Assembly

David calls together the secular leaders of Israel, the priests and the Levites. The latter are differentiated into ordinary Levites (24,000), officers and judges (6,000), gatekeepers (4,000) and singers (4,000).

The Levites are counted from thirty years and upwards (v. 3). It was from the age of thirty that priests and Levites took up their religious responsibilities, according to Numbers 4. Similarly, the New Testament portrays Jesus as about thirty years old when he begins his public ministry (Luke 3:23). The letter to the Hebrews explores the idea of Jesus as our great high priest. Note, however, that verses 24 and 27 refer to twenty years, not thirty.

Gershon, Kohath, Merari

The family lines of the three sons of Levi are now given (vv. 7–23): ten lines for the family of Gershon, nine lines for Kohath and five for Merari.

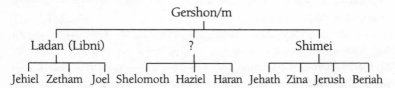

There is a problem over the middle group of three names. According to the opening of verse 9, they are sons of Shimei. However, at the end of the verse they are reckoned as belonging to Ladan, and the names of Shimei's sons are given in verse 10. It is probably best to include them as sons of Ladan. Elsewhere, Gershon is spelled Gershom, and his eldest son is called Libni rather than Ladan (1 Chronicles 6:17).

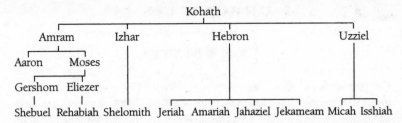

The next chapter will trace the priestly line of Aaron. His brother Moses is not a priest and so the lines of Moses' descendants are to be reckoned among the Levites (vv. 13–14).

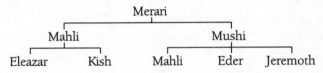

Thus it is possible to count twenty-four levitical houses, 10+9+5. These correspond to the 24,000 'ordinary Levites' of verse 4. However, verses 11 and 22 indicate that the exact counting of these lines was problematic, reducing the numbers to 23 or 22 houses.

The Levites' duties

By the end of David's reign, the land finally had 'rest'. The ark of the covenant had also come to rest and God now resided in Jerusalem for ever (v. 25). The Levites' former task of carrying the ark was now at an end (v. 26). New duties, new responsibilities, have to be found within the temple complex. Some will serve as gatekeepers (v. 28), some as ordinary Levites assisting the priests (v. 29), and others as singers and musicians (v. 30). In this way both the seasonal festivals and the daily offerings may be observed (v. 31).

Religious systems and structures do not stand still. The past twenty or thirty years have seen great changes in church orders as each denomination has sought to adapt to new times. Clergy and laity will have to adjust accordingly in this new millennium. New times mean new duties. The Chronicler was wise enough to realize that—let us pray that our church leaders and congregations will realize it too.

PRAYER

Pray for the individuals who lead the churches and for the assemblies, synods and conferences which make policy decisions.

The PRIESTS

The previous chapter outlined the twenty-four levitical divisions, though we saw that the exact counting of them was not straight-forward. Chapter 24 presents the priestly divisions that were familiar to the Chronicler. Here, too, there was undoubtedly a period of some fluidity before arriving at the final figure of twenty-four.

Aaron's family

The previous chapter concentrated on the non-priestly Levites. The present one focuses on that branch of the family of Levi that was descended from Aaron and claimed the privileges of priesthood. Aaron himself was the son of Amram, the son of Kohath, the son of Levi.

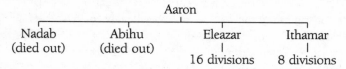

The death of the two oldest sons is recounted in Numbers 3:1–4. One possible way of understanding that story is that it represents the extinction of some older priestly lines and their replacement by younger ones. The Chronicler links the names of the two senior priests of David's time with each of the surviving lines. Zadok takes priority and his name is linked to the elder and more numerous group of Eleazar. Ahimelech's line is traced to the younger son, Ithamar.

By the time of the Chronicler, the priesthood had been divided into its twenty-four divisions and he is keen to show that this has its origins in the time of David. In the priestly list contained in Nehemiah 12, twenty-two names are given. That list probably comes from the century before Chronicles. It is therefore likely that the lists in this chapter reflect the final development of the priestly houses. These twenty-four divisions were to continue right up to the destruction of the temple by the Romans in AD70.

The twenty-four divisions

How the twenty-four priestly houses were divided by lot is not explained (vv. 7–19). With twenty-four divisions, sixteen for Eleazar and eight for Ithamar, it could be done in two ways. The first would entail one division from Eleazar and one from Ithamar in turn up to number 16, then numbers 17 to 24 from Eleazar. The second would entail two divisions from Eleazar followed by one from Ithamar. Whichever way it was done, the implication of this chapter is that all the divisions were of equal standing (v. 5).

The first book of Maccabees in the Apocrypha mentions the division of Jehoiarib. 1 Maccabees 2 tells the story of how a priest of this division, called Mattathias, began the rebellion against Greek culture. This war of independence, begun in 167BC, was led by his sons, including the most famous of them all, Judas Maccabeus. The division of Abijah is mentioned in the New Testament. Zechariah, John the Baptist's father, was of this family (Luke 1:5). The first chapter of Luke gives a vivid picture of how the priestly divisions operated. There was a rota system, with each of the divisions serving in turn. While Zechariah's section was on duty at the temple, he was chosen by lot to go in and burn incense. An angel appeared to him and announced the birth of his son. When his period on duty was over, he left Jerusalem and returned to his village. In the story of the good Samaritan, we should perhaps imagine the priest and the Levite coming up to Jerusalem to fulfil their duties on the temple rota.

The rest of the Levites

The information in verses 20–31 repeats that given in the previous chapter, though there are some differences. Most noticeable is the fact that the line of Gershon or Gershom has dropped out—probably as a result of faulty copying of the lists. Secondly, changes seem to have been made to the Merari family line in verses 26–27. Eleazar the son of Mahli, whose position was in jeopardy in chapter 23, has been downgraded, and in comes a new son of Merari called Jaaziah and his family. Thirdly, in some instances the genealogies have been extended by one generation. It is possible, therefore, that this section is a slightly later addition to the book of Chronicles which brings the situation up to date, a generation later than the time of the Chronicler himself.

REFLECTION

Consider the role of the priests in ancient Israel's religion. What was their function? Why does the letter to the Hebrews use the image of Christ as our supreme priest?

The SINGERS

Following the description of the Levites and priests, we are introduced to the temple singers or musicians. They too are divided into twenty-four sections. However, although the priests were on duty for two weeks at a time, we do not know how the rota for the musicians was organized. Perhaps their duties would vary according to the religious calendar and they would be called on to perform extra duties during the great festivals, just as church or cathedral choirs are today. 1 Chronicles 6 gave the names of the three guilds of singers. They are named after Asaph, Heman and Jeduthun/Ethan. In that chapter, each of their family lines was traced back through the younger sons of the three main levitical groups:

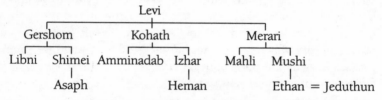

The singers' families

The Chronicler clearly placed a high value on the role and work of the guilds of singers. He describes their task as to 'prophesy' (v. 1), and Heman is further designated as 'the king's seer' (v. 5). The link between music and prophecy is actually very old. In Exodus 15: 20–21, Miriam sings a song to the accompaniment of a tambourine. The song celebrates the deliverance of the Israelites at the Red Sea, and Miriam is called 'the prophetess'. Furthermore, in 1 Samuel 10, we have one of the earliest Old Testament descriptions of a band of prophets. They meet Saul and he falls into a prophetic trance as the music of their harp, tambourine, flute and lyre swirls around him. In 2 Kings 3:15, the prophet Elisha asks for a musician in order to be able to prophesy.

By the time of the Chronicler, writing in about 350BC, the phenomenon of prophecy had virtually ended. Prophecy was believed to have come to an end with the books of Haggai, Zechariah and Malachi. For the Chronicler, the temple musicians were the successors to the prophets. Music and singing were often seen as inspired by God's Spirit. So now, in place of the spontaneous, charismatic phenomenon of prophecy, the Chronicler sees God's Spirit at work in the more formal and regulated manner of the temple choirs and musicians.

The twenty-four divisions

The singers are made up of the familiar twenty-four divisions, each with twelve people, making a total of 288 (v. 7). The groups include both teachers and pupils (v. 8), so there must have been a training programme, a school of temple music which handed on the sacred traditions. Unlike the other lists of the Levites, priests and gatekeepers, the Chronicler gives both the family lines and the order of the divisions of the singers. They are organized as follows:

- Asaph—four lines—division numbers 1, 3, 5, 7

- Jeduthun—six lines—division numbers 2, 4, 8, 10, 12, 14

- Heman—fourteen lines—division numbers 6, 9, 11, 13, 15–24

Two points emerge from this. The line of Asaph seems to have priority, even though it is the smallest of the groups. On the other hand, the line of Heman is the one most abundantly blessed by God, having fourteen of the twenty-four lines. Perhaps this reflects the steadily growing influence of the Heman group.

We do not know exactly how the psalms were sung in the temple, or how the musicians accompanied them. In the book of Psalms, some of the headings attribute authorship of certain psalms to Asaph, Heman and Jeduthun/Ethan. No doubt particular ones were sung at each of the special festivals in the temple. So, for instance, we know that Psalms 113—118 were sung at Passover in the time of Jesus, and 121—134 were associated with the feast of Tabernacles in the autumn. The Jewish law book known as the Mishnah, which was edited around AD200, suggests that of the twelve musicians in each group, nine played lyres, two harps and one the cymbal. We can be sure that music held a significant place in worship, from the temple's beginnings under David through to its last years in the first century AD.

PRAYER

Pray by name for musicians and singers you know, asking that their ministry may be blessed by God.

The GATEKEEPERS

The list of the various levitical duties ends with the gatekeepers (vv. 1–19) and finally other administrative officials (vv. 20–32).

The gatekeepers' families

The gatekeepers are divided into three families (vv. 1–11). The first is that of Meshelemiah, belonging to the sons of Korah and comprising eighteen family members in total (v. 9). A significant group of psalms has the heading 'of the sons of Korah' (Psalms 42—49; 84—89). So perhaps the Korahites once belonged among the temple singers. If so, they may have fallen on hard times and been 'relegated' to the position of gatekeepers. Nevertheless, it is in one of these psalms that we find the lines, 'I would rather be a doorkeeper in the house of my God than live in the tents of wickedness' (Psalm 84:10).

Second comes Obed-edom, whose story we encountered in 1 Chronicles 13, 15 and 16. Although not explicitly stated, it is probable that he too is to be seen as belonging to the sons of Korah. His is the largest contingent of gatekeepers, with sixty-two members (v. 8).

Third comes Hosah of the sons of Merari, whose numbers total thirteen (v. 11).

Once more, there seems to be an attempt to construct twenty-four divisions by counting the sons and some grandsons of these three family groups. Meshelemiah has seven sons (v. 3), Hosah has four (v. 11). Obed-edom has eight sons and six grandsons, through his eldest son Shemaiah. If Shemaiah's sons are counted in his place, we get thirteen (8 minus 1, plus 6), and 7 plus 4 plus 13 gives us twenty-four divisions.

Gatekeepers' duties

While there are three families of gatekeepers, there are four sides of the temple precincts to watch (vv. 12–19). Meshelemiah, as the senior family, gets a 'double portion'. It watches over the east side, which was the most prestigious position, and the eldest son, Zechariah, watches over the north. Meanwhile, Obed-edom gets the south end and Hosah the west. The gatekeepers would be responsible for maintaining good order within the temple—which was not always easy. A number of stories in the New Testament show how difficult temple security could be, with Jesus overturning the money-changers' tables in Mark 11:15–19, and Paul being almost lynched by a mob in Acts 21.

Verses 17–18 give details of the various positions at which the gatekeepers were situated. Unfortunately many of the details remain obscure to us, but it looks again as if a system of twenty-four different 'stations' for the gatekeepers has been followed.

Officers and judges

In the introduction to the lists in chapter 23, the Chronicler mentioned among the subgroups of Levites not only singers and gatekeepers but also 'officers and judges'. These other roles are now explained and can be roughly divided between the tasks of temple treasurers (vv. 20–28) and those of administrative officials who worked away from Jerusalem (vv. 29–32).

While verses 20–21 mention some of the Gershonite families responsible for the temple treasuries, the main interest seems to be on the four Kohathite families mentioned in verse 23.

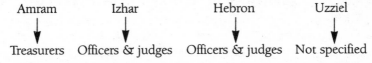

Amram	Izhar	Hebron	Uzziel
↓	↓	↓	↓
Treasurers	Officers & judges	Officers & judges	Not specified

Amram was the father of Moses, and it would appear that the descendants of Moses had a particular flair for the keeping of the temple accounts. As often in Chronicles, a distinction is made between the area to the west of the Jordan and that to the east. The Hebron line of officers and judges is divided between the two administrative parts of the kingdom. It would seem, then, that some Levites were involved in duties well away from the Jerusalem temple. Perhaps they involved collecting taxes or otherwise assisting with the royal bureaucracy. However, the details are extremely sketchy.

PRAYER

Pray by name for those people who welcome people at the church door on Sundays, and for your church secretary and treasurer. Consider the significance of their ministries.

COURT OFFICIALS

The list of David's arrangements ends with details of the non-religious appointments made by the king. David is shown to preside over a well-run, efficient system of government. It provides protection for the people through the conscript army and ensures favourable economic progress.

Military commanders

In ancient Israel, there was no such thing as a large-scale professional army. Some groups, such as the 'Thirty' or the Pelethites and Cherethites, who formed David's personal bodyguard, were undoubtedly organized, professional and paid. For the most part, however, men would be called up to fight on a much more irregular basis.

With no regular standing army, a system of conscription was set up, whereby 24,000 men were set apart for each month under a commander. Whether we should envisage them as on active service for that month, or merely on standby in case of emergency, is not clear.

The names of the commanders in verses 1–15 are taken from the list of the valiant warriors in chapter 11. Additional information is given about the ancestry and geographical origins of some of the commanders. Genesis 38 tells the story of the birth of Perez (v. 3), the son of Judah, while Judges 3:7–11 recounts the exploits of the hero Othniel (v. 15). Asahel, the brother of Joab, is mentioned in verse 7, but he was killed early in David's reign, as told in 2 Samuel 2. The name of his son is therefore given as his successor. The village of Tekoa (v. 9) was the birthplace of the prophet Amos (Amos 1:1), while Anathoth (v. 12) was the home of the prophet Jeremiah (Jeremiah 1:1).

Other officials

Virtually all the information in verses 16–34 is exclusive to the book of Chronicles. Since Chronicles was not written until six hundred years after the time of David, there seem to be only two options regarding these lists. Either the Chronicler composed them himself, and they are a pure literary invention, or they contain genuine information from old archives preserved in Jerusalem. Although six hundred years is a long time, it is possible that some material was preserved. The system described by the Chronicler was certainly not in operation in his own day, when the Persians ruled Judah. Therefore, it cannot be a reading back of the situation in his own day.

Verses 16–22 give the names of the leaders of the tribal groups. There are a number of peculiarities about this list. Not surprisingly, the Chronicler includes a separate leader, the priest Zadok, for the sons of Aaron. There is also a named leader for the remainder of the Levites. The Joseph tribes are divided into three—Ephraim, West Manasseh and East Manasseh. However, the tribes of Gad and Asher are left out. Was this by accident, through careless copying? Or was it in order to retain the number of the tribes at twelve?

Verses 23–24 give a brief summary of the notorious census episode recounted in chapter 21. However, the summary here is a little different, in that everything is done to absolve David from responsibility and to put the blame on Joab. David, in line with the census in Numbers 1, only counts those over the age of 20. It is when Joab extends the count to the under-20s that the Lord's anger is roused. In the account in chapter 21, it was Joab who was reluctant to count the people at all. This little section seems intent on exonerating David from all blame.

Verses 25–31 give details of the economic administration of David's reign. Not surprisingly, twelve officials are named—two treasurers, five overseers for the agricultural produce, and five overseers of the herds and flocks. The antiquity of these lists appears to be confirmed by the inclusion of two non-Israelites among them. Obil, a descendant of Ishmael, and Jaziz, a descendant of Hagar (v. 30), are both of Arab descent. In the post-exilic world of Judaism, such foreign names would scarcely be invented.

Finally, verses 32–34 include details of some of David's closest counsellors. Jonathan (v. 32) is not to be confused with the son of Saul, or with the nephew of David mentioned in 20:7. It seems that even in those far-off days there was a tutor for the royal children, in the person of Jehiel (v. 32). 2 Samuel 16—17 tells the story of Ahithophel, who defected to the rebellious Absolom, along with the account of how Hushai undermined his good advice and so proved himself David's 'friend'.

REFLECTION

If these lists bore you to tears, try to imagine creatively the personal stories behind each name. Remember, God knows each one by name.

DAVID'S FINAL SPEECH

The opening verse of this chapter links in very neatly with the previous one. There we were given the names of the great and the good in David's kingdom. Now he gathers together the leaders of all Israel for a final assembly. In many ways, the material in his speech is very similar to that in chapter 22. However, the context is different. The earlier chapter depicted a private occasion between David and his son Solomon. In contrast, this address is given a public setting.

There is a vivid contrast between the last days of David in Chronicles and the description in 1 Kings 1. The Chronicler depicts David rising to his feet to address the assembly in verse 2. There is no hint here of the enfeebled, bedridden David, manipulated by the court intrigue swirling around him, which we find in Kings. David remains in control and the accession of Solomon is publicly announced as the will of God and not the result of political manoeuvring.

David's words to the people

The speech in verses 2–8 repeats many of the fundamental themes of the book of Chronicles. If there is not much that is new, perhaps it is because the Chronicler appreciates how important it is to reinforce the message to his hearers. In verse 2, the theme of 'rest' comes to the fore once again. God has given rest to his people, and now the ark of the covenant will find rest at the temple. The ark is described as 'the footstool of our God', a notion that is also found in Psalm 132:7. Indeed the Chronicler will quote from this psalm at Solomon's dedication of the temple (2 Chronicles 6).

Verse 3 repeats the idea that David, as a 'man of blood', cannot build the temple. The following verses, however, emphasize more clearly than ever before the belief in the divine election of David and his line to be kings over Israel. In the story related in Joshua 7, a guilty culprit is identified by the process of casting lots. First the tribe is identified, then the clan, the family, and finally the individual. Here, God's positive choice is likewise narrowed down: first the tribe of Judah, then the family of Jesse, then David, and finally Solomon of all David's sons. Despite this glowing presentation, there are words of warning. The promise is conditional—'...if he continues resolute in keeping my commandments and my ordinances, as he is today' (v. 7). God does not offer a blank cheque to the line of David.

Verse 8 makes it clear that the people too have a responsibility to observe all the commandments. For the Chronicler, David's words are not spoken simply to that one assembly. They are words for every generation to take to heart. David's speech is, in effect, a sermon for all succeeding generations, since the Chronicler firmly believed that each new generation had to learn to be obedient. It could not simply depend on the faith of a previous generation. This theme will be prominent in the story in 2 Chronicles.

David's words to Solomon

Turning publicly to Solomon, David addresses his son with words of advice and exhortation (vv. 9–10). His message is a catalogue of themes dear to the Chronicler's heart. If he is to rule wisely, then Solomon must observe the following instructions.

- Know God: a personal relationship with the Lord is essential.

- Serve wholeheartedly: there is to be no lukewarm attitude or grudging service.

- Seek him: observe the commandments for living that God has supplied.

- Do not forsake (by turning aside to other pagan deities): the results will be disastrous.

- Be strong and act: put this programme into operation—have the courage to act boldly.

The Chronicler applies these criteria to all Solomon's successors. Some will win his approval, but many more will fail the test.

The phrase in verse 9 that God 'understands every plan and thought' is an echo of Genesis 6:5. Indeed, the language employed in this address is filled with echoes from elsewhere in the Old Testament. The Chronicler knew the sacred scriptures and expected his readers to catch the allusions.

MEDITATION

Each generation must learn the truth for itself. We cannot depend on the faith of our fathers and mothers to sustain us for ever.

The TEMPLE PLANS

The book of Chronicles depicts David handing over detailed plans to Solomon. This is no rough sketch, but clear and precise instructions for the building programme. Two other places in the Old Testament give detailed descriptions of preparations for building. In Exodus, meticulous details are given for the construction of the tabernacle to be built by the Israelites for the desert wanderings. Moses is shown a plan of the work in Exodus 25—31, and Exodus 35—40 repeats the details of the construction. Secondly, in Ezekiel 40—44, the prophet is given a vision of the restored temple and told to write it down (Ezekiel 43:11). So here in Chronicles, the idea of a divine plan for the temple resonates with the Exodus episode, and the idea of its being put into writing is paralleled in Ezekiel. The Chronicler gives an overall account here of the preparation David made, and then in 2 Chronicles 3—4 he gives a more detailed account of the execution of the design.

Temple architecture

Verses 11–13 give details of the various parts of the temple complex. Worshippers entered the temple by stairs leading into a vestibule or porch. Beyond that was the heart of the temple buildings. First was the Holy Place, which only the priests could enter. Then came the Most Holy Place or Holy of Holies. This could only be entered by the high priest on the Day of Atonement, and then only after proper preparation. Attached to the temple buildings were the ancillary rooms for storage, administration and the temple treasuries. Around the buildings were the open temple courts, where lay-Israelites gathered for their worship. This pattern was to be followed for the second temple, built after the exile and dedicated in 515BC. It was the second temple that was standing in the days of the Chronicler. Finally, this second temple complex was magnificently rebuilt by Herod the Great. Work started on this project in 19BC and was still in progress during the ministry of Jesus (see John 2:20). Though much more magnificent, Herod's temple still followed the outline plan of Solomon's project. For a diagram of the temple complex, see the notes on 2 Chronicles 3.

Gold and silver

Within the Holy Place, there were three important objects.

- The gold lampstand or *menorah* (v. 15). This seven-branched candle-stick is still used as a symbol among the Jewish people today.

- The table for the shewbread or 'bread of the presence' (v. 16). The twelve loaves of bread represented the twelve tribes of Israel.

- The altar of incense (v. 18).

It was the task of the priests to keep the lampstand burning, to change the loaves on the table regularly, and to offer incense on the altar. This third duty is what John the Baptist's father, Zechariah, was doing when the angel appeared to him in Luke 1:8–11.

Inside the Holy of Holies there was, in Solomon's temple, the sacred ark of the covenant. This was a box that contained the tablets of stone given to Moses by God on Mount Sinai. The lid of the ark was known as the mercy seat (that is, the place of forgiveness, atonement or cover-ing) (v. 11) and two golden cherubim overshadowed it with their wings (v. 18). Elsewhere in the Old Testament, God is described as 'enthroned upon the cherubim' (Psalms 80:1; 99:1), and Ezekiel 1 pictures these cherubim as part of a mobile throne-chariot. God sits enthroned in the Jerusalem temple, but is not confined there. This aspect will come out clearly in Solomon's prayer of dedication in 2 Chronicles 6.

A united enterprise

As Moses had handed over responsibility to Joshua, so now the aged David hands over to the young man Solomon (vv. 20–21). Everything is in place and David speaks words of encouragement to his son. All the priests, Levites and officers, whose names were meticulously given in chapters 23—27, are there in support. So too are the skilled crafts-men and indeed all the people. Once more, the Chronicler emphasizes that the enterprise of temple building has the full support of the whole nation. It is not for the personal aggrandisement of the king but is to be a genuine community enterprise.

REFLECTION

How far have the ideas of temple architecture affected the way Christian churches have been built? Does your church have a 'Holy of Holies' and how is this understood?

THANK OFFERINGS

David's words to the assembly continue as he exhorts and encourages them to give generously. No doubt, too, the Chronicler hoped that this message of generous giving to the temple project would not be lost on his own audience. Once a building has been erected, it takes considerable amounts of money to maintain it. The Bible writers are not unaware of these issues, which loom so large in the debate about the upkeep of church buildings today—particularly historic ones. Keeping ancient sacred buildings in good repair is not just a modern problem.

David's generosity

In verses 1–5, David outlines the measures that he has already taken to provide for the temple. As well as the resources available from the royal revenues, David will add to it a gift from his own personal treasure (v. 3). We are reminded of his words when he purchased the plot for the temple from its original Jebusite owner in chapter 21. He will not offer to God that which does not cost him personally. It is all too easy to be generous with other people's money, but David digs into his own private fortune. Whereas the previous chapter emphasized the provision of gold and silver, this passage highlights that the enterprise involved far more. Other less precious metals, wood, gemstones and marble are all provided for the Lord's house.

David the preacher knows how to tug at the heartstrings of the people. The task is great, and Solomon is young and inexperienced. The lad will need their help if the project is to be completed. In verse 5, the old king therefore asks the people to 'consecrate themselves' for the undertaking. This is a strong term, used elsewhere only of priests set apart for sacred duties. While standing firm in his emphasis on the separateness of priesthood, this is the nearest the Chronicler comes to a doctrine of the priesthood of all believers. It is in line with the promise to Israel that 'you shall be for me a priestly kingdom and a holy nation' (Exodus 19:6).

The people's response

The people do not need coaxing or chivvying along. Instead they respond enthusiastically with their freewill offerings (vv. 6–9). Huge quantities of material are provided, which are measured in the standard biblical measure of the 'talent'. Although all weights and measures in the Old Testament must be approximate, a talent is generally thought to be the equivalent of 30kg. Verse 7 mentions 'ten thousand darics of gold'. The daric was a Persian coin that was not minted until the reign of Darius 1 (522–486BC), after whom it was named. The Chronicler is therefore using the terminology familiar to his contemporaries. In the same way, modern translations convert the talents, shekels and minas of the Bible into metric measurements. There is a stress here on the joy of giving, which is typical of Chronicles. In a later period, Paul will encourage the church in Corinth to be open-handed and generous, 'for God loves a cheerful giver' (2 Corinthians 9:7).

Doxology

In verses 10–13, David utters a prayer of praise in which he extols the incomparable goodness of God. He piles up a string of words to portray the grandeur of the Lord in verse 11. These words of David, together with the second half of verse 14, are often used in churches at the dedication of monetary gifts or of the offertory at the eucharist. They are fitting words, for they emphasize that God is the ultimate source of all goodness. In the end, as the words of the hymn put it, 'we give thee but thine own, whate'er the gift may be'.

PRAYER

Use verses 11–13 as a prayer and then add your own special thanksgiving for God's goodness and mercy.

DAVID'S FAREWELL

1 Chronicles draws to a close at a very significant moment. It is the hinge point between the reigns of David and of Solomon. Together, these two reigns represent the ideal of a united monarchy ruling over all Israel. The transition between the rule of father and son is smooth. Solomon is publicly seated on the throne of the kingdom before his father dies peacefully and 'full of years'.

David's last prayer

The theme of David's prayer now changes. In the earlier part, he had spoken of the incomparable greatness of God. Now, in verses 14–19, his thoughts turn to the place of humankind. In services of worship, prayers of adoration often lead into prayers of confession as we acknowledge our failings in the sight of God. So David asks, 'Who am I, and what is my people?' His prayer therefore turns to petition. Verse 15 is a reminder of the fragile and transitory nature of human life. No doubt the words would ring true for the Chronicler's audience in the often depressing days of the post-exilic period. Despite this, however, verses 16–17 remind God of what the people have achieved, and it is no mean achievement. With upright hearts and generous hands they have shown themselves willing to glorify God. Solomon will need the same single-mindedness of purpose if the great enterprise is to be completed. So David's prayer ends with a fervent petition for Solomon's welfare and continuing obedience to the Lord (v. 19).

Solomon's coronation

At last Solomon is publicly crowned king (vv. 20–25). The ceremonies associated with the event are extremely lavish, with an abundance of sacrifices. The sacrifices would have included not only whole burnt offerings to God but also peace offerings. Parts of these offerings were burnt on the altar, but the bulk of them was made available to provide food for celebrations. So the feasting in verse 22 is part of the religious ceremonial. As usual, the emphasis on joy and festivity in worship is to the fore of the Chronicler's presentation.

Along with the anointing of Solomon, the Chronicler also records the anointing of Zadok, presumably not just as priest but as high priest. The legitimacy of the lines of Solomon the king and Zadok the priest are thus confirmed, side by side. In the post-exilic period, nearer to the Chronicler's own time, there would be further examples of this sharing of leadership in the community. The rebuilding of the temple in 515BC is achieved thanks to the joint effort of Zerubbabel the prince and Joshua the high priest. In the following century, the reform of life in Jerusalem is championed by the layman Nehemiah and the priest Ezra. Perhaps it is not surprising, therefore, that the community who wrote the Dead Sea Scrolls should look forward to two Messiahs or Anointed Ones: one royal—the Messiah of David— and one priestly—the Messiah of Aaron.

The harmony at this coronation is emphasized in verse 24. All the significant leaders, and particularly all the rest of David's sons, acknowledge Solomon as the rightful king. There is no hint here of the struggle for the throne depicted in 1 Kings 1. There Adonijah is a powerful rival for the throne, supported by Joab the warrior and Abiathar the priest. Solomon's faction, led by his mother Bathsheba, included Nathan the prophet and Zadok the priest.

Forty glorious years

A final summary is given of David's life in verses 26–30. A distinction is made between the seven years' reign over all Israel in Hebron and the thirty-three years in Jerusalem. David's peaceful death at the end of a long and prosperous life is similar to the epitaphs we find for characters such as Abraham, Isaac, Moses and Job.

The Chronicler refers to other sources of information for the reign of David. The prophets Samuel, Nathan and Gad were active in David's time and have entered the Chronicler's story. Whether any of these records or chronicles are the same as our 1 and 2 Samuel is impossible to tell. The Chronicler's readers would be aware that there were other versions available of the story of David. The Chronicler, however, is sure that he has been faithful in his retelling of the story of Israel's great king.

PRAYER

We give you thanks, O God, for the life of your servant David.
May we learn from his story and follow him in his devotion to you.
Amen

A PORTRAIT *of* DAVID

The picture that the Chronicler paints of David is a very distinctive one. While it contains much material in common with the story in 1 and 2 Samuel, it nevertheless gives a decidedly new presentation. Sometimes it omits things, and sometimes it adds greater detail. Like all great works of art, it will not be to everyone's taste. After all, not everyone appreciates the work of the Impressionists or of Picasso!

In 1885, a German scholar called Julius Wellhausen made this rather sour comment about the representation of David in 1 Chronicles.

See what Chronicles has made out of David! The founder of the kingdom
has become the founder of the Temple and public worship, the king and
hero at the head of his companions in arms has become the singer and
master of ceremonies at the head of a swarm of priests and Levites; his
clearly cut figure has become a holy picture, seen through a cloud of incense.

Perhaps that tells us as much about the author Wellhausen as it does about the Chronicler. He was a German Lutheran theologian with a clear dislike of anything to do with priests! Nevertheless, it is a comment that may well find sympathy among many readers of Chronicles today. Is the Chronicler's portrait a true likeness of David, or is it a dangerous distortion?

Perhaps it is important to realize that what the Chronicler has produced is a portrait. It is an artist's impression and not a photograph. The two are quite different things. Furthermore, every genuine artist and author will put something of themselves into their work. They will seek to bring out the things that they consider significant and which they wish their viewers or readers to see.

There is a famous story of Oliver Cromwell sitting to have his portrait painted. He is reputed to have told the artist not to flatter him but to paint him 'warts and all'. It can hardly be said that the Chronicler has painted David in this way. Compared to 1 and 2 Samuel, all the warts seem to have been painted out! Indeed, any film maker having to choose between the story of David in Samuel or in Chronicles would be unlikely to choose the latter. It misses out most of the things interesting to a modern audience—all the sex and most of the violence! It could be argued that the portrait of David has become bland, idealized, too good to be true.

These criticisms will only hold if we assume that ancient historians like the Chronicler were trying to produce realistic 'photographs' rather than evocative 'portraits'. Instead we ought to accept that the David of 1 Chronicles is a portrait. It is not the only portrait of David that could be painted, but it is a legitimate one. The Chronicler has chosen to work with a limited number of colours on his palette. He has produced this work of art for a new generation of readers, living in a very different situation from that of the first readers of 1 and 2 Samuel. Here is a new portrait for a new age; one that highlights those things which the Chronicler considers most important for his readers. The monarchy is gone, its restoration only a dream; but the temple remains, with its priests, Levites, singers and gatekeepers. This part of David's work has endured down to the fourth century BC when the Chronicler is writing. He focuses on those things, therefore, which will help his contemporaries to feel 'in touch' with the life of David. He wishes to demonstrate that the faithfulness and dedication of David were crowned with God's blessing. Here are lessons for every generation to learn, not only the original readers of Chronicles. If sometimes he provides additional information on David's life from other sources or archives, that is a bonus for us readers today. It was hardly his main concern, and we should learn to appreciate the artistry with which the author of Chronicles has worked to produce his 'new portrait' of an 'old master'.

REFLECTION

Try to get hold of a portrait of David,
for example, Michelangelo's famous sculpture of the young David.
Study it and ask yourself:

What is the artist trying to portray?
What is the aspect of the character that is most prominent?
What can you learn about the artist from the picture?

WISDOM & WEALTH

The first nine chapters of 2 Chronicles are concerned with the reign of Solomon. The Chronicler stresses the unity between the reigns of David and Solomon. There is no hint of the struggle for the throne described in 1 Kings 1—2. Nor will the Chronicler offer any of the criticisms of Solomon's foreign wives that are found in 1 Kings 11.

To Gibeon

Gibeon was a city five or six miles north of Jerusalem in the territory of Benjamin (vv. 2–6). In the version of the story in 1 Kings 3, Solomon visits Gibeon alone. In Chronicles, he is accompanied by representatives of all Israel. This is not a private affair but a very public occasion. Solomon goes there because it is the site of the tent of meeting and the bronze altar—the place to receive communication from God, through dreams or oracles. Until the temple is built, Gibeon will continue to be the home of the tent of meeting and the place for offering sacrifice to the Lord. The ark at Jerusalem is served by the temple musicians. Only a service of song, not of sacrifice, takes place there as yet. Once the temple is built, sacrificial worship will transfer to Jerusalem and will cease at Gibeon. Thus the Chronicler explains to his audience how Solomon could legitimately offer sacrifice at Gibeon when his hearers knew that, for them, only Jerusalem was a proper place to offer sacrifices.

The bronze altar made by Bezalel is described in Exodus 38. The craftsmanship of Bezalel, along with that of his assistant Oholiab (Exodus 31:6), had become justly famous. Soon the Chronicler will describe the artistic work of those who were to furnish the Jerusalem temple with its own array of beautiful objects.

The wisdom of Solomon

At Gibeon, Solomon is offered his heart's desire (vv. 7–13). Anything he chooses can be his, rather like those stories in the *Arabian Nights* in which the genie offers to make Aladdin's every wish come true. The temptation to ask for personal gain, whether of money, power or pleasure, must be very great. Solomon resists the temptation and, conscious of his responsibilities as monarch of all Israel, asks for the gift of wisdom and understanding. We may be reminded of the words of Jesus, 'Seek ye first the kingdom of God and his righteousness and all these things shall be added unto you' (Matthew 6:33, KJV). This passage from the Sermon on the Mount follows on from the description of 'Solomon in all his glory' (Matthew 6:29), so this chapter on Solomon was clearly in the mind of Jesus as he gave his teaching.

Solomon was regarded as the patron of wisdom, as his father David had been the patron of psalm-writing. No less than three 'Wisdom' books in the Old Testament are credited to Solomon—Song of Songs, Proverbs and Ecclesiastes. The rabbis taught that he wrote Song of Songs as a young man, Proverbs in middle age, and Ecclesiastes in his last years. Among the books of the Apocrypha, a further work, called the Wisdom of Solomon, was attributed to him.

Imports and exports

Solomon presided over an unprecedented time of peace and pros- perity for Israel (vv. 14–17). Considerable building programmes were begun, not only in Jerusalem but throughout the land. In particular, the cities where the chariot troops were stationed gave visible expres- sion to a sense of 'national security'. For the first time, chariots became an important part of the professional army. In the time of Saul and David, such things were unknown. When David captured quantities of chariots, he hamstrung most of the horses (1 Chronicles 18:4).

With an exuberant flourish, the Chronicler depicts gold and silver as being as common as stone, and beautiful cedar wood as common as ordinary sycamore (v. 15). This sycamore, like the one that Zacchaeus climbed in Luke 19, was a common type of fig (*ficus sycomoros*). We should not confuse it with the tall sycamore tree of more northerly climes. A lucrative export and import trade created a thriving economy. Chariots and horses were imported from Egypt and from Kue. This latter is probably Cilicia in south-eastern Turkey. In New Testament times, Tarsus, the home of Paul, was capital of Cilicia. These most up-to-date means of military might were controlled by Solomon in his trade dealings with the Hittites and the Syrians. The Chronicler approves of this international trade. Today, many Christians are rightly concerned over the issue of 'fair trade' between rich and poor countries.

MEDITATION

What are the characteristics of a truly wise person? Can you identify any among your own circle of friends?

KINGS & CRAFTSMEN

David had earlier made contact with Huram (or Hiram) regarding the building of his own palace (1 Chronicles 14:1–2). Furthermore, he had begun the process of gathering non-Israelites into labour gangs to work on his projects (1 Chronicles 22:2). Once more, continuity between David and Solomon is stressed.

Solomon's request

Solomon asks Huram to continue the favourable trading relations established in the time of David and to assist him in his grand project (vv. 3–10). Verse 4 outlines the main purpose of the temple in ancient Israel. Worship includes:

- the offering of incense as prescribed in Exodus 30.

- the offering of the shewbread (or bread of the presence) com-manded in Leviticus 24.

- the offering of sacrifices at the appropriate times. These times would include every morning and evening, each sabbath, each new moon, and the pilgrimage festivals of Passover, Pentecost and Tabernacles, according to legislation in Numbers 28—29.

Solomon needs a skilled artisan to work in all kinds of materials, including precious stones and delicate fabrics. The raw materials required in particular are the trees of Lebanon. The Holy Land has plenty of stone but supplies of timber for building purposes are scarce. Hence the need for the trade agreement between the two monarchs, which is mutually beneficial. Solomon will pay well in supplying provisions to the workers (v. 10).

King Huram and Master Huram

King Huram's response begins by acknowledging Solomon as the Lord's appointed king and praising the God of Israel who has blessed him. Huram's words are similar to those of the Queen of Sheba in 2 Chronicles 9. The Chronicler is keen to show that Gentile rulers recognize the sovereignty of Solomon and the power of God that lies behind his throne. It is noticeable how verse 12 explicitly links the wisdom of Solomon with the building of the temple. This, for the Chronicler, is the supreme evidence of Solomon's famed wisdom.

King Huram responds to Solomon's request for a skilled worker by sending an artisan who has a similar name to the king. Most translations give his name as Huram-abi, but the second part of this word may be a title rather than part of the name. Literally, *abi* means 'my father', and it may be used to designate someone who is the finest in his field, a master craftsman.

Huram's list of skills is very impressive indeed. In the book of Exodus, the names of the two skilled workers who built the tabernacle are Bezalel and Oholiab. Bezalel was of the tribe of Judah (Exodus 31:2) and Oholiab was of the tribe of Dan (Exodus 31:6). Now the work on the temple is supervised by Solomon, who is of the tribe of Judah, and Huram, whose mother is of the tribe of Dan. Later Jewish rabbis would conclude that not only was Huram of the same tribe as Oholiab, but that he was actually a direct descendant.

The plan to float the timbers along the coast to Joppa and then take them by land up to Jerusalem would be a sensible one. Roads were poor, so bulky transport would be a problem. Joppa was the only decent port on the coast of Israel in Old Testament times. It was from there that the prophet Jonah sought a ship to try to escape from the Lord (Jonah 1:3).

Labour force

According to the Chronicler (vv. 17–18), the labour gangs were made up entirely of non-Israelites, the so-called 'resident aliens'. 1 Kings 9:20–23 identifies them as the remnants of the nations that inhabited Canaan prior to the conquest by Joshua. Chronicles is keen to stress that Israelites were not included. However, the reference in 1 Kings 5:13–18 makes us wonder. Among the grievances that led to the division of the kingdom after Solomon's death was the complaint about the 'hard service' Solomon had imposed (2 Chronicles 10). The grandiose project to build the temple was completed on the back of a forced labour programme. Are there similar high-profile projects today? What is their cost to communities and individual human lives?

PRAYER

Give thanks to God for those who have skills in design,
in engineering, in engraving. Rejoice in the ability of human beings
to create great works of art.

The TEMPLE PLAN

In the opening verse, the Chronicler explains carefully where the site of the temple was. Firstly, it was Mount Moriah; secondly, it was the place where the Lord appeared to David; and thirdly, it was the threshing floor of the Jebusite farmer Ornan (or Araunah). He has told the story of the angel appearing to David above the threshing floor in 1 Chronicles 21. The Chronicler is the first writer explicitly to link the temple site with Mount Moriah. It was to 'the land of Moriah' that Abraham went when he was commanded by God to sacrifice his son Isaac (Genesis 22). Jewish tradition has therefore linked the place of Isaac's near sacrifice with the altar of the Jerusalem temple. Today, the beautiful Muslim shrine of the Dome of the Rock stands on the site of the temple mount.

Archaeological digs on the temple mount are not allowed, so fixing the exact location and layout of the temple is difficult. However, the description given of the plan of the temple fits with what we know of other sanctuaries in the ancient Near East. These include some sanctuaries excavated in other parts of the Holy Land. Scholars do not unanimously agree about the exact date of Solomon's accession to the throne. Almost all, however, date the beginning of his reign to somewhere between 970 and 960. After so much preparation, building finally gets under way in the fourth year of his reign.

Size and shape

The information given in this chapter is shown in the diagram overleaf. The length of the 'old cubit' was about 45 centimetres, so the dimensions of the temple building at sixty by twenty cubits would be about 27 by 9 metres.

Porch (v. 4): The whole temple complex faced east towards the rising sun, and overlooked the Valley of the Kidron, beyond which was the Mount of Olives. According to 1 Kings 6:3, the porch was ten cubits (4.5 metres) long.

Holy Place (v. 5): This area, sometimes translated as the nave or sanctuary, could be entered only by the priests. According to 1 Kings 6:2, it was thirty cubits (13.5 metres) in height. Its furnishings are described in the next chapter.

Holy of Holies (vv. 8): The most holy place at the heart of the temple complex was a perfect cube, twenty cubits (9 metres) long, wide and high. In Solomon's temple, it housed the ark of the covenant and the figures of the cherubim. In the second temple of the Chronicler's time, it was entirely empty. Only the high priest could enter here, and even he dared to enter only after much preparation on the Day of Atonement.

Cherubim (v. 10): These were probably fierce-looking winged creatures like sphinxes. Perhaps they were intended as guardians of the throne room of God, for the ark was seen as the footstool of God's throne. They too disappeared with the destruction of Solomon's temple.

Veil (v. 14): The author of Kings does not mention the veil, but it formed part of the tabernacle and also of the second temple, so the Chronicler is probably right to include it. It was a beautifully worked piece. It was the equivalent of this veil that was torn in two at the time of Jesus' death (Matthew 27:51). For Christians, this tearing represents the ending of separation between human beings and God. An eternal atonement has been made. Now all who believe in Christ may enter into the Holy of Holies, the very presence of God.

Pillars (v. 15): We should probably imagine these pillars as free-standing, rather than as part of the structure of the temple itself. Their significance is something of a mystery. Jachin means 'he establishes' and Boaz means 'in him is strength'. These too were a feature of Solomon's temple only, and were not part of the second temple rebuilding.

Temple Courts: It was in these open-air courts that the worshipping Israelites gathered.

Solomon's temple was beautifully furnished with gold and gems. It provided a model for future buildings on the site. The second temple, which was standing at the time of the Chronicler, was a rather modest affair by comparison. Eventually the second temple was replaced by the magnificent buildings of Herod the Great. It was this final remodelled temple that was familiar to Jesus. Both Jesus and Paul use the image of the temple to describe what the Christian community is meant to be. We must admit that, like the Jerusalem temple, we often fall short of the ideal. Consequently we fail to be the living temples of the Holy Spirit that we could and should be.

MEDITATION

'Do you not know that you are God's temple and that God's Spirit dwells in you?' What do these words from 1 Corinthians 3:16 mean for you?

Plan *of* Solomon's Temple

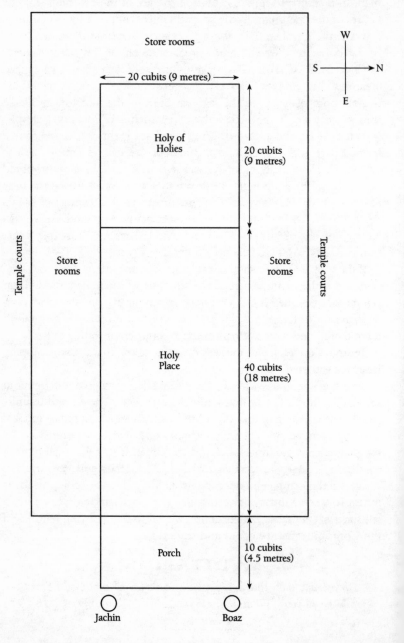

Furnishings *of the* Temple

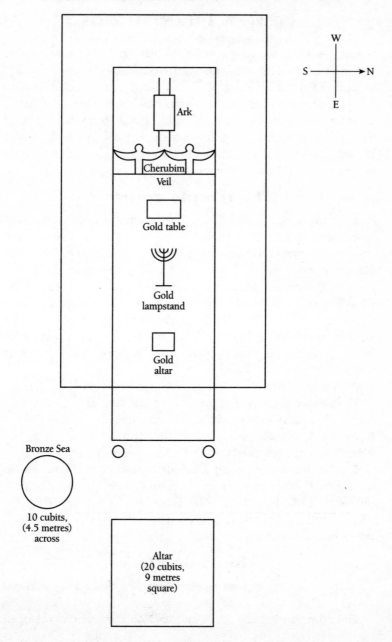

TEMPLE FURNISHINGS

Having described the temple buildings, the Chronicler now goes on to outline the main objects associated with Solomon's new sanctuary. He largely follows the description in 1 Kings 7, but is also keen to show the continuity between Solomon's building and the desert tabernacle furniture fashioned by Bezalel and Oholiab in Exodus. The best way to get an overall perspective on the objects within the desert tabernacle is to read the summary in Hebrews 9:1–5. The diagram on the previous page may help to place things in perspective.

The temple courts

It was in the open temple courts that the main acts of public worship took place (vv. 1–6). It was here that the majority of Israelites would observe the religious ceremonies prescribed in the Law of Moses. The Chronicler distinguishes between the court reserved for the priests and the 'great court' which was open to all Israelites. In Herod the Great's remodelled temple, there were even more courtyards. These included the Court of the Gentiles open to everyone, the Court of the Women, the Court of Israel for male lay Jews, and the Court of the Priests. The idea of increasing spheres of holiness lies behind this scheme.

Within the Court of the Priests, there were two large structures:

The bronze altar (v. 1): The base of this altar measured twenty cubits (9 metres) square, which was the same size as the Holy of Holies. Steps probably led up to the top of the altar, on which the various offerings of animals, grain and wine were offered.

The bronze sea (vv. 2–6): A bloody business like animal slaughter required plenty of water for cleansing. It was also necessary for priests to be ritually clean in order to perform their duties. Thus, the huge bronze sea and the accompanying ten basins were provided for the ceremonial washing within the temple compounds.

The Holy Place

The furnishings of the nave or Holy Place are all made of gold (vv. 7–22).

The altar: This was a much smaller altar than that in the open courts. Its purpose was also different. It was for the burning of fragrant incense, not for the offering of sacrifices.

The lampstands (v. 7): In the wilderness tabernacle, there was just one large seven-branched lampstand called the *menorah*. It is described in Exodus 25. Similarly, the second temple also contained just one lampstand, according to 1 Maccabees 1:21 and 4:49. However, both 1 Kings 7 and the Chronicler speak of ten lampstands in the sanctuary, in two rows of five. These would provide light for the building, since there were no windows. Later Jewish rabbis harmonized these traditions by claiming that in Solomon's temple the seven-branched *menorah* was surrounded by the ten lampstands.

The tables (v. 8): In similar fashion, Exodus 25 mentions one table for the bread of the presence in the tabernacle, and 1 Maccabees refers to one table in the second temple. 1 Kings 7:48 also speaks of only one table in the sanctuary of Solomon's temple. The Chronicler is therefore the only writer to speak of ten tables. There are two ways of interpreting what he means. The ten tables may be for the ten lampstands, in which case they are not the same as the table for the bread. This would mean that the Chronicler makes no mention of the table for the bread. Alternatively the Chronicler may indeed intend us to understand that there were ten tables for the bread, in which case he is following a tradition of his own.

The references to ten lampstands and ten tables are mysterious. The diagram therefore simply has one of each. In fact, the Chronicler himself seems to envisage just one of each in Solomon's temple, in 2 Chronicles 13:11.

The Holy of Holies

The ark: The ancient, sacred ark of the covenant would be placed within the Holy of Holies. There is no description of the ark being made, since it had been preserved from the time of Moses. The next chapter will describe how it was brought to the temple and placed in the Holy of Holies.

REFLECTION

Can you make any connection between the furnishings of Solomon's temple and those of your own church (for example, candles, communion table or altar, font or baptistry)?

FILLING *the* TEMPLE

According to 1 Kings 6:37–38, the temple took seven years to build, from the fourth to the eleventh year of Solomon's reign. As yet, the temple is only an empty shell of a building, waiting to be filled by the divine presence.

The ark at rest

The description in verses 2–10 of the ark being installed in the new temple has many parallels with the story of David bringing it to Jerusalem. As David had assembled 'all Israel' for the purpose in 1 Chronicles 13, so his son does likewise in verse 2. The ceremony takes place in the seventh month of the Jewish calendar, the month Tishri. This is the month in the autumn when the feast of Tabernacles is celebrated.

The process of moving the ark to its final resting-place is very carefully choreographed. It follows the instructions given in Numbers 3 and 4. There the priests are responsible for going into the tent and dismantling it, but the Levites are responsible for actually carrying the ark and the equipment of the tent of meeting. So the Chronicler now describes how the Levites carry the ark (v. 4), but when they arrive at the sanctuary it is, of course, only the priests who can take the ark into the temple buildings (v. 7).

Though the ark itself could not be seen from the Holy Place, the poles projecting out were visible. Verse 9 contains the phrase that 'they are there to this day'. Now in fact, in the time of the Chronicler they were not, for the Holy of Holies was empty. The phrase may have simply been taken over rather carelessly by the Chronicler from his source material in 1 Kings 8:8. Alternatively, perhaps, we should not take the phrase literally but as meaning something like 'from that time onwards'.

In verse 10, the Chronicler follows 1 Kings 8:9 in stating that the ark only contained the two tablets of stone with the Ten Commandments. There do seem to be variant traditions about what was actually in the ark. According to the summary in Hebrews 9:4, the ark also contained the jar of manna and Aaron's staff. This is based on the stories in Exodus 16:33 about the manna, and

Numbers 17:10 concerning the staff. Both texts speak of these objects being preserved in the tabernacle before the presence of God, but do not say specifically that they were kept inside the ark. The author of Hebrews is concerned with the wilderness tabernacle rather than the temple of Solomon. By the time of Solomon, these objects may have disappeared, or were kept elsewhere.

The glory of the Lord

For this grand ceremonial occasion, absolutely all the temple personnel are present. The rota of twenty-four divisions is forgotten and all the priests are present (v. 11), as are all three groups of levitical singers (v. 12). The 120 trumpeters may represent five from each of the twenty-four divisions. The whole thrust of these verses is to emphasize the joy and united celebration of the moment.

Once the ark is in place, then the glory of the Lord descends in a cloud, filling the house. In just such a way had the cloud filled the desert shrine in Exodus 40. It is a sign that God's very presence has also 'come to rest' in the Jerusalem temple. Here, more than anywhere else on earth, God promises to meet with his people. So, almost four hundred years after these events, the prophet Ezekiel has a vision of God's glory departing from the temple and city prior to their destruction by the Babylonians (Ezekiel 10:18–19; 11:22–23). God's presence is not automatic and cannot be guaranteed. It is a matter of grace, and what is given can also be taken away.

The New Testament often uses the image of a cloud to denote the presence of God. At the incarnation, Mary is told that 'the power of the Most High will overshadow you' (Luke 1:35). At the Transfiguration, when the three disciples witness the glory of Jesus, a cloud overshadows them on the mountain top (Mark 9:7). Finally, at the Ascension Jesus re-enters the glory of heaven in a cloud (Acts 1:9). In gracious love, God identifies his presence in special times, places and people; God is truly there, but never confined. This, perhaps, is the message of the cloud to believers in every age.

PRAYER

The presence of God filled the temple in Jerusalem.
Pray for the infilling of the Holy Spirit in your life, that you
may be a 'spiritual temple'.

DEDICATION

Perhaps it is the appearance of the cloud which prompts Solomon to say that the Lord will dwell in 'thick darkness' (v. 1). This is further stressed by the dimensions of the Holy of Holies. Such a relatively confined space without windows would indeed be a place of real darkness. God may be present and accessible to human beings, but there is still an eternal mystery at the heart of the temple. God's presence is real, but is in many ways impenetrable. The words of the hymn proclaim:

Immortal, invisible, God only wise,
In light inaccessible hid from our eyes (W.C. Smith, 1824–1908).

In the central part of the temple, it is not the dazzling light but the mysterious deep darkness that hides God from our sight. Still, as the psalmist remarks, 'Darkness is as light to you' (Psalm 139:12).

Solomon's speech

The bulk of chapter 6 consists of words spoken by Solomon at the dedication. Thus the Chronicler has devoted as much space to Solomon's words as he did to the description of the building of the temple itself in chapters 3 and 4. He is less interested in giving minute attention to the details of Solomon's temple, which, after all, was no longer standing in his day. Rather, he is concerned to emphasize what the Jerusalem temple is for, and to point up its continuing relevance to his readers.

It is in Solomon's speech in verses 4–11 and the following prayer that the theology of the book of Chronicles comes through most clearly. The speech points to God's election of the Davidic dynasty and of the holy city Jerusalem. It emphasizes the radical new departure in the history of Israel that came about as a result. Nothing like this had happened since the time of the exodus from Egypt (v. 5). Alongside the treasured names of Moses and Mount Sinai must now be set those of David and Mount Zion.

Solomon's prayer

Solomon stands on a specially built platform to address the people (v. 13). Since he addresses all the congregation from it, we must assume it is situated in the outer 'great court' rather than in the inner 'priests' court'. Solomon, though a king, could not enter this priestly preserve. Solomon kneels to pray, but is clearly visible to the whole congregation. He is the model of a pious monarch, leading the people in prayer. Kings cannot offer sacrifice, but they can lead in prayer, as could any devout Israelite.

Solomon begins by stressing God's faithfulness in the past, and goes on to pray that God will continue to be faithful to the promises made to the line of David (vv. 15–16). He is aware, however, that the promise is conditional. God has not signed a blank cheque for the house of David. There remains an 'if only...' clause. The wording is very close to the Chronicler's heart and to his theology—'if only your children keep to their way, to walk in my law as you have walked before me' (v. 16). There is here the stress on obeying the Law, the Torah of Moses. There is no doubt that, for the Chronicler, this meant the written laws which we find in the Pentateuch (the first five books of the Bible). For the Chronicler, it was the failure of Solomon's descendants, the later kings of Judah, to walk in God's ways that led to the disaster of exile in Babylon.

The heart of Solomon's prayer is found in verses 18–21. Here, above all, his theology of grace is spelled out. The temple may be called 'God's house' or 'the place of God's name', but such terms, like all religious language, should not be taken in a wooden, literal way. God cannot be confined, certainly not in a space twenty by twenty by twenty cubits, however magnificent the decor! Not even heaven itself can contain God, for God is beyond time and space, even if God chooses to be available to us through time and space.

Above all, the temple is to be a place of prayer. The sacrificial ritual was only a means by which to worship God. The true end of all worship is the encounter with the loving and forgiving nature of God. Therefore, prayer, intimate and passionate, is at the centre of temple worship and at the heart of the Chronicler's theology. Without that personal encounter, the gaudy trappings of the temple ritual count for little. The Chronicler knew that just as clearly as did radical prophets like Amos, Micah or Jeremiah.

REFLECTION

What would be an appropriate prayer to use at the dedication of a new church building today?

PETITION

Solomon's prayer at the dedication of the temple continues. He gives a catalogue of specific instances in which prayer may be spoken at the temple or directed towards it. He rounds off his prayer with a short burst of song taken from the psalms.

'Hear from heaven'

The specific instances of prayer can be parallelled from texts elsewhere in the Old Testament.

Oaths (vv. 22–23): Exodus 22:7–11 describes the procedure when two parties are involved in a dispute. To lie under oath was a serious offence, and Solomon prays that in these disputes right may prevail.

Defeat (vv. 24–25): Defeat in battle was often regarded as a sign of God's displeasure and a consequence of sin. Psalm 60 is typical of the kind of liturgical prayer that may have been sung at this time, with its plaintive cry, 'You do not go out, O God, with our armies' (Psalm 60:10).

Drought (vv. 26–27): Israel depended on the coming of the early rains in autumn and the latter rains in springtime for the sowing and harvesting of its crops. Unlike Egypt with its River Nile, the land was entirely dependent on rainfall. 1 Kings 17 records a time of drought that lasted for three years. It was finally ended by Elijah's prayer on Mount Carmel (1 Kings 18:45).

Disease (vv. 28–31): Failure of crops leading to famine, and human-borne diseases such as plague, were terrible killers. Remember that the four horsemen of the Apocalypse in Revelation 6 include famine and pestilence. Psalm 91 is the kind of prayer that might be offered in order to avert 'the pestilence that stalks in darkness' (Psalm 91:6).

Foreigners (vv. 32–33): Jerusalem and its temple are to be a focus for prayer, not only for Jews but for Gentiles too. This is in line with the vision expressed in Isaiah 56:7, that 'my house shall be called a house of prayer for all peoples'. In Herod's temple there was a 'court of the Gentiles'. Unfortunately this was also the area occupied by the traders and money changers. When Jesus upsets their tables in his cleansing of the temple, he quotes the words of Isaiah. The Chronicler's positive attitude to foreigners displayed in these verses contrasts with the more nationalistic attitude found in the books of Ezra and Nehemiah.

War (vv. 34–35): While similar to the theme of verses 24–25, there is a difference. The earlier text spoke of defeat brought about as a consequence of sin, and followed by repentance. Here, the emphasis is on prayer before the onset of war. Elsewhere, the Chronicler has given accounts of David's military victories, and he will include details of the military successes of some of the later Jerusalem kings.

Exile (vv. 36–39): At the time the Chronicler was writing, many Jews still lived in foreign lands, far away from the temple. This petition would mean much to them. Though they were far from 'home', nevertheless Jerusalem could still be a focal point for their prayers. An example of this kind of prayer can be found in Jonah 2, where the prophet looks longingly towards the temple. Similarly, Daniel kneels in prayer with his face turned towards Jerusalem (Daniel 6:10). In a similar way, millions of Muslims today offer their prayers facing the direction of Mecca. The Chronicler is conscious of the universality of sin, from which there is no escape (v. 36). In the New Testament, Paul expresses this idea with the words, 'All have sinned and fall short of the glory of God' (Romans 3:23).

'Arise, O God'

The Chronicler departs from his source in 1 Kings 8 here by closing Solomon's prayer in verses 41–42 with some words from one of the psalms. He does not quote exactly, but these verses are clearly based on Psalm 132:8–10. This is an altogether appropriate choice, for the psalm recalls the action of David in bringing the ark to Jerusalem, and God's subsequent promise to the Davidic dynasty. It echoes the theme of 'rest' which is important to the Chronicler. God has given rest to his people in the peaceful time of Solomon. Now the ark finds a 'resting-place' in the Jerusalem sanctuary. Thus, Solomon's prayer comes to an end with a final personal petition that God will not turn away from his anointed one.

REFLECTION

In place of the seven categories in verses 22–40,
compose your own list of petitions for use today.

PAGEANT & PROMISE

The long section on Solomon's temple-building exploits comes to an end with a description of the festivities associated with the dedication. The section began in chapter 1 with God appearing to Solomon by night. Now it closes with a second appearance in which concluding words of promise and warning are addressed to king and people.

Festival

Chapter 5 ended with the manifestation of the Lord's glory in the sanctuary. Following the lengthy report of Solomon's words in chapter 6, the opening verses of chapter 7 repeat the details of the presence of God's glory. We should not see this as a 'second helping' of the glory of the Lord. Rather, the divine presence has been filling the temple throughout Solomon's prayer. However, two new elements are now introduced. Firstly, the divine fire burns up the sacrifices on the altar. Secondly, the divine glory is now recognized by all the congregation. Previously it had been seen only by the priests, who consequently had to leave the sanctuary. The coming of the fire and the visible presence of God in the cloud echo the events at the wilderness tabernacle described in Leviticus 9:23–24.

The Chronicler makes the point that the Jerusalem temple is the true and legitimate successor to the tabernacle. He reinforces this by having present representatives from all corners of Israel. There is, perhaps, a deliberate cutting edge to this remark. In the Chronicler's day the division between Jews and Samaritans was growing ever wider. The Jewish historian Josephus, writing in the second half of the first century AD, supplies further information about this. He says that the Samaritans built a temple on their holy mountain, Mount Gerizim, during the time of Alexander the Great (333–323BC), close to the period when Chronicles was written. So all the pro-temple statements in Chronicles may also have an anti-Samaritan bias.

The Chronicler is much more precise about the date of the festivities than is his source in 1 Kings 8:65–66. In the earlier text, the seven-day festival seems to coincide with the seven-day feast of Tabernacles. The Chronicler distinguishes between them, however (vv. 8–10). The festival of dedication lasts seven days (the 8th to the

14th of the seventh month, Tishri). The seven days of the feast of Tabernacles (15–21 Tishri) follow. The festivities conclude with an assembly on the eighth day (the 22nd) and then the people depart on the 23rd of the month. This would be in accordance with the calendar that was observed in the second temple period. Leviticus 23: 34–36 gives instructions for the observance of Tabernacles, and Nehemiah 8:18 shows how these rules were carefully followed.

'If my people...'

By and large, the Chronicler follows his source text in 1 Kings 9:1–9, but he makes a few changes. He adds the very significant and stirring words in verses 13–15, including, 'If my people who are called by my name...'. In these verses the Lord responds specifically to Solomon's petitions by referring to times of distress caused by drought, locust or pestilence. The promise is given that God will indeed hear the prayers of the people. However, the nation must show itself truly penitent by four actions. The people must humble themselves, pray, seek God's face, and turn away from wicked ways. The promise is given that if they genuinely repent, God will hear them and turn away the disaster. In subsequent chapters the Chronicler will show how, when these conditions were met, God was faithful to his promise to later generations. For many Christians today, the words of verse 14 provide a rallying cry for a programme of national renewal. God's demands to modern nation states and their political leaders are still the same— a genuine turning away from evil and a turning towards the 'right paths' of God.

While verses 12–18 are addressed directly to Solomon, verses 19–22 are spoken to the whole people. They are words of warning about what will happen if the nation turns away from the true worship of God. They warn of ruin and exile, and of a glorious exalted temple reduced to a heap of ruins. Solomon's magnificent building will become a proverb or byword for ultimate disaster. The Chronicler's readers knew that this had all come to pass. These words would stand not just as a reminder of past history but as a warning for the future. The message to them was clear: 'Do not let history repeat itself and the second temple share the fate of the first.'

PRAYER

Read verse 14 again. Use it to pray for your own country's needs.

ECONOMIC BOOM-TIME

The Chronicler is primarily interested in Solomon's work on the temple. He omits or abbreviates much of the material about Solomon found in 1 Kings. However, this chapter does contain some information about Solomon's other activities, including commercial ventures.

Northern expansion

The Chronicler includes a note (vv. 1–2) that the combined period of building by Solomon was twenty years. Elsewhere we learn that this comprised seven years on the temple and thirteen years on his palace. In 1 Kings 9:11–14, Solomon gives twenty cities in Galilee to the king of Tyre. Here in Chronicles, it is Huram who presents the cities to Solomon. Perhaps we should combine the two texts and see the cities as originally being leased to Huram by Solomon and subsequently recovered. It is important for the Chronicler to show the king of Tyre as the subordinate and junior of the great king Solomon.

We last heard of the towns of Hamath and Zobah (vv. 3–6) during David's reign (1 Chronicles 18). At that time, Tou, king of Hamath, was on friendly terms with David and seeking an alliance against the king of Zobah. Perhaps political circumstances had changed in the ensuing years, and it became necessary for Solomon to mount an expedition to the north. If so, then Solomon's reign was not entirely the peaceful time presented in Chronicles. Nevertheless, by this brief note the Chronicler is able to portray Solomon not only maintaining David's empire but even extending it northwards. The same is true of the reference to Tadmor in verse 4. In later times, the name of this city was Palmyra. It was a great oasis city in the middle of the desert, about 120 miles north-east of Damascus. To control this city would mean controlling the important camel-train routes across the desert. Much nearer to Jerusalem were the cities of Upper and Lower Beth-horon, important fortifications north-west of the capital.

Administration

The use of forced labour for Solomon's building projects was mentioned earlier in 2 Chronicles 2:17–18. In verses 7–10, the

Chronicler goes out of his way to stress that only non-Israelites were used as forced labourers.

Whereas the author of Kings has quite a lot to say about Solomon's foreign wives, the Chronicler barely mentions the matter. In verse 11, he briefly refers to Solomon's marriage to a daughter of Pharaoh. Unfortunately we cannot be sure which pharaoh it was. Solomon built her a special palace, and the Chronicler explains why. It was because of Solomon's religious sensibilities that he did not wish his wife to dwell near to the place of the ark. Firstly as a foreigner, and secondly as a woman, her presence might be considered polluting. Remember that in the later post-exilic temple there were points beyond which no foreigner and no woman could go. Therefore, Solomon behaves as a model of religious orthodoxy.

Verses 12–16 give a brief account of how careful Solomon was to oversee the temple worship. All the appointed persons (priests, Levites, singers, gatekeepers) and all the appointed times (daily, sabbath, new moon, three pilgrim feasts) are scrupulously observed. Thus Solomon is seen to put into operation both the ancient Law of Moses and David's reforms of temple personnel. He does not offer up the sacrifices himself, but is ultimately responsible for their supervision.

Southern commerce

Ezion-geber (vv. 17–18) was the only port on the Red Sea in Israel's possession. Today the modern town of Elath stands there at the head of the Gulf of Aqaba. Huram, the king of Tyre, was a Phoenician and the Phoenicians were renowned as seafarers. By contrast, the Israelites were landlubbers, with no history of seamanship. Therefore, a joint trading operation makes commercial sense for both Solomon and Huram. The king of Tyre supplies the know-how, with ships and expert sailors. Solomon provides access to lucrative trade routes. It is not clear whether the ships were transported overland from Tyre to the southern port, or whether they sailed up the Nile and along a canal to the Red Sea. Ophir is a rather mysterious, faraway place whose exact location is not known. It has been identified with India, Somaliland in Africa, or with a part of Arabia.

PRAYER

*Offer a prayer for the modern land of Israel
and its relations with its neighbours.*

The QUEEN of SHEBA

The visit of the famous Queen of Sheba is one of those biblical stories that has excited the imagination of poets, artists, storytellers and film-makers down the ages. A whiff of the exotic wafts through the story like the romantic fragrance of the spices the queen brought with her.

'Take my breath away'

Sheba was one of the kingdoms in the far south of Arabia, modern-day Yemen. The lavish, impressive qualities of Solomon's court and entourage are breathtaking to the queen. The literal translation of the end of verse 4 is 'There was no more breath/spirit left in her.'

The wealth of the land of Sheba came from its trade, especially in valuable spices and aromatic gums such as frankincense and myrrh. Thus the queen brings these precious gifts to Solomon, along with a large quantity of gold and jewels. It is worth comparing the sentiments in Psalm 72, a psalm which is traditionally linked to Solomon.

> May the kings of Tarshish and of the isles render him tribute,
> may the kings of Sheba and Seba bring gifts.
> May all kings fall down before him, all nations give him service...
> Long may he live! May gold of Sheba be given to him.
>
> (Psalm 72:10–11, 15a)

In time, this psalm was taken to refer to the coming Messiah. Matthew's Gospel recounts the visit of the magi from the east at the birth of Jesus. Like the Queen of Sheba nearly one thousand years before, they bring gold, frankincense and myrrh to the 'king of the Jews'. Yet for the Gospel writers, 'something greater than Solomon is here' (Matthew 12:42)—the very embodiment of Wisdom. For Matthew, the Gentile Queen of Sheba stands as a reproof against the unbelieving cities of Galilee who fail to recognize Jesus' true greatness.

The queen's speech

In her speech to the king (vv. 5–8), the Queen of Sheba expresses her admiration and wonder. The queen praises Solomon in extravagant terms, but her speech also includes words of praise to God (v. 8). The grandeur of Solomon's court is not mere ostentation and extravagance. It is a sign of the wisdom granted him by the Lord, and above all of the love that God has for his people Israel. Like Huram before her, this Gentile visitor recognizes the hand of God behind the glory that is Solomon's.

Fair exchange

Wherever the land of Ophir was, whether in India or Africa, Sheba would be an important trading-post *en route*. Therefore, although the Bible presents the queen's visit primarily in terms of her admiration for Solomon's wisdom, we should not preclude the possibility of commercial incentives too. The exchange of gifts might represent the fruits of these lucrative trade agreements. There was mutual benefit to be gained—access to the valuable spices and resins of the east for Solomon, and access to wider markets for the queen.

Among the specific items mentioned in verses 10 and 11 is the mysterious 'algum wood'. This has tentatively been identified with red sandalwood from India or Sri Lanka. It was clearly of a type unknown to Israel and was highly prized.

Verse 12 concludes the story of the queen's visit. The enigmatic phrase 'Solomon granted the queen of Sheba every desire' has been much debated, and popular legends have made much of it. According to ancient traditions, Solomon and the queen became lovers and the queen returned home expecting Solomon's child. In Ethiopia, the story was told that this child was Merelik I, the founder of the Ethiopian dynasty. That may well be an exotic fantasy, but it shows how one nation sought to link its 'story' with that of the Bible. British people do exactly the same with the legends of Joseph of Arimathea and the site of Glastonbury. Joseph is supposed to have brought the boy Jesus to England. This legend is commemorated in William Blake's poem, 'And did those feet in ancient time walk upon England's mountains green?' Somehow each of us would like to feel that our story connects with the biblical narrative. The story of the Queen of Sheba is one of the biblical tales that sets the imagination running in overdrive.

REFLECTION

Why do some stories excite our imaginations and become the 'stuff of legend'? Can you think of others that do the same?

'In ALL HIS GLORY'

When speaking of the wild flowers of the field, Jesus comments, 'Even Solomon in all his glory was not clothed like one of these' (Matthew 6:29). In the time of Jesus, Solomon's glory had become proverbial, on the basis of texts such as the present one listing the wealth and honour of the king. The Chronicler was not the first to produce such a list; it had already been catalogued by the author of 1 Kings.

The previous work of history was largely favourable towards Solomon. However, it was not one hundred per cent in favour, and in 1 Kings 11 the author brought together all his criticisms of the king. He mentioned his many foreign wives and their corrupting influence on Solomon in his later years. He mentioned rebellions by various peoples living under Solomon's rule, as his great empire began to fray at the edges. Finally, he recorded the internal dissatisfaction over Solomon's forced labour and the figure of Jeroboam from the northern territories as a rebel against Solomon's autocratic rule.

By contrast, the Chronicler says nothing about any of these things, and we must assume that his silence is deliberate. The peaceful years of Solomon continue to the very end, for there are no blemishes on his character. As with his picture of David, the Chronicler has given us an idealized portrait of the king. Perhaps Solomon is even more idealized than David, for David was a 'man of blood' who made mistakes. For the Chronicler, Solomon is the model king and, as such, represents the ideal of the perfect king to come. In the Chronicler's day, there was no king in Jerusalem. The only monarch was the all-powerful Persian emperor. The Chronicler and his readers never gave up hope, however, that one day David's line would be restored, for God had made an 'everlasting covenant' with the house of David. We could compare this portrait of Solomon with those visionary, messianic passages we find in the Old Testament prophets. Solomon is the model for the king to come. Foreign rulers make their way to him and acknowledge his greatness, and the wealth of nations flows to him. His wisdom is of a supernatural quality and he is the embodiment of righteousness and faithfulness. Compare what the prophet Isaiah says of the coming Messiah in passages such as Isaiah 9:7 and 11:2.

The vision of Solomon in all his glory, Solomon the king of *shalom*, is not just a question of looking back through rose-tinted spectacles. It provides the Chronicler and his audience with a vision of what shall be in the future. We need to read history and prophecy together.

Untold riches

Verses 13–28 provide a catalogue of Solomon's stupendous wealth: image piles upon image in order to create effect. Our heads reel as we try to take in the golden shields, ivory throne with its lion decoration, and ships laden with exotic animals from faraway places. Tarshish appears in a number of biblical texts. It is most famous as the place the prophet Jonah tried to run to. It is usually identified with the Greek place name Tartessus, perhaps referring to the Straits of Gibraltar or a city in Spain. For the Hebrews, it was the very edge of the known world in the distant west. There, too, Solomon and Huram's ships ply their trade. Verses 25–28 repeat the information given in 2 Chronicles 1:14–16. This is not a careless slip by the Chronicler but part of his literary technique. He gives this information at the beginning of his account of Solomon and now again at the end. It provides emphasis and a sense of completion to the narrative.

Forty glorious years

Typically, the account of the king's reign ends with a brief summary and a tantalizing mention of some other sources to read if we want more information (vv. 29–31). If only we could! These works are now lost to us. In his summary of David's reign in 1 Chronicles 29:29, the Chronicler mentioned three works by Samuel, Nathan and Gad, all prophets active during David's time. Now he mentions 'the history of the prophet Nathan, the prophecy of Ahijah the Shilonite and the visions of the seer Iddo'. Again, these are the names of prophets active during Solomon's time. We cannot identify any of these works now, but it is noteworthy that they were all written by prophets. There is no doubt about it—the Chronicler believed that history and prophecy should be read together.

MEDITATION

Read Isaiah 9:7 and 11:2. How well do they fit the character of Solomon the king and Jesus the Messiah?

DIVISION

The Chronicler now begins his account of the rest of the kings of David's line, down to the time of the exile. He gives notes about the length of reign of each king and a summary of whether the king was 'good' or 'bad', according to his own perspective. Given the data we have, it ought to be possible to build up an agreed chronology for the reigns of the kings. Unfortunately there are several problems that affect the arithmetic and so there is no unanimous consensus about the dates of the kings. A number of schemes operate, all of which give similar dates, but with some variations. I will use a scheme which dates the death of Solomon and Rehoboam's accession to the year 932. Other schemes date it slightly later, down to 922, but by the time we reach the end of Chronicles the gap has almost disappeared. All scholars agree that Jerusalem fell to Nebuchadnezzar's Babylonian army in the summer of either 587 or 586.

Confrontation

When David became king of all Israel, there was a gathering of the tribal leaders at Hebron in order to endorse him (1 Chronicles 12). It is noteworthy that when his grandson becomes king a similar assembly takes place (vv. 1–5). This time, the venue is not the southern city of Hebron but the town of Shechem in the central highlands. Shechem was an important centre in the north of the country, associated with the patriarchs and with Joshua. It was close to the mountains of Ebal and Gerizim, and on this latter mountain the Samaritans, much later in history, would build their temple as a rival to Jerusalem. The northern tribes had their own sturdy independence and their own traditions. They did not expect to be taken for granted, and there were, no doubt, those who were suspicious of the southern power base of the Davidic dynasty. This assembly would need careful, tactful handling—which is just what Rehoboam seems incapable of giving.

A rebellion during the time of Solomon by the ambitious Jeroboam is recorded in 1 Kings 11:26–40. Now he tries again with more success and Jeroboam's name becomes a rallying cry for the disaffected people of the north.

Bad advice

Rehoboam does not possess the strength, wisdom or flair of his illustrious father. Unsure what to do following the request for a less oppressive administration and taxation system, he approaches two groups of advisors (vv. 6–15). The old men offer cautious advice to accommodate the people's demands. The younger men rashly encourage him to brag about his intentions. The scene depicts in story form a message that is often found in the Wisdom writings of the Old Testament. The message is that older people's advice should be heeded, and one should beware the impetuosity of youth. However, we ought to note that Rehoboam was forty-one years old when he came to the throne, so he and his advisors were hardly mere callow youths! A combination of Rehoboam's stupidity and Jeroboam's ambition will break the united kingdom in two. From now on, there will be two separate kingdoms, 'Israel' in the north and 'Judah' in the south. Rehoboam threatens to make the *yoke* on the people heavier. What a contrast with Jesus' comforting words—'Come to me, all you that are weary and are carrying heavy burdens, and I will give you rest… For my yoke is easy, and my burden is light' (Matthew 11:28, 30).

A foolish son

Ezekiel 18 tells a parable of three generations—a righteous father, a sinful son, and a righteous grandson. The theme of Ezekiel's parable is that each generation will be held accountable for its own actions. The Chronicler holds a similar philosophy of history. Each generation is accountable for its deeds and will be commended or condemned accordingly. Solomon was wholly blameless and Israel prospered. Now his feckless son will spoil it all, and the nation will bear the consequences.

Rehoboam compounds his insensitivity by sending a hated taskmaster to preside over the Israelite work-gangs. Without a strong, charismatic king, the united kingdom of David and Solomon could not hold together. The words of verse 16, 'What share do we have in David?' are a sad contrast to the refrain sung in 1 Chronicles 12:18, 'We are yours, O David; and with you, O son of Jesse!'

PRAYER

Pray for Christian parents who find it hard to come to terms with their children turning away from the faith.

REHOBOAM

Compared to the last chapter, this one paints a rather different picture of the character of King Rehoboam (932–916). It is typical of the Chronicler's method of dealing with his material to present the reigns of kings in this way. Instead of viewing aspects of good and bad inter-woven throughout a reign, he presents his information in blocks of good and bad periods. The good is rewarded immediately and the bad is punished immediately. So in this chapter, the first three years of the king's reign are seen as positive (v. 17). Consequently Rehoboam is blessed with success in building, with popularity and with the gift of many children. We need to recognize that what we have here is a theo-logical presentation rather than a chronological one. We should not assume that all the building work went on in these first three years, any more than we should place the birth of all his children in this one period!

Uneasy peace

Rehoboam musters the troops of the two remaining loyal tribes in order to attack the north (vv. 1–4). He is prevented, however, by the words of a prophet called Shemaiah. Verse 4 makes the point that the division of the kingdom, sad though it is, is within the will of God. It must there-fore be accepted rather than resisted, as Rehoboam discovers. Others down the ages have had to learn these hard lessons of history too.

Tension remains high and relations between Rehoboam in the south and Jeroboam in the north are sour throughout their reigns (2 Chronicles 12:15). Furthermore, Jeroboam had sought refuge in Egypt and the pharaoh had granted it. This caused a deterioration in Judah's relations with Egypt, to the extent that the country will soon face an invasion by the pharaoh. The description of Rehoboam's fortifications is therefore perfectly understandable. Many of the fifteen towns listed in verses 6–10 were on strategic routes guarding the valleys that led up to the hill country of Judah and its capital Jerusalem.

Migration

1 Kings 12:26–33 mentions Jeroboam's fear that people in his north-ern kingdom would still be drawn to the temple in Jerusalem in order

to worship the Lord. He therefore established rival sanctuaries in Bethel and Dan, equipped them with his own priests and set up bull images. All this is completely abhorrent to the Chronicler, who portrays Jeroboam in the worst possible light (vv. 13–17). He describes how faithful priests and Levites, along with some lay Israelites, did indeed leave the north to settle around Jerusalem.

Rehoboam may not have been the best king the country ever had, but he was of the legitimate line of David. For the Chronicler, Jeroboam had committed a double sin. He had rebelled against God's anointed and he had abandoned the true place of worship at the temple, filling his own shrines with his own appointed priests. The Chronicler presents the worship at the northern shrines as totally unacceptable. The bull images are an abomination and the sacrifices are offered to goat demons (satyrs) and not to the true God.

Family matters

Rehoboam's large family is seen as a sign of God's blessing upon him, and evidence of God's continuing faithfulness to the house of David. One thing we learn from the information here is that within the large extended family of David, intermarriage between cousins and second cousins was a regular occurrence. Mahalath, Rehoboam's wife, was his cousin and could trace both paternal and maternal lines to David's father, Jesse. Jerimoth is otherwise unknown. Perhaps he was a son of one of David's concubines. Maacah is called a *daughter* of Absalom, presumably David's rebellious son. However, according to 2 Samuel 14:27, Absalom's only daughter was called Tamar. Perhaps Maacah was her daughter and therefore a *granddaughter* of Absalom. The idea of inheritance passing automatically to the eldest son of the king was not yet established. Solomon was not the eldest surviving son of David, but the son of his favourite wife. So the same principle applies here in the case of Abijah, the son of Rehoboam's favourite wife.

PRAYER

Lord, give me the serenity to accept the things I cannot change,
the courage to change the things I can,
and the wisdom to know the difference.

Reinhold Niebuhr (1892–1971)

INVASION

In this chapter, the Chronicler demonstrates his belief in the theory of immediate retribution. For three years, Rehoboam, strengthened by the faithful who had flocked to Jerusalem, had walked in the ways of the Lord. However, the strengthening of his position leads only to pride and arrogance rather than to an acknowledgment of God's mercy. In the fourth year, he turns away from following the true path. Punishment is swift. In the fifth year of his reign (around 928BC), his land is devastated by the invasion of Pharaoh Shishak.

Pharaoh Shishak

Verses 1–12 provide the first instance in the Bible where an individual pharaoh is named, and this enables us to make connections between the biblical account and Egyptian records. The records from Egypt corroborate what the Chronicler says. Though there is no pharaoh called Shishak, there is a pharaoh whose name in Egyptian is pronounced 'Shoshenk', who ruled from about 945 to 924. He was a powerful, energetic Libyan nobleman, who founded the 22nd dynasty of Egyptian pharaohs. The Chronicler describes him invading the Holy Land with a large army of chariots and horsemen. As well as native Egyptians, his army also comprises Libyans (like Shoshenk), Sukkiim (another tribe from the desert of Libya) and Cushites (from Ethiopia or possibly Sudan). Clearly the power balance in the ancient world has shifted. David and Solomon were able to expand their empire during a time of Egyptian weakness. Now, that empire is fragmented and a resurgent Egypt is back on the scene.

It is not the Chronicler's intention, however, to catalogue the interplay of power politics. He is writing a theological work, not a modern piece of journalism. Therefore, Shishak is, for him, the first in a line of foreign kings who act as agents of God's judgment on his disobedient people. At the dedication of the temple, God had spoken to Solomon, warning of the disaster that would ensue from disobedience. Yet his words had included a promise too (2 Chronicles 7:14). This is the first occasion on which we see that promise fulfilled. As a response to the words of Shemaiah, the people do indeed 'humble themselves' (v. 7). The nation has had to learn a hard lesson, and verse 8 makes the point very clearly. By refusing to live as servants of God, they have become servants of one of the 'kingdoms of other lands'. The Chronicler's readers, living under Persian domination, would duly take note. Rebellion against the God 'whose service is perfect freedom' leads only to servitude under the hard taskmasters of foreign empires.

Fortunately we can corroborate details of this military campaign in the 920s from the Egyptians' own accounts. After the campaign, the pharaoh set up a royal inscription at a temple in the city of Karnak. It does not mention King Rehoboam by name, but it does give a list of one hundred and fifty places in Palestine which were captured by Shishak/Shoshenk. Among the fortified cities Rehoboam had built (2 Chronicles 11:6–10), the city of Aijalon is mentioned on the pharaoh's inscription. Jerusalem, however, is not mentioned, and this supports the view that it did not fall. Solomon's fabulous golden shields were probably enough to buy off the pharaoh. It was a common tactic and later, in King Hezekiah's time, more temple treasures would be sold off to keep away the Assyrian king (2 Kings 18:15). In the place of the gold shields, poor bronze replicas are positioned. The gold of Ophir no longer flows to the Jerusalem treasuries.

Summary

Comparing the end of Rehoboam's reign with its beginning (vv. 13–16), one is tempted to use the lament of David: 'How the mighty have fallen' (2 Samuel 1:19). The glorious united empire of his father and grandfather is shattered for ever. Bronze hangs in the place where gold once glittered. Arrogance, stupidity and pride have taken their toll on the nation's life. It is hardly surprising that Rehoboam's reign gets a negative verdict from the Chronicler in verse 14. However, compared to the assessment in 1 Kings 14, the Chronicler is less harsh on Rehoboam. The king was willing to listen to the voice of the prophet Shemaiah and thus avoided full-scale war with Jeroboam. He and his people humbled themselves before the Lord at the prophet's prompting. In the end, the real tragedy of Rehoboam's reign is of potential wasted and opportunities lost.

PRAYER

Ask God's forgiveness for times of wasted potential and lost opportunities in your own personal life.

NORTH *versus* SOUTH

This chapter provides information on the short reign of Abijah (916–914), including details not found in the earlier historical work of Kings. Verse 2 gives the name of the king's mother as Micaiah, daughter of Uriel of Gibeah, whereas in 2 Chronicles 11:22 it is Maacah, daughter of Absalom. Probably Maacah and Micaiah are variations on the same name, and some translations smooth out the spelling difference. A similar variation of spelling occurs with the name of the king. In 1 Kings it is spelled Abijam, but in Chronicles it is Abijah. The latter name means 'My father is the Lord' and so expresses a positive faith. Indeed, the Chronicler presents not only more detail but also a much more positive assessment of the reign of Abijah than the negative summary found in the Kings version.

Abijah's speech

The skirmishing that previously went on between Jeroboam and Rehoboam now flares up into full-scale hostilities. Unlike his father, Abijah would not accept the reality of a divided kingdom. As so often in Chronicles, it is through the speeches of the characters in the story that the theology of the book is most clearly visible. Abijah's speech in verses 4–12 is a comprehensive denunciation of the northern king and his religious policy. Jeroboam is an upstart and a usurper of the throne, a mere servant, in rebellion against the true son of David (v. 6). He is surrounded by 'worthless scoundrels' and has taken advantage of the weakness of Rehoboam (vv. 7).

The rest of the speech catalogues the difference between the religious policies of the two kingdoms. The north has its golden calves, as false and useless as the golden calf the Israelites worshipped in the desert (Exodus 32). The priesthood has been corrupted and sold off to whoever pays the going rate to be a priest (v. 9). Against such idolatrous practices and phoney priesthood, Abijah contrasts the scrupulous worship performed at the true sanctuary in Jerusalem (v. 11) by the true descendants of Levi and of the house of Aaron (v. 10).

Here, the Chronicler's pro-southern attitude is clearly to the fore. However, he is also making an important theological point. There may have been many reasons to support the division of the kingdom during the weak times of Rehoboam's reign, but they are no longer valid. A true descendant of David is now on the throne. He is strong in character and orthodox in worship. Meanwhile, the north has strayed into error through idol-worship. The rift between north and south ought not to continue. It is time for the separated northern tribes to 'come home'. Sadly, history teaches us that schisms are not so easily ended. This is true not only of splits between nations but of divisions between churches too. Very soon, they harden into unbridgeable gulfs and become institutionalized. Think of the division between eastern (Orthodox) and western (Catholic) churches in the Middle Ages, or between Protestant and Catholic at the Reformation. Nor do calls for one group to 'come home' and admit their error really achieve very much. The work of building bridges and achieving reconciliation is a long, slow process.

Pitched battle

Abijah's words therefore fall on deaf ears and the crafty Jeroboam even uses the opportunity to set an ambush (v. 13). Yet despite being outnumbered two to one, the southerners win a famous victory. Verse 19 mentions three towns that were captured by Abijah's troops. The most important of these was Bethel, since it was a principal shrine for the northern kingdom. The three towns are in the borderland between the tribal territories of Ephraim and Benjamin. So they were in the front line in the battle between north and south. During his short reign, Abijah succeeded in pushing the southern kingdom's frontiers further to the north. By the time of 2 Chronicles 16, the land had been lost again to the aggressive King Baasha of Israel, who pushed the frontier south beyond Bethel to the town of Ramah. Nevertheless, during his lifetime Abijah had checked Jeroboam and dealt him a serious blow.

The final summary in verses 21–22 emphasizes the positive evaluation of Abijah's reign in the Chronicler's account. He believes that there is no need for the division of the kingdom to continue. If it does, the schism is the fault of the obstinate northern kings.

PRAYER

Lord, how easily differences and divisions become permanent and harden into bitterness. Forgive us when, in the life of the church itself, we continue to hide behind our denominational barricades.

KING ASA

Following the short reign of Abijah comes the long rule of King Asa (914–874). Once more, the Chronicler has considerably expanded the material on Asa's reign, compared to his source in 1 Kings. In fact, his policy seems to be to supplement material on the first four kings of the divided kingdom and to be more positive towards them. By contrast, as he moves towards the end of his work, he severely curtails the information on the last four kings. They are all summarily dealt with in the final chapter of 2 Chronicles, and all are written off as bad kings.

Reformation

The biblical writers consistently oppose many of the religious practices that were taken for granted in neighbouring lands. During the opening years of his rule, Asa pursues a vigorous policy of religious reformation (vv. 2–8). Foreign altars are removed from the land. These may have been altars built for the foreign wives of the kings to worship their gods. Similarly, the 'high places' are suppressed. These were alternative sanctuaries to Jerusalem. The Chronicler regarded them as tainted and not legitimate places to offer sacrifices. Two ceremonial objects are mentioned—the pillar and the sacred pole. In ancient Near Eastern religions, the stone pillar represented the male fertility god, while the wooden pole, called an *asherah*, represented the female deity. Indeed, one of the goddesses of the Canaanites was called Asherah. In the account in 1 Kings, the development of these cults is blamed on the lax attitude of the previous kings, Solomon, Rehoboam and Abijah. In Chronicles, their existence is not ex-plained, since the Chronicler gives all these kings a high approval rating. Perhaps he saw them as the evidence for the persistence of native Canaanite religious practices. Similar and far more sweeping reforms will eventually be carried out by pious monarchs like Hezekiah and Josiah.

The Chronicler depicts Asa's reign in positive terms. This is in keeping with his view of the relationship between faithfulness and the reward of prosperity. It is a time of 'rest', a favourite word in Chronicles. In this period of peace and tranquillity, there is further opportunity for building projects. This too is a regular sign of approval in the Chronicler's scheme. Verse 8 describes the state of the army in Judah and Benjamin and the different roles assigned to the warriors.

Zerah the Cushite

The tranquillity of Asa's early years is finally broken by a massive invasion by Zerah the Cushite (vv. 9–15). Cush is the name of a land somewhere to the south of Egypt, though its exact location is disputed. Some English translations describe Zerah as an Ethiopian, while others make him a Sudanese.

Who was Zerah? And what is his relation to the Egyptian pharaoh, since he invades Asa's territory through Egypt? Two possibilities have been suggested. The first is that Zerah was, in fact, the Egyptian pharaoh. However, on the death of Pharaoh Shoshenk the throne had been taken by a pharaoh called Osorkon I. The second suggestion is that Zerah was one of Osorkon's generals. By this time, Osorkon was quite old and so may have sent his army under his general, Zerah. These are only guesses, however, so the identity of the Cushite commander remains something of a mystery.

Some scholars think Zerah may have been the leader of a small local group of Bedouin raiders and that the Chronicler has exaggerated the numbers involved. Certainly the figure of one million (1000 times 1000) seems very high. Some people try to bring these large figures down by arguing that the term 'thousand' designates a military unit, rather than being a straight number. Theologically, the huge numbers serve to heighten the miracle: only God's power can defeat such an enemy.

Just as Abijah's army was outnumbered two to one against Jeroboam, so now Asa's forces are outnumbered two to one against Zerah. The king therefore cries to the Lord for help, in verse 11. Asa's words echo those of Paul in Romans 8:31: 'If God is for us, who is against us?' With trust in God, the weak may become strong and overturn their lack of numbers. So victory ensues, and the great host flees back towards Egypt.

REFLECTION

Martin Luther said that 'the church is always in need of reformation'. What kind of reformation do we need today?

WORDS & ACTIONS

The sweeping victory over Zerah and the success of the king's reform movement go hand in hand. They are confirmed by the words of a prophet who encourages 'more of the same'.

Azariah's sermon

2 Chronicles mentions a number of prophetic figures who are otherwise unknown. Azariah, the son of Oded, is one of these. Azariah's sermon in verses 2–7 provides an interpretation of history. It is an interpretation relevant not only to Asa's generation but to that of the Chronicler as well. The sermon can therefore be heard at two levels. For King Asa, the time of lawlessness and anarchy (vv. 3–6) would be the turbulent period before the monarchy. The last verse of the book of Judges describes this period as a time when 'all the people did what was right in their own eyes'. With the establishment of the Davidic monarchy this had changed, and with Asa's reforms there was now access to the true God, to teaching priests and to the Law of Moses (v. 3). The Chronicler's readers could also be expected to make a connection with their own situation. The sixth-century period of the exile, with all its traumas and uncertainties, had come to an end. Now they too had the security of the Jerusalem temple and its priesthood, and the Law was being taught with integrity and authority. Azariah's sermon therefore interprets two periods of history at once: the period of the judges followed by the monarchy and the period of exile followed by restoration.

Covenant

Encouraged by the prophet, Asa's reforms continue. The altar of burnt offerings would need regular repair (v. 8) because of wear and tear. There is no indication that it had been neglected or desecrated. The gathering together of not only Judah and Benjamin but also representatives from three of the northern tribes is very significant. Clearly the Chronicler does not 'write off' the northerners as a hopelessly lost cause. He portrays loyal followers of the Lord defecting to Asa in Jerusalem and abandoning the northern shrines (v. 9).

So in Asa's fifteenth year, following the defeat of Zerah, offerings are made on the altar and the covenant is renewed (v. 12). This all takes place in Sivan, the third month of the Jewish year around May or June. In the Jewish calendar, this is the month of the festival called 'Weeks' in the Old Testament and 'Pentecost' in the New Testament. It is the time of the wheat harvest, but it also came to commemorate the giving of the Law at Mount Sinai. According to Exodus 19:1, the Israelites arrived at the holy mountain in the third month. There at Sinai they entered into a covenant with God. So it is highly significant that Asa's ceremony to renew the covenant also takes place in the third month.

Further reforms

A final reference is made in verse 16 to the name of Maacah (or Micaiah?). She was the wife of Rehoboam (2 Chronicles 11:20) and the mother of Abijah (2 Chronicles 11:20; 13:2). The literal description of her as the 'mother' of Asa is therefore difficult. All the evidence points to Asa being the son of Abijah, not his brother. There are three possible solutions to the difficulty.

• There were two Maacahs.

• Micaiah and Maacah are really two different people, but the similarity of names led to confusion.

• The term 'mother' can include the meaning 'grandmother'.

All in all, the third option seems to be the best solution, and is adopted by the Good News Bible and New International Version. The main point, however, is that the reforms of Asa touched even his own family.

Since Abijah ruled for only a short time, he probably died at a relatively young age. Asa may have been a child or a teenager when he came to the throne. The position of queen mother could be a very powerful one, and Abijah's mother may well have continued to hold that position when her grandson inherited the throne. Perhaps Asa's sweeping reforms were made at his 'coming of age' when he began to exercise authority for himself.

REFLECTION

How can stories from other periods of history help to throw light on our own period?

ASA'S LAST YEARS

Once more, we are given a picture of a reign of two halves. Chapters 14 and 15 depicted security and peace. Now Asa's last days are clouded with all kinds of trouble.

Political manoeuvres

The reference to King Baasha's attack in the thirty-sixth year of King Asa creates a problem. According to 1 Kings 16:8, Baasha died in the twenty-sixth year of Asa's reign. How can he be fighting him ten years after he died? Three solutions have been offered:

- **Scribal:** the signs for 16 and for 36 have been confused by a scribe and the war really took place in Asa's sixteenth year.

- **Historical:** the thirty-sixth year is counted from the time of the division of the kingdoms. This would also make it the sixteenth year of Asa's reign.

- **Theological:** the Chronicler works with a theory of cause and effect. Reward follows goodness and retribution follows badness. Since Asa was known to be sick for the last couple of years of his life, his act of disobedience must have been immediately before he fell ill. This is perhaps the most likely explanation.

The town of Ramah, captured by Baasha, is only about five miles north of Jerusalem. So Baasha has won back territory that the northern kingdom lost to Abijah, and he poses a real threat to King Asa. As a young man in his prime, Asa had taken decisive military action against Zerah. Now in his last years, he resorts to a political solution. With Baasha campaigning in the south, Asa negotiates with the ruler of Damascus to open a new front in the north.

Politically Asa's action seems to make sense. Northern towns and villages in the Galilee area are devastated and Baasha of Israel has to withdraw in order to deal with the invasion of his territory. Asa, without engaging in battle, has secured a victory.

A prophet's rebuke

What seemed to the king to be a brilliant political move is viewed very differently by the prophet Hanani (vv. 7–10). He sees it as signi-fying an unwillingness to trust in God. In exactly the same way, more than a hundred and fifty years later, the prophet Isaiah will confront King Ahaz when the armies of Israel and Aram are once again ranged against Judah. Then Isaiah warns Ahaz, 'If you do not stand firm in faith, you shall not stand at all' (Isaiah 7:9). Instead of trust in a foreign alliance he offers the sign of Immanuel (Isaiah 7:14).

So Hanani is in good company in his opposition to foreign alliances. He is also one of the first prophets to suffer for his message (v. 10). He is put in the stocks, as years later the prophet Jeremiah will be (Jeremiah 20:2). In the New Testament, John the Baptist suffers impris-onment and execution for his brave stand against Herod Antipas (Mark 6:14–29). Similarly John, the author of Revelation, is banished to the island of Patmos (Revelation 1:9). The little-known prophet Hanani stands at the head of a long line of prophets who suffer for standing up to the political authorities.

Nor was Asa's move such a political triumph. Ben-hadad, the king of Aram (or Syria), would be a significant opponent for years to come. The power of the Arameans was growing ever stronger, and both the north-ern and southern kingdoms would feel the pressure. Hanani believed it could all have been so different. As the Lord had defeated the Ethiop-ians and Libyans combined, so he could have defeated the forces of Israel and Aram combined (v. 8).

Sad decline

The Chronicler operates with the iron law of retribution. On the heels of the events of the thirty-sixth year comes news of Asa's sickness in his thirty-ninth year. The disease of the feet is not specified further, but it may have been a form of gangrene. It is a sad end to a long, positive reign, and the king dies in his forty-first year on the throne. The funeral arrangements are given in detail. The spices would be a regular feature of state funerals and need not relate to the king's last illness. The fire is not a funeral pyre, for the kings were buried, not cremated. Rather, it is part of the mourning ceremonies. Asa's has been a reign of two parts—a feature that will be found in other reigns too.

PRAYER

Like Asa, most of us are the same curious mixture of good and bad, faith and doubt, trust and unbelief. Lord, have mercy.

JEHOSHAPHAT SUCCEEDS

In Chronicles, the treatment of Jehoshaphat's reign (874–850) is similar to the presentation of his father's rule. Asa's reign was depicted as reform and building followed by battle, further reform, and another battle. The same sequence occurs in the story of Jehoshaphat. We have reform and building in chapter 17, a battle report in chapter 18, further reform in chapter 19 and another battle in chapter 20.

King Jehoshaphat

Jehoshaphat succeeds to the throne, perhaps after ruling alongside his ailing father during Asa's last two troubled years. Jehoshaphat also 'succeeds' in the sense of being a winner in the eyes of the Chronicler. He is undoubtedly one of the Chronicler's heroes. The second half of verse 1 is a good example of how difficult it can be to translate a quite straightforward Hebrew sentence. The literal translation says that Jehoshaphat 'consolidated his power with regard to Israel'. But what is meant by Israel here?

- Is it the northern kingdom? In that case it refers to Jehoshaphat's strengthening the border fortifications against the threat from the north, and this would fit with what is said in verse 2.

- Does 'Israel' mean the southern kingdom of Judah? Sometimes the Chronicler uses the term in that way, to refer to the 'legitimate' kingdom ruled from Jerusalem. Perhaps it was necessary after the rumblings of discontent at the end of Asa's reign to consolidate his hold on the throne (2 Chronicles 16:10).

Maybe the phrase is deliberately ambiguous. When a ruler builds up his military might, it may be because of an external enemy, but it may also be a sign of internal trouble. In many parts of the world, it is still true that the large standing army is to stifle dissent in the country as much as to fight another nation.

In his religious policy, Jehoshaphat follows the reforms of his father. He too removes the high places and the *asherah* poles (v. 6). The god Baal is specifically mentioned for the first time (v. 3). Baal is actually a title which means 'lord' or 'master'. It was the name of the chief fertility god of the Canaanites, who was thought to be in control of the rains. Jehoshaphat's loyalty to the Lord God is to be seen as a deliberate contrast to what was happening in the north. There Ahab and Jezebel were encouraging the worship of Baal, while the prophets Elijah and Elisha opposed them. The Chronicler does not tell the stories of the goings-on in the north, but he expects his readers to know them from the older sources in 1 Kings 17—22.

Teaching ministry

A unique feature of Jehoshaphat's reforms is the policy of sending out teachers to instruct the people (vv. 7–9). A group of five lay officials, along with Levites and priests, is sent around the country to ensure knowledge of 'the book of the law of the Lord'. During the period of the monarchy, priests had a particular responsibility for interpreting the Law. The position of scribes and rabbis, who were experts in the Law, would develop much later, close to New Testament times. In Nehemiah 8, the Levites also have a particular role in translating the Law to people. How much of this legal code was actually written down in the ninth century, we do not know. By the Chronicler's time, in the fourth century, certainly all of the Pentateuch (the first five books of the Bible) was in written form. The wandering ministry of teaching exercised in Jehoshaphat's reign may remind us of a Gospel parallel. Jesus similarly sends out first the twelve disciples and then the seventy-two on a teaching mission to the villages of Galilee (Luke 10).

Military records

The Chronicler presents the standard description of prosperity and peace accompanying the reign of Jehoshaphat (vv. 10–19). Arab tribes bring tribute, and 2 Chronicles 21:16 states that they live 'near the Ethiopians'. Perhaps those living in the south-west of the land, near Gerar where Asa defeated Zerah, are meant. The description of the military commanders, their names, numbers and 'regiments', is very precise and matter-of-fact. Perhaps this is one instance when the Chronicler had access to written documents that helped him to compile his work. Such 'muster rolls' may have survived down into his time.

PRAYER

*Give thanks for those who exercise a teaching ministry
in the church today, and pray for them.*

FOUR HUNDRED *to* ONE

This chapter of Chronicles is taken almost word for word from 1 Kings 22. The Chronicler only recounts stories about the northern kings when they have a direct impact on the reigns of the Davidic rulers in Jerusalem. The battle of Ramoth-gilead is one such incident.

Alliance

As the years went by, the power of the kings of Damascus grew and posed a real threat to the northern kingdom. King Ahab, now on the throne of Israel, sought to forge alliances with other nearby states in order to counter the Syrian threat (vv. 1–3). He married Jezebel, a princess of Tyre, and arranged for his daughter, Athaliah, to be married to Jehoshaphat's son, Jehoram. This marriage alliance brought to an end the conflict between north and south which had erupted sporadically ever since the division of the kingdom in the previous century. For a time, therefore, the two royal houses were linked in marriage. Once more, it made sense politically. However, in religious terms it was disastrous for Judah, and almost ended with the annihilation of the royal line of David. The story of the wicked Queen Athaliah will be told in chapter 22.

Ramoth-gilead was a town to the east of the Jordan river, in the territory of East Manasseh. It had become disputed territory between Syria and Israel as the kingdom of Damascus expanded. Ahab now calls upon his ally, Jehoshaphat, to help him recapture the city.

Yes men

It was common practice in the ancient world for kings to consult prophets before making major policy decisions such as going to war. Ahab assembles an impressive array of four hundred prophets, who all urge him on in his venture in verses 4–11. Prophets acted as advisors to kings and, in time, there grew up a category of 'professional prophets' or 'court prophets'. How easy it must have been to fall into the trap of becoming 'yes men', and saying what you thought the king wanted to hear! It is an ever-present danger for organized religion in every day or age. How easy it can be for chaplains to institutions to go along with the ethos of that institution. How hard it can be to stand over against it. Similarly, how much easier it is for preachers to offer words they know will please the congregation, or at least to avoid saying anything that might cause offence. It is far easier to play it safe. When that happens, religion can become a mere tool of the state or other institution.

The four hundred prophets are unanimous in their encouragement, and they make an impressive sight. One of them, named Zedekiah, performs an action of prophetic symbolism (v. 10)—the equivalent of a visual aid in a sermon today! The use of such visual aids was very common. The great prophets, Isaiah, Jeremiah and Ezekiel, all used prophetic actions. Jeremiah 28 tells a similar story of a false prophet using such symbolism. In that instance, the prophet Jeremiah is confronted by the false optimism of the prophet Hananiah.

The lone voice

In verses 12–17, one prophet in all Israel stands out against the 'yes men'. Micaiah, the son of Imlah, has got himself a bad reputation with Ahab. The king's messenger comes to him and begs him to be cooperative. Micaiah's words are forthright. He will speak only what God tells him to speak, no more and no less (v. 13). It is surprising, then, that when he meets the two kings he gives them the same optimistic message as the four hundred. His tongue is firmly in his cheek, however, and the note of sarcasm in his voice must have been obvious. Ahab is no fool, and he commands the prophet to speak the truth (v. 15).

Micaiah describes his vision of a defeated and scattered army. He sees them 'like sheep without a shepherd'. The same phrase is used in Mark 6:34 to describe Jesus' compassion on the crowds in Galilee. 'Shepherd' was a common title for the king. Therefore the message is stark and clear. It spells doom for Ahab.

How often today do we hear the lone voice of the one against the many? The person who is willing to become unpopular or even to suffer for the sake of speaking the truth can often be a difficult and uncomfortable presence. Who are such people today, and how do we tell the voice of the 'true' prophet from the 'false'?

PRAYER

*Pray for chaplains to the armed forces, to industry, education
and prisons, that they may have the courage to offer challenge
as well as support.*

DECEIT & DISGUISE

Micaiah's words continue as he vividly recounts the vision he has seen. Ahab, none the less, thinks that he can cheat his fate. On the battlefield he discovers how wrong he is, for his true enemy is not the king of Aram but the king of Heaven. From God there is no hiding-place, and no disguise will frustrate the will of the Almighty. Jonah learned that lesson the hard way, while the psalmist takes comfort in it: 'Where can I flee from your presence?' (Psalm 139:7).

The heavenly court

With a few brush strokes, Micaiah depicts the vision of God's heavenly council chamber (vv. 18–22). About one hundred years later, another prophet will describe a similar scene. In Isaiah 6, the prophet also feels that he has 'listened in' to the debate in heaven. He sees the throne of God and the heavenly attendants, the fiery seraphim. Micaiah does not use the term 'angels' or 'seraphim' to describe the heavenly hosts. Instead he uses the simple term 'spirits'. The earthly king was surrounded by attendants and servants who did his bidding. So ancient visionaries pictured the heavenly king surrounded by his ministering spirits (see Psalm 103:20–21).

Micaiah's vision confronts the issue of the 'true' and 'false' in prophecy. Here it would seem that the four hundred prophets were not simply making up their message in order to please the king. Rather, God had sent a 'lying spirit' to deceive them. This is a different way of thinking about the nature of God compared to our own. Today we tend to see only good coming from God, but the ancients thought differently. Job recognized this when he cried out, 'Shall we receive the good at the hand of God, and not receive the bad?' (Job 2:10).

In its own way, this story is teaching that sometimes God uses 'mysterious ways' to achieve his purposes. It also raises the vexed issue of free will versus fixed destiny. Ahab now has two messages, and both come from God! Still, he has a choice of whether to fight or not—and he chooses to go into battle. So this curious story raises very powerful issues about the nature of God and human beings. God is in ultimate control, and yet human beings must make their own choices. A theological paradox lies at the heart of this ancient tale.

Accident or design?

Ahab makes his choice and the die is cast. The king still hopes to cheat fate, by going into battle in disguise (v. 29). This is a tragic tale in the making. It reminds me of the final scenes in Shakespeare's great tragedy of the Scottish king Macbeth. Like Macbeth at the battle of Dunsinane, so is Ahab at Ramoth-gilead.

Ahab's crafty disguise has the effect of leaving Jehoshaphat of Judah perilously exposed. He appears to be a sitting target, dressed in his royal robes. The Chronicler is teaching the lesson that if you ally yourself with wickedness you put yourself in mortal danger. He makes one small but theologically significant change in verse 31. In the version in 1 Kings 22:32, Jehoshaphat simply cries out in panic and the enemy soldiers realize he is not their prime target, the king of Israel. In the Chronicler's version, this cry becomes a cry of prayer. God responds to the appeal of his anointed one and rescues him. Once more the promise made to Solomon, 'If my people...', has been honoured.

Meanwhile, the battle is going badly for Ahab's forces. In the heat of the battle, a stray shot pierces the king's armour (v. 33). The Authorized Version has the memorable phrase, 'A certain man drew a bow at a venture'. It is random, pure chance—or is it? There really is nowhere to hide, nowhere to escape from the will of God. Ahab's crafty disguise is, in the end, the cause of his own downfall. The Bible has many verses which speak of such poetic justice. The image of people snared by their own nets or falling into pits they have dug for others is common. Proverbs 26:27 is typical: 'Whoever digs a pit will fall into it, and a stone will come back on the one who starts it rolling.' As Ahab discovers to his cost, sometimes you can be too clever for your own good!

REFLECTION

What do you make of this 'alternative picture' of God as the source of all things, both bad and good? How do we reconcile such ideas with statements like 1 John 1:5 that 'God is light and in him there is no darkness at all'?

REBUKE & REFORM

This chapter concludes the story of the disastrous alliance Jehoshaphat had made with the northern kingdom. The king of Judah receives a firm rebuke from the prophet Jehu and acknowledges that he has learnt his lesson. He does not venture north again but concentrates on reforming the administration in his own territory. In Hebrew, the king's name, Jehoshaphat, means 'the Lord judges'. Now we learn how the king lived up to his name by a thorough reform of the Judean legal system.

A prophet's reprimand

The statement in verse 1 fulfils the words of Micaiah's prophecy in 2 Chronicles 18:16. Jehoshaphat has learned a painful lesson, but at least he is able to return home to Jerusalem in peace. Jehu comes from a prophetic family. It was his father Hanani who had rebuked King Asa in chapter 16. Now history repeats itself as Hanani's son, Jehu, confronts Asa's son, Jehoshaphat. Father and son represent a faithful line of prophets not afraid to criticize the powers-that-be.

Jehu was probably a very old man at the time. We should not confuse him with another biblical character called Jehu, whose story is told in 2 Chronicles 22:1–9 and 2 Kings 9. This other Jehu was notorious for his bad driving! He led a *coup d'etat* which brought an end to Ahab's dynasty by killing both Ahab's wife Jezebel and their son Joram.

Magistrates' courts

The information in verses 4–7 about the reform of the judicial system is found only in Chronicles and not in Kings. The first part of the reform concerns the local courts in the provinces. Verse 5 makes particular mention of the fortified cities as places where honest judges were appointed. In the earliest days, responsibility for the administration of justice lay with the local elders in each town or village. With the establishment of a central monarchy, responsibility for overseeing justice passed to the king. Therefore, Jehoshaphat's reforms show how the growth of a more centralized system of government affected the process of law. Judges are now appointed directly by the king and are answerable to him.

As the king reminds them in verses 6–7, however, they are also answerable to God. Bribery and corruption were an ever-present threat to the system of law. He therefore stresses the need for complete impartiality in making judgments. Some later prophets, like Amos, would complain that the system was indeed being abused. The system of local courts described here is very similar to that outlined in Deuteronomy 16:18–20. For the biblical writers, one of the ways of judging a 'good' king was in how well the legal system performed in practice.

Court of appeal

The higher court of appeal is in Jerusalem itself (vv. 8–11). It is used in particular for deciding difficult cases, and seems to have had two divisions. The first deals with religious or ceremonial matters, 'the matters of the Lord'. The chief priest Amariah and his later successors preside over this court. On the other hand, more secular affairs, 'the matters of the king', are dealt with by the court presided over by Zebadiah, the governor of Judah. So there is a two-stage process of higher and lower courts, with the higher court divided into two sections.

In Exodus 18, Moses' father-in-law Jethro advises him to operate such a two-tier system. He is not to try to deal with every minor case himself but to appoint honest representatives to do the bulk of the work. Only especially difficult cases should be brought to Moses himself. Deuteronomy 17:8–11 also makes provision for a two-tier system. Therefore, Jehoshaphat's reform is not a total innovation but is applying principles found elsewhere in the Old Testament. This account shows how one particular monarch sought to put into practice a proper, efficient legal system. Such a system lies at the heart of God's will for any nation.

PRAYER

Pray for all those involved in the legal system, especially those who have to make decisions in complex ethical cases.

COALITION

Like the story of Zerah the Cushite, the details of the present invasion are only found in Chronicles. The material is not in Kings, though 2 Kings 3 tells a story of a threefold alliance of Israel, Judah and Edom against Mesha, the king of Moab. In the nineteenth century, an inscription called the Moabite Stone was discovered. It tells how Mesha regained independence for Moab during the time of King Ahab. An invasion by a resurgent Moab and its allies therefore fits well into this time-period.

Danger from the east

Previously in Chronicles, the invaders had come from the west—Philistines in David's time, Pharaoh Shishak in Rehoboam's reign, and Zerah the Cushite in Asa's. Now the threat comes from the east, from the other side of the Dead Sea (v. 2), the country that today is called Jordan. According to the story at the end of Genesis 19, the Moabites and Ammonites were descendants of Lot. The third group, the Meunites, are rather more obscure. Verse 10 links them with the territory around Mount Seir, and this is part of Edomite land. There is a town called Ma'an about twelve miles from Petra, so perhaps the Meunites were a local tribe from that area. The coalition forces advance from south of the Dead Sea and camp at the fertile oasis of En-gedi on the western shores. They are then ready to move westwards, up through the rugged valleys into the hill country of Judah. In a time of crisis, king and people turn for help to God.

The king's prayer

In many ways, the pious prayer of King Jehoshaphat in verses 6–12 recalls the words of Solomon at the dedication of the temple. In particular, the sentiments of verse 9 immediately suggest the promise 'If my people...' in 2 Chronicles 7:14. Now that the country is facing the specific threat of invasion, Jehoshaphat and the people respond in precisely the way they should, according to the Chronicler's theology. In fear and trembling, they turn to God as the only source of hope.

The king's prayer begins by cataloguing the Lord's deeds in the past, stressing in particular the sovereignty of God (v. 6) and his kindness to their ancestors. Abraham is singled out and called God's 'friend'. Exactly the same title is given to him in Isaiah 41:8. It emphasizes the especially close relationship between God and the first of the patriarchs. In verse 10, attention is also drawn to events during the wanderings in the wilderness. Deuteronomy 2 describes how the Israelites avoided conflict with Edom, Moab and Ammon. Now these nations are repaying them by treacherously invading the promised land. Jehoshaphat's prayer is very similar to some psalms, which may have been sung at times of national distress. Psalms such as 44 and 83 also recall past events in history and call upon God to act now as he once did in days of old.

The prophet's reply

Once more we hear a prophetic voice addressing king and people (vv. 13–19). Jahaziel is a descendant of Asaph, so he belongs to one of the groups of temple singers established by David. He is given a long pedigree of five generations, which would take his line back to the time of David. This link between prophecy and the temple musicians may well be significant. By the time the Chronicler wrote in the fourth century, the phenomenon of prophecy had almost disappeared. Could it be that the singers in the second temple, with their responses in the liturgy, preserved a memory of other more spontaneous forms of prophecy in bygone days?

Jahaziel has words of reassurance for king and nation. He speaks an oracle of salvation, promising that, ultimately, the battle is the Lord's (v. 15). Once more, we can compare his words with some of the forms we find in the psalms. In verses such as Psalm 12:5 or Psalm 60:6–8, a voice like that of a prophet suddenly speaks out in the middle of the psalm. These voices speak of God's intention to act to restore the desperate situation, just as Jahaziel does. Finally, in verse 17, the prophet pronounces forthcoming victory. His words echo in a remarkable way those spoken by Moses beside the Red Sea in Exodus 14:13. God's people must simply stand still and watch, and the Lord will deliver them from their enemy.

MEDITATION

Does the prophetic voice of God still speak to us through hymns, songs, anthems, and choruses in our worship?

ROUT & WRECK

This passage recounts the conclusion of the battle against the coalition, and gives a summary of Jehoshaphat's reign. The king is clearly among the 'good' kings in the Chronicler's estimation. Nevertheless, as with his father Asa, there are reservations. He does not reach the stature of his ancestors David and Solomon.

Victory on land

Prayers in the psalms often look for God's saving help to come early in the morning (so Psalm 30:5; 46:5). It is hardly surprising, then, that Christ's resurrection victory is discovered by those who come early in the morning to the tomb. Jehoshaphat's words in verse 20 are similar in some respects to those that the prophet Isaiah will address to King Ahaz in Isaiah 7:9. A clear connection is made between standing firm in faith and being established by God. Here in Chronicles, however, an additional element is stressed—the need to believe in the prophets. By the Chronicler's time, the prophetic books were written down and preserved. They were increasingly regarded as inspired scriptures with an abiding message for each generation of readers.

The details of the battle itself are only sketchily drawn (vv. 22–23). The coalition forces find themselves in an ambush—and the Judean wilderness provides plenty of scope for ambush. This trap, however, is not set by the soldiers of Jehoshaphat's army, but by the Lord himself. Perhaps the Chronicler envisaged the army of heaven, or 'heavenly host', fighting on behalf of God's people, but he does not say so explicitly. What is clear is that panic and confusion set in among the invaders. The triple alliance disintegrates and in their panic they turn on one another. There can sometimes be a self-destructive element in the forces of evil.

The king's soldiers are reduced to the role of spectators while the invaders turn against each other. When the slaughter is over, there is plenty of scope for the victorious Judeans to gather plunder (vv. 24–30). The return to Jerusalem was no doubt accompanied by appropriate psalms of thanksgiving for deliverance—the sort of songs we find in Psalms 68 and 118. The remarkable events are commemorated by giving a new name to the valley. It is called the Valley of

Beracah or 'blessing' (v. 26). The valley itself is in the region of Tekoa, which was to be the birthplace of the prophet Amos.

Shipwreck at sea

The Chronicler now gives a concluding summary of Jehoshaphat's reign, including personal details about him (vv. 31–34). On the whole, the verdict is positive, like that on his father Asa. However, it is not a one hundred per cent endorsement. Despite his reforms, some of the high places remain, though according to verse 33 the fault lies with the people rather than the king. Perhaps the lesson here is that corruption, especially in the public domain, cannot be erased overnight. Wickedness is deep-seated and ingrained, and good intentions alone will not remove it. Verse 34 may refer to one of the lost sources which the Chronicler used. The writings of Jehu are now lost to us and do not seem to be part of the biblical books of 1 and 2 Kings. Perhaps the Chronicler had access to a work which included a number of stories linked to prophetic figures such as Jehu.

In contrast to the stirring victory on land, Jehoshaphat experiences complete defeat at sea (vv. 35–37). The victory had come through utter reliance on God. The defeat comes by trusting in human alliances, especially with a dubious character such as Ahab's son Ahaziah. According to the account in 1 Kings 22:48, the ships do not even leave the port of Ezion-geber but are wrecked by storms. Who is it who controls the winds and the waves but God alone? The God who set an ambush against the enemies of Judah now ambushes the plans of the kings of Israel and Judah. God's 'messengers' of wind and storm wreak havoc among the great ships. Jehoshaphat is no Solomon, and Ahaziah is not Huram of Tyre. Wonderful trading and maritime ventures of the past will not be repeated.

PRAYER

Offer a prayer 'for those in peril on the sea'.

A Dismal Reign

Jehoshaphat is succeeded by his son, Jehoram (850–843). The Chronicler's assessment of this ruler is the most negative yet of all the kings of Judah. A king who begins his reign with a massacre is destined to come to a very unpleasant end indeed.

Repression

By this stage in Judah's history, it was accepted practice that the eldest son should succeed to the throne. So Jehoram rules not because he is the best but because he is the eldest. Jehoshaphat seems to have given lands and responsibilities to his other sons in different parts of the country. Jehoram, however, sees them not as brothers but as rivals. Consequently he eliminates them all (v. 4). It is the beginning of a process that will put the very survival of the line of David in jeopardy. It will precipitate the greatest crisis the royal house has yet had to face.

Jehoram was married to King Ahab's daughter, Athaliah, and it is her malign influence which reinforces his own evil character. Jehoram and Athaliah are the Macbeth and Lady Macbeth of the Bible. Yet, for all his wickedness, Jehoram is of the line of David. Verse 7 recalls how God keeps covenant with David's house, even when the light of the lamp flickers very low indeed.

Revolt and rebuke

Both the Old and New Testaments warn that we reap what we sow (Job 4:8; Galatians 6:7). In his wickedness, Jehoram has sown the wind, and he will reap the whirlwind (see Hosea 8:7). The political gains of previous reigns are squandered. The Edomites rebel, and despite the king's military campaign the territory is lost (vv. 8–10). At the same time, the territory around the city of Libnah revolts (v. 10). This is land on the border with the Philistines. So Jehoram faces rebellion in the east and in the west.

The religious gains of his father's and grandfather's policies are reversed as the worship on the high places is once again encouraged. Jehoram earns a stinging rebuke and a dire warning from the old prophet Elijah, whose story is found in 1 Kings 17—2 Kings 2. The prophet is a major figure in the history of the northern kingdom of Israel. He is a fierce opponent of Ahab, Jezebel and their line, and is equally scathing in his condemnation of their son-in-law, Jehoram (v. 12). The king has chosen to walk in the ways of his father-in-law, Ahab, rather than his own father Jehoshaphat. The prophet warns him that his cruelty to his brothers will lead to the near extinction of his own children (vv. 13–15).

Retribution

The conflict spreads even further, with attacks from the west and south by Philistines and Arabs (vv. 16–17). We are not told that the marauders reached Jerusalem. However, they may have captured some of the fortified towns of Judah, and with them the wives and children of the king. Only one son, Jehoahaz (or Ahaziah), is left alive. The future of the line of David hangs by a thread, for Jehoahaz himself will survive his father by just one year.

The grisly details of the king's final illness (vv. 18–20) are meant to convey a sense of God's wrath directed against him personally. His dismal reign is a low point in the history of Judah. When he dies, he is unmourned (v. 20). No memorial fires are lit for him as they had been for his grandfather Asa (16:14). He is not even buried in the royal tombs, nor does the Chronicler refer to any other accounts of this king's rule. For the Chronicler, it is a reign best forgotten. It has brought the country and the kingship to the brink of disaster and the tragedy is set to deepen even further in the next chapter.

PRAYER

Jehoram's attitude to his brothers and sisters was malicious and cruel in the extreme. Families can sometimes bring out the worst in us rather than the best.

Pray for families torn apart by jealousy, greed or fear.
Pray for any members of your own family with whom you have argued or fallen out.

HANGING *by a* THREAD

In this chapter, the crisis facing the house of David threatens to extinguish the dynasty completely. By the end of the chapter, all that survives of the male line is a nursing infant, and for six years there is no descendant of David on the throne.

Ahaziah

For a single year (843–842), the throne is occupied by King Ahaziah. He is the youngest son of King Jehoram, and is the same man who was called by the name Jehoahaz at the end of the last chapter. Hebrew personal names often include an element based on the special name for God, which is rendered in English as 'Yahweh' (or misrendered as 'Jehovah'). At the end of names it is spelled 'iah' and at the beginning 'jeho'. So Ahaz-iah and Jeho-ahaz are one and the same.

In the Hebrew text, verse 2 states that Ahaziah was forty-two years old when he began to rule. This cannot be right, since his father had been only forty-one when he died. A copying error must have occurred in the text of Chronicles at an early stage. 2 Kings 8:26 gives Ahaziah's age as twenty-two, and this is preferable. Both the Good News Bible and the New International Version amend the Chronicles text to bring it in line with Kings. As a relatively young man, the king is understandably influenced by his mother and his counsellors. The power of the queen mother was considerable in ancient kingdoms. Furthermore, the family ties established by King Jehoshaphat when he married his son Jehoram to Ahab's daughter Athaliah are now at their strongest. Athaliah has a son (Ahaziah) on the throne of Judah in Jerusalem, and a brother (called Joram) on the throne of Israel in Samaria. Soon both kings will be swept away in Jehu's revolt.

The story of Jehu's *coup d'etat* in verses 7–9 is told in detail in 2 Kings 9–10, following his anointing by the prophet Elisha. The Chronicler is not interested in the details of the northern dynasty, and so he abbreviates the story considerably. He also makes some changes to the description of the death of Ahaziah. In 2 Kings 9, Jehu assassinates Joram, king of Israel. Ahaziah is wounded in the fighting, flees to the city of Megiddo, and dies of his wounds there. By contrast, in 2 Chronicles 22:9 Ahaziah is found hiding in Samaria and is summarily executed by Jehu. So his death is more ignoble than in Kings. Nevertheless, for the Chronicler, these events are all 'ordained by God' (v. 7). Although the Chronicler concedes that Ahaziah received a decent burial for the sake of his grandfather Jehoshaphat, he does not state, as Kings does, that the burial took place in Jerusalem. Instead he implies that the king was buried in the north where he died. With such small details, the Chronicler builds up the negative picture of Ahaziah.

Athaliah

The fate of Judah and of the line of David now hangs on the actions of two women. On the one hand is the dowager queen mother, Athaliah, who seeks to wipe out the Davidic line altogether. On the other side stands Jehoshabeath, daughter of King Jehoram of Judah, and therefore sister or half-sister to Ahaziah. Miraculously this member of the house of David has survived all the massacres and turmoil. Perhaps Athaliah did not consider the female descendants of the royal line to be a threat, or perhaps Jehoshabeath's position as wife of the high priest protected her. In the midst of all the confusion, she is able to smuggle her young nephew, Joash, into the temple area (v. 11). He will be brought up in the safety of the temple precincts, just like the boy Samuel at the shrine at Shiloh.

Joash is only an infant of about a year old, and for six years Athaliah is able to impose her authority. It seems as though God's promise to David has come to nothing. Nevertheless, as Paul says in 1 Corinthians 1:27, it is often through the weak and powerless that God achieves his purposes. The end of the Davidic royal line has not come yet; it will rule for another 250 years. For the readers of Chronicles, living in the post-exilic days without a king, the stories in this chapter may have held out a message of hope. It is a messianic hope, the hope of a new branch of David's line. As the infant Joash was hidden in the temple, so even now the Messiah of the royal house might yet appear.

MEDITATION

'Unto us a boy is born, unto us a son is given' (Isaiah 9:6).
Try to imagine how these words stirred up hope for people in the darkest, bleakest of times.

RESTORATION

By and large, the author of Chronicles follows his source in 2 Kings 11 here. As usual, however, he makes a number of small changes or additions which bring out his own particular viewpoint. We should not see the material in Chronicles as the simple retelling of older material. It becomes something new and distinctive under the Chronicler's editing.

'Long live the king'

One of the changes that the Chronicler makes is to emphasize from the beginning the popular support for the restoration of Joash. There is a parallel here with his accounts of the coronations of David and Solomon and the support given by all Israel. So now, in verse 2, the five named commanders together gather support from the whole countryside. According to the account in 2 Kings 11, the conspiracy was a much more secret affair, involving only the members of the temple guard. Once accomplished, it was welcomed by the general populace. This scenario of secret plotting and the queen mother taken by surprise does seem more realistic. The Chronicler's version makes it difficult to think how Athaliah could have been kept in the dark for so long. All the indications are that she was an astute political operator. Nevertheless, her attempt to occupy the throne in Jerusalem was ultimately doomed. She was a foreigner and she was a woman, both factors which would count against her. Her own family had been removed from power in the northern kingdom, to be replaced by Jehu's implacable hostility. Her religious policies would antagonize all true worshippers of the Lord.

Two other additions that are typical of the book of Chronicles should be noted. Verse 6 emphasizes that religious protocol is to be strictly observed. Only the temple clergy could enter the sanctuary itself. The crucial role of the priests and Levites in the conspiracy is therefore emphasized. Verse 9 refers to the shields and spears that David had dedicated as gifts to the temple. Symbols are important, and the use of these ancient weapons forges an all-important link with David, the founder of the royal line.

'Death to the queen!'

Queen Athaliah meets her end defiantly, just like her infamous mother Jezebel. The story of the death of Jezebel during Jehu's purge is told in 2 Kings 9:30–37. Seven years on, Jezebel's daughter follows her mother, swept away in a popular rebellion. So now the line of Ahab is no more. The shedding of human blood in the temple would cause ritual pollution of the sanctuary, so Athaliah is led out of the temple courts to meet her end. Typically, the Chronicler finds an opportunity to mention the presence of the temple singers in verse 13. They too have their part to play, and mention of them reinforces the sense of popular rejoicing at the queen's downfall.

Verses 16–21 portray the extent of the religious corruption in the land. The old regime had given full support to the worship of Baal. A rival sanctuary dedicated to this god had been established in Jerusalem itself. The installation of Joash as king, with Jehoiada as the boy's counsellor, provides the opportunity for a thorough reform programme. The temple to Baal is destroyed, and worship in the Lord's temple is restored. Verse 18 makes it clear that Jehoiada is a devout follower of the old Hebrew traditions. He reorders things according to the instructions of Moses the law giver and of David the founder of the temple.

Again we should remember the situation in which the Chronicler is writing in the period after the exile. Proper worship of the Lord in the sanctuary at Jerusalem was of supreme importance. The nation still needed courageous and faithful priests like Jehoiada, who would steer a course during the time when there was no king of David's line. Perhaps some day, if they remained faithful, the King Messiah would appear in his temple, just as, centuries before, the young King Joash had been presented to his people. So, centuries on, the old story could inspire hope for a new generation of readers.

MEDITATION

Compare these stories:

the young King Joash being brought into the temple;
the presentation of the infant Jesus in the temple (Luke 2:22–38);
the adolescent Jesus coming to the temple (Luke 2:41–51).

REBUILDING

It is quite common for the Chronicler to divide the reign of a king into two distinct parts. In the one, the king is faithful and blessed, and in the other, he departs from the path and is subsequently punished. This was the pattern in the account of King Asa, where Asa begins well (2 Chronicles 14 and 15) but ends badly (2 Chronicles 16). The Chronicler now follows the same process in his account of the reign of Joash. It is the high priest, Jehoiada, who keeps the king on the straight and narrow way. After the old priest's death, the situation deteriorates. The rebuilding that takes place is not just that of the physical structure of the temple. The dynasty too is rebuilt, as verse 3 indicates. Now the sole survivor, Joash, has many sons and daughters to carry on the line of David. Joash himself rules from 836 to 797BC.

Finance

As verse 7 makes clear, there had been extensive damage to the temple buildings, and its furnishings had been looted to provide objects for use in the temple of Baal. Interestingly, it is the king who takes the initiative rather than the priesthood. Perhaps this is an indication that Joash has 'come of age' and is a child no more. The Levites are instructed to go all around the land collecting revenue for the restoration programme, and reference is made to the tax levied by Moses (vv. 6, 9). The story in Exodus 30:12–16 recounts how Moses received payment of half a shekel from each adult. This was used to provide the furnishings for the wilderness tabernacle, according to Exodus 38:25–28.

Joash's order reintroduces this payment to secure the restoration of the temple. In a later period of time, Nehemiah will do something similar (Nehemiah 10:32). By New Testament times, the half-shekel temple tax had become a regular annual payment. It is referred to in the curious story in Matthew 17:24–27 when Peter is asked whether Jesus pays the tax or not. He finds that Jesus does, but as a free-will offering, not as a compulsion.

Although the people here appear to pay willingly, such religious taxes can become unpopular—like all taxes! In England in the

Middle Ages there was a tax called 'Peter's Pence' which was paid to the Pope in Rome. At the time of the Reformation, it was the grand scheme to rebuild St Peter's basilica in Rome that led to the notorious sale of 'indulgences'. Grievances such as this led Martin Luther to begin his 'protest' against the medieval church and so usher in the beginnings of Protestantism. Any church today with a large building scheme will know full well the thorny ethical issues involved in deciding how to raise the money required.

Repairs

After some delay by the priests and Levites in implementing the scheme, the king decides to take over responsibility personally (vv. 8–14). Historically, of course, the temple was right next door to the royal palace, and during the period of the monarchy the king may have exercised considerable influence over temple affairs. This is one of the few places in Chronicles where criticism of the clergy is implied. They should surely not have needed the king to spur them on in this way.

The description of the joyful offerings made by the people is no doubt intended to recall similar stories. These would include the gifts for the tabernacle at the time of Moses, and also the generosity of the populace at David's plan to build the temple (1 Chronicles 29). The response this time provides not only for the repairs to the temple structure but also for the various temple utensils. As a result, proper worship can be offered once more at the Jerusalem shrine. The proper observance of the regular daily burnt offerings signifies a new beginning. The nightmare of the Athaliah years is over and it would seem that all is destined to end happily. However, life is rarely as straightforward as that.

PRAYER

Lord, worries about finance, buildings and repairs seem to take up so much time in church business. This story teaches us that they have their rightful place. Help us to get things in proper perspective so that church buildings may become an asset rather than a liability.

ASSASSINATIONS

The death notice for Jehoiada in verses 15 and 16 is unique for a high priest. It reads much more like the traditional statements about the death of kings. His great age is stressed, and at 130 he outlives some of the great biblical characters such as Moses (120 in Deuteronomy 34:7) and Joseph (110 in Genesis 50:26). He receives the special honour of being buried among the kings in the royal tombs.

A martyred prophet

A pattern familiar to readers of Chronicles is about to repeat itself, as Joash turns away from the true path after the high priest's death. Some of the blame is put on false counsellors, just as it was in the case of Rehoboam. According to Chronicles, however, God does not allow the king or nation to get away with it. As ever, he sends them a prophet with a message of warning—in this case, none other than Jehoiada's son, Zechariah (v. 20).

We would very much like to know what was really going on behind the scenes during the reign of Joash. Some people have speculated that there were different groups or factions at his court. Increasing tensions may have developed between the priestly group in the temple and the royal officials in the palace. The words of Zechariah, who is both priest and prophet, are too general to give us much of a clue. The fact that he was stoned to death is very significant, however. It indicates that it may have been a public execution, performed on the orders of the king.

For the Chronicler, the most shocking aspect of the affair is that the execution takes place in the temple courts themselves. How ironic that Zechariah's father had forbidden the execution of Athaliah in the temple courts when raising Joash to the throne. Now this same king puts Jehoiada's son to death in the same temple courts.

Jesus refers to the events of this story in Luke 11:50–51 when speaking about the tombs of the prophets. He speaks of innocent martyrs down the years, and begins with Abel, whose story is told in Genesis 4, the first book of the Bible. He ends with Zechariah, whose story we find here in 2 Chronicles, which is the last book of the Bible in the Hebrew order of books. So from Abel to Zechariah is the A to

Z of Old Testament martyrs—from beginning to end of the Hebrew Bible. We should note that there was sometimes a tendency to confuse this Zechariah with the author of the Old Testament prophetic book, who was Zechariah the son of Berechiah. This mis-identification is made in Matthew 23:35.

A murdered king

As usual in the Chronicles narrative, retribution follows swiftly (vv. 23–27). An army sent by the king of Damascus wreaks havoc in the country and the guilty advisors to the king are singled out for particular mention. Previously the Chronicler has told stories of how a small army of Israel and Judah had won famous victories over far superior forces (2 Chronicles 14 and 20). Now positions are reversed and a small army from Syria sweeps all before it.

King Joash too comes to an inglorious end. He is wounded in battle and murdered on his sickbed (v. 25). The Chronicler is able to give details about the two assassins which are not found in Kings. Did he get this extra information from another source than the book of Kings? Does he perhaps refer to this other source in verse 27 when he speaks of 'the Commentary on the Book of the Kings'? Unfortunately we have to admit that we do not know as the evidence is lost to us.

No doubt, a deliberate contrast is intended between the deaths of Jehoiada and of Joash. The one dies at 130, the other at 47; the one passes away peacefully, and the other violently. Jehoiada finds a resting-place among the royal tombs, although he is not a king. King Joash is not buried among his ancestors, though he does receive honourable burial in the city of David. This ambiguity emphasizes the Chronicler's mixed feelings for the reign of Joash. The infant who represented the whole house of David ends his life as the victim of others' political intrigue and of his own religious backsliding. He is a sad disappointment.

PRAYER

Pray for martyred prophets of our own time, whose words proved too uncomfortable for rulers or people. Light a candle in memory of such servants of God in every age.

SUCCESS & FAILURE

The assassination of Joash was not aimed at removing the royal house of David, for his son Amaziah immediately succeeds to the throne. This is one of the main differences between the kingdoms of Israel and Judah. In the northern kingdom, a *coup d'etat* always leads to the establishment of a new dynasty on the throne, and often the elimination of the old one. In the south, despite many tribulations, the line of David continues to sit on the throne in Jerusalem.

King Amaziah

Amaziah takes a firm grip on the throne at the beginning, and the assassins are put to death (v. 3). According to the practice of those times, however, the king is considered lenient. The punishment does not extend to the families of the killers, and the Chronicler notes this with approval. In verse 4 he quotes the law of individual responsibility from Deuteronomy 24:16.

On the whole, however, the Chronicler is not impressed with Amaziah's reign (797–769). The king's half-hearted commitment receives in turn a lukewarm response from the writer. Amaziah's is to be a reign of two parts, like that of his father before him. In the first part he is obedient and meets with success, but in the second he is disobedient and pays the price.

Amaziah and Edom

In biblical stories of warfare, it is usually men of twenty years and over who are summoned for battle. The number who gather on this occasion is 300,000. Although this sounds a lot, it is in fact the smallest number that a king has been able to muster so far. Perhaps this explains Amaziah's action in recruiting 100,000 mercenary troops from the kingdom of Israel.

Once again, a prophet comes on to centre stage. He warns the king not to rely on these troops from the north (v. 7). It is the presence of God with the army, not the additional numbers, that will prove decisive. At this point, Amaziah heeds the words of the man of God, though with a rather penny-pinching attitude toward the money he has spent on them (v. 9). Unfortunately for the king and country, the disgruntled mercenaries, having been deprived of their share in the spoils of war, respond by plundering the cities of Judah (vv. 10, 13).

Amaziah does prove to be victorious in the battle, which takes place somewhere in the area south of the Dead Sea. Warfare in any age is cruel and brutal, but the execution of 10,000 prisoners of war surely cannot be justified (v. 12). We may be tempted to denounce Amaziah, and biblical writers like the Chronicler, as barbaric. Before we do, however, we should remember the civilian casualties of the wars of the twentieth century. The massacre takes place at Sela. This name means 'the rock' and is often identified with the site of the later city of Petra. It stands as one of the many places that have witnessed brutality and massacre down the ages.

Amaziah and Israel

Verse 14 is the turning point of the chapter, as Amaziah foolishly offers worship to the gods of the Edomites. Perhaps he credits his victory as much to these deities abandoning their people as to the Lord God supporting him. It is time for another unnamed prophet to speak (v. 15), but this time the king pays no heed and silences the man of God. He turns away from the counsels of the Almighty and, like kings before him, prefers the counsel of human advisors. As ever in Chronicles, this is a policy doomed to disaster. Yet verse 20 emphasizes the fact that the Sovereign Lord is still in control of history.

Perhaps it was the action of the marauding mercenaries that prompted Amaziah to go to war against the king of Israel. By now, a new king is on the throne of Israel. He bears the name Joash (or Jehoash), but he should not be confused with Joash of Judah (Amaziah's father). The parable of the thistle and the cedar (v. 18) highlights the pride of Amaziah, but it is pride that comes before a fall. He suffers defeat and capture. The walls of Jerusalem are broken down and both royal and temple treasuries are looted. So much for Amaziah's penny-pinching!

The chapter closes with a typical summary of the reign. In many ways it mirrors that of his father—and like his father he meets his death at the hands of conspirators (v. 27).

PRAYER

Pray for all those whose lives have been scarred by warfare,
whether soldiers or civilians.

A LONG REIGN

Uzziah's 52-year reign is the second longest in the history of the kings. Giving precise dates for it is difficult as different historians follow slightly different schemes. It is possible that Uzziah may have come to the throne while his father was still alive. Furthermore, Uzziah's own son ruled for the last years when the king had leprosy. So both at the beginning and end of Uzziah's reign he may have over-lapped, with the son acting as regent for the father—just as the Prince Regent did in Britain at the beginning of the nineteenth century during the madness of King George III. Uzziah probably died towards the end of the 740s.

As often before, the Chronicler divides the reign into two distinct parts. It begins well, with a time of prosperity and a wise counsellor, but ends badly. In this respect Uzziah follows closely in the footsteps of his father Amaziah and his grandfather Joash.

Building a reputation

The Chronicler is ready to acknowledge the good aspects of Uzziah's reign. The fact that he reigned so long would have been seen as a sign of God's blessing upon him. Further signs of a good king in Chronicles are building achievements, prosperity, and conquest of land and enemies. All of these Uzziah achieves: as long as he sought God, he was successful (v. 5). He regains the strategic port of Eloth (modern Elat) on the Red Sea, and extends his territory at the expense of the Philistines in the west and Arab tribes in the south (v. 7). Expansion northwards is not possible with the powerful king Jeroboam II on the throne of Israel.

Uzziah is also credited with the rebuilding and fortification of the walls of Jerusalem which had taken such a battering during his father's reign. The king is praised as an organizer of the army and as a lover of the soil (v. 10). Archaeological evidence seems to support both of these claims. Verse 15 makes special mention of the ingeni-ous devices used to protect the walls of Jerusalem. These may have been catapults of some kind, although the invention of catapults may not have occurred until several centuries later. All in all, the long reign of Uzziah seems to have restored the reputation of the Davidic house.

The ominous threat from the powerful Assyrian empire only began to emerge at the very end of Uzziah's reign.

Overstepping the mark

2 Kings 15:5 mentions in passing that the king (there known by his other name of Azariah) was a leper. The author of Kings gives no details, so we are dependent on the Chronicler to fill in the gap for us. This he does with a vivid account of the king's spectacular fall from grace (vv. 16–23). Throughout his work, the Chronicler is a champion of priestly rights. Kings and priests are both set apart by God. Nevertheless, they have quite separate functions and should not interfere with one another's roles and privileged spheres. This is what King Uzziah foolishly does when he enters into the Holy Place itself in order to offer incense. This area and this action were purely for the priesthood (v. 16).

In Chronicles, a foolish king is always warned of his folly, usually by a prophet. In this case it is the high priest, Azariah, who confronts the king (v. 17). When he persists in his arrogance, the king is struck down by a form of leprous skin disease. He becomes unclean and so unable to perform his kingly duties. His son has to step in to take over the royal administration. The fact that the leprosy breaks out on the king's forehead is significant (v. 19). Not only is it a very visible place, it is also an unfortunate contrast with the plate of gold worn by the legitimate high priest, as described in Exodus 28:36–38. The idea of a mark on the forehead signifying blessing or curse is also found in the book of Revelation. There the mark of the Lamb (Revelation 14:1) is vividly contrasted with the mark of the beast (Revelation 13:16).

We do not have Isaiah's account of the reign of Uzziah. He did begin his prophetic ministry in the year that King Uzziah died (Isaiah 6:1), but all the stories we have in the book of Isaiah are from the later reigns of Ahaz and Hezekiah. For a king who reigned so long, we know surprisingly little about Uzziah, and most of the details we do know come from this chapter in 2 Chronicles.

REFLECTION

In many ways, Uzziah's reign is like a classical Greek tragedy.
One moment of arrogance and stupidity undoes so much good.
A basic flaw in a personality leads to nemesis (judgment).

STORM CLOUDS

The shortest chapter in Chronicles covers the reign of Jotham. As usual, the name of the king's mother is given, but this time the Chronicler also tells us that she was of the line of Zadok. Presumably this means that she was a descendant of the Zadok who was high priest during David's time. In many respects, the details of Jotham's reign follow those of his father—with the exception of his father's invasion of the temple. In contrast to the last three reigns, which have all been a mixture of good followed by bad, Jotham is given a wholly positive evaluation (v. 2).

He continues the positive work of his father through the rebuilding programme both in Jerusalem and beyond (v. 4). A successful campaign is waged against the Ammonites across the River Jordan, and they pay a large amount of tribute for three years. However, the information about Jotham's reign is very general and very sketchy. Consequently, of all the kings so far, Jotham appears the most colourless character we have met. The sixteen years of his reign may include the period of his father's illness, so that the time during which he was sole ruler may be much shorter (741–734, perhaps). The Chronicler was often able to use additional information to supplement the information from Kings, but he has no such stories about Jotham. So we have the phenomenon of a basically good king who somehow fails to make any impression on us.

The Assyrian threat

By the time we reach this period in the history of the kingdoms of Israel and Judah, we are able to supplement our knowledge by using other sources, both inside and outside the Bible. Some of the major prophetic figures of the Bible appeared in the second half of the eighth century. The prophets Amos and Hosea spoke their messages of warning primarily to the northern kingdom of Israel. In the south, Isaiah and Micah directed their prophecies primarily at Judah and Jerusalem. Isaiah began his ministry at the end of Uzziah's reign. Micah began a few years later, in the reign of Jotham. Unfortunately there are no stories or messages that can be precisely dated to the reign of Jotham. However, the opening chapters of both books give a vivid impression of how they saw the state of the country during the following reigns of Ahaz and Hezekiah.

Jotham's reign saw the end of a period of relative peace and prosperity. Over in the east, in Mesopotamia, a new superpower was rising up, in the shape of the Assyrian empire. Around 742, the new and vigorous ruler of Assyria, Tilgath-pileser III, led an expedition west to conquer and subdue. Increasing pressure began to build on small states such as Syria, Israel and Judah. Attempts were made to form a coalition to ward off the Assyrian threat. By now, however, the northern kingdom of Israel was beginning to fall apart. Military coup followed military coup, as kings were deposed or assassinated, sometimes after only one month on the throne. The details of this sorry decline can be found in 2 Kings 15.

Although the threat from Assyria was not yet acute during the reign of Jotham, it was building up, and would break over the two kingdoms. In 722, the northern kingdom of Israel would be destroyed and the ten tribes of the north would disappear into exile, never to return. Judah would survive, but would take a heavy pounding. For the next hundred years, the pressure of the Assyrian military machine would dominate all of the Near East. There were dark days ahead.

REFLECTION

Why do some people, even good people like Jotham, fail to make much impression? Does it matter?

A REIGN *of* EVIL

The Chronicler presents the reign of Ahaz (734–715) as uniformly evil. The picture painted in 2 Kings 16 and Isaiah 7 is of a weak king, dithering under pressure. In Chronicles, Ahaz is a king who deliberately leads his people into sinful practices.

The fires of hell

The most horrendous of these practices is the burning of his sons in the Valley of Hinnom (v. 3). Later, this place would serve as the smouldering rubbish-dump of the city. In the New Testament, its Hebrew name, Ge-hinnom, would give rise to the name Gehenna as a symbol for hell. In the reign of Ahaz, the Chronicler depicts a deplorable turning away to foreign gods and to forbidden cultic practices. The north had turned away two hundred years before, in the time of Jeroboam. Now Ahaz will lead the southern kingdom down the same degrading route.

Good Samaritans

The Chronicler describes two separate attacks on Judah. The first, in verse 5, is by Rezin, the king of Damascus, and the second (v. 6) by Pekah, who had seized the throne of Israel in a military coup. In other biblical texts, such as 2 Kings 16 and Isaiah 7, Rezin and Pekah form an alliance against Ahaz. The fighting that follows is usually called the Syro-Ephraim war, as Syria and Ephraim (or Israel) form an anti-Judah coalition. This brief but nasty war forms the original background for the famous words in Isaiah 7:14 about the child Immanuel.

The details of the story in verses 8–15 are found only in Chronicles. Captivity is a major theme of this chapter. The Chronicler's readers would see these events as a foretaste of the greater captivity to come during the exile in Babylon. The Judean captives are brought to Samaria to be sold as slaves, only to be saved from their fate by the words of the prophet Oded (vv. 9–11). He acknowledges the sin that the northern kingdom has fallen into and warns against making the situation worse. He stresses the ties of kinship between north and south. There is no doubt that these sentiments are also those of the writer of Chronicles. Although he is based in Jerusalem, he is not 'anti-northern'. He seeks the ultimate restoration of unity between Jerusalem and Samaria.

The captives are treated well. They are given clothes, food and drink, and oil for anointing wounds, and are brought safely to Jericho (v. 15). In his famous parable in Luke 10:30–37, Jesus tells of another 'good Samaritan' who does all these things for a wounded man on the way down to Jericho. Could this episode in Chronicles have provided Jesus with some of the details for his well-loved story?

Perils on every side

Ahaz' situation now deteriorates further (v. 19): 'The Lord brought Judah low.' Edomites raid from the east, no doubt aiming to recapture the port of Eloth. Philistines from the west encroach deep into Judean territory. As a result, the territorial gains of Uzziah's reign are lost. Ahaz responds in panic and seeks help from the king of Assyria. This is despite the warnings from Isaiah not to enter into any military alliances, and certainly not with a land-hungry empire like Assyria. Isaiah 8:5–8 gives a warning to Ahaz of what will happen to Immanuel's land if the king relies on the Assyrians. If you pay tribute to an oppressive power, it will only come back demanding more next time.

In verses 22–25, the sins of Ahaz go from bad to worse. His offering of sacrifice to the victorious gods of Damascus echoes the story of Amaziah and the Edomite deities (25:14). The spoiling of the temple is not just in order to pay tribute money to the Assyrian king, Tilgath-pileser. It involves the closing down of worship in the Lord's temple altogether (v. 24). The rule of Ahaz has proved to be a political, moral and religious disaster. It is hardly surprising that the Chronicler finds no place for such a king among the royal tombs.

In this chapter of Chronicles, cherished assumptions are turned upside down. The favoured southern kingdom has become a place of faithlessness and of religious corruption. Meanwhile, the inhabitants of the northern kingdom listen to the word of a prophet from God. The Chronicler is often accused of painting everything in black and white, but in fact his world-view is more complex than that. There is room for surprises.

MEDITATION

Have you ever been surprised by a kindness from someone
unexpected? Who have been the 'good Samaritans' in your life?

ABOUT TURN

Once more, a change of ruler brings about a complete reversal of policy as Hezekiah ascends the throne (715–697). Sons do not invariably follow the lead of their fathers—whether for good or ill. In Ezekiel 18, the prophet tells a parable of three men. The first is a righteous man, the second is his son who turns to evil ways, and the third is a grandson who turns back to the right path. Each one, says the prophet, will be judged according to his own deeds, not those of his father. In his portrait of the kings of this period, the Chronicler follows the same line. His story of the pious father (Jotham), the wicked son (Ahaz) and the righteous grandson (Hezekiah) brings the message of the parable to life.

A call to repent

The negative consequences of Ahaz' religious policies are swiftly undone. The closed, neglected temple is soon alive again with the sounds of activity (v. 3). The restoration programme has to deal not just with the effects of neglect but also with the systematic ritual pollution of the temple. Before true worship can be offered to the Lord, all evidence of the defilement must be removed.

At significant moments in the past, the Chronicler has portrayed the kings preaching powerful sermons to the people. Kings such as David, Solomon and Abijah have all done so. Hezekiah stands up to deliver a forthright address to the people, a call for national repentance. Hezekiah's sermon stresses the consequences of disobedience, and in particular he singles out captivity (v. 9). This would relate well to the Judeans' recent experience of defeat during Ahaz' reign. It would also 'ring bells' for the Chronicler's own readership in the fourth century. Hezekiah is not just delivering a 'one-off' sermon but proclaiming lasting truths. His words apply not only to the time of Ahaz but to all the times of impiety that led to the calamity of exile in 587. As ever in Chronicles, the sanctuary is the centre of attention (v. 7) and the role of the priests and Levites (v. 11) is crucial. Hezekiah concludes his sermon by addressing the clergy by the term 'my sons'.

Purification

The term 'Levites' is used in two senses in this chapter. Sometimes, as in verses 5 and 12, it is used in the broad sense to mean all the clergy, including the priests. At other times, as in verse 16, a distinction is made between the priests (of Aaron's line) and the rest of the Levites. In the list of names in verses 12–14, we should understand that the priests are included among the sons of Kohath (see 1 Chronicles 6). The list of names mentions fourteen individuals, two representatives from each of seven different families. The first three families we have met before. Kohath, Merari and Gershon are the three levitical groups descended from the ancestor Levi (1 Chronicles 6:1). The last three are also familiar, being the three groups of temple singers, Asaph, Heman and Jeduthun (see 1 Chronicles 15:17 and 16:37–42). The unusual addition is the middle family of Elizaphan. The genealogy of Levi in Exodus 6 includes an Elzaphan, who is a grandson of Kohath. Perhaps this branch of the Kohathites became particularly strong and so is included here in the list.

Eight days are spent removing pollution from the outer courts, and a further eight attending to the temple buildings themselves (v. 17). Naturally only the priests could enter there, and so they bring the pollution out to the temple courts and then the Levites deal with it by taking it out to the Kidron Valley. The whole process is reminiscent of the decontamination process at a nuclear plant following an accident. In many senses, the Chronicler viewed pollution of the holiness of the temple as being as deadly and dangerous as any radioactivity. In verse 5, he uses a particularly strong word, 'filth', to describe it. The concepts of holiness, purity and cleanness all belong together in the Hebrew mind. In the New Testament, Jesus is described as the one who comes to transform us into a holy temple. Jesus himself would come to the temple of his own day to 'cleanse' it from the 'pollution' of the money changers (Mark 11:15–18). How easily, too, we can let our 'spiritual temples' (1 Corinthians 3:16–17) become polluted, either by careless neglect or sometimes by our own very deliberate fault.

PRAYER

Create in me a clean heart, O God,
and put a new and right spirit within me.
(Psalm 51:10)

ECHOES *of* SOLOMON

The description of the restoration of the temple and its worship is reminiscent of the account of Solomon building the sanctuary. Hezekiah the reformer is clearly one of the great heroes of the book. For the Chronicler, he is none other than a new Solomon.

Dedication

The Chronicler gives graphic details of all the sacrifices that accompanied the reopening of the temple (vv. 20–24). Different animals were used for differing kinds of sacrifice. The bulls, rams and lambs were used for the whole burnt offerings. On the other hand, he-goats were often used for sin offerings, such as that made on Yom Kippur (the Day of Atonement). The basic idea behind the word translated 'atonement' is 'to cover over'. The blood of the slain beast was thought to cover the sin of the believer. Different animals could be used depending on whether the individual who sinned was a high priest (bull: Leviticus 4:3), ruler (he-goat: Leviticus 4:23) or ordinary Israelite (she-goat or sheep: Leviticus 4:28, 32). As well as the sins of individuals, the sins of the community could also be removed by the communal offering of a bull (Leviticus 4:14) at any time, or of a he-goat on the Day of Atonement (Leviticus 16:15).

It is important to note that the sacrifices described in this chapter are for 'all Israel'. Since the year 722, the northern monarchy had ceased to exist, wiped out by the Assyrians. So Hezekiah now has no rival in the north. Not since the time of Solomon has the legitimate Davidic king reigned in Jerusalem without a rival claimant in the north. We know from archaeological evidence that Hezekiah extended the walls of Jerusalem, probably to make room for refugees from the north. Perhaps there were hopes in his time that, with the demise of the northern monarchy, the whole land could be reunited. That would be another echo of Solomon's reign.

Verses 25–30 introduce a common theme in Chronicles, that of the active participation of the temple musicians. Typically, they have a leading role to play in the celebrations. As in previous episodes, the playing of the trumpets is reserved for the priests alone, while the Levites play the rest of the instruments. These other instruments are specifically linked with the name of David in verse 26. Trumpets, on the other hand, were used in Israelite worship as early as the time of Moses. Is it possible, given his obvious interest in them, that the author of Chronicles was himself a musician?

Celebration

The 'official' sacrifices are now complete, but the celebrations do not stop there. The people continue to bring offerings in thankfulness for the restoration of legitimate worship. Different types of offerings are mentioned in verses 31–35:

- **Sacrifices:** A general term for offerings of slaughtered animals.

- **Thank offerings:** A more specific name for a sacrifice expressing relief and thanksgiving for God's mercy.

- **Whole burnt offerings:** The whole carcass was consumed on the altar.

- **Peace or fellowship offerings:** Only parts of the carcass were burnt on the altar, the rest was eaten by the worshippers.

- **Drink offerings:** Liquids that accompanied the animal sacrifice.

Verse 34 introduces a note of reproof for the priests and praise for the Levites. Whole offerings had to be skinned or flayed before the carcass was burnt, as described in Leviticus 1:6. On this occasion, not enough priests had gone through the cleansing ceremonies required for them to participate in the worship. As a temporary measure, some of the Levites helped out with these duties. It is quite surprising for the Chronicler to be critical of the priesthood. By contrast, the Levites come out very well from this episode. Again it seems that the Chronicler is basically sympathetic to the Levites. Was he perhaps a Levite himself? During the post-exilic period, the role of the priests grew at the expense of the Levites. Perhaps, in his own way, the Chronicler is maintaining the importance of the role and ministry of the Levites against those who would diminish it. The chapter ends with a note of praise for all that God has done for his people (v. 36).

REFLECTION

In what ways can we recapture a genuine sense of joy and celebration in our worship?

A REMARKABLE FESTIVAL

In this chapter, the comparison between Hezekiah and his ancestor Solomon is made very clear, as the Passover is celebrated with great rejoicing in the purified temple.

Proclamation

Springtime is the season for the two related festivals of Passover and Unleavened Bread. They take place in the first month of the Jewish year, the month Nisan. The Passover meal is eaten on the evening of the 14th day of the month, followed by the week-long festival of Unleavened Bread, from 15 to 21 Nisan. Hezekiah's Passover was to prove unusual and irregular in many ways (vv. 1–12). The work of cleansing the temple was not completed until 16 Nisan (29:17) and so it proved impossible to observe Passover on the 14th. Also, the majority of the people were not assembled in Jerusalem, as verse 3 indicates. Help was at hand, though, through an earlier biblical precedent. A passage in the Law of Moses provided a solution to the dilemma. Numbers 9:9–13 makes provision for those individuals who, for legitimate reasons, have not been able to observe the Passover. They may do so in the following month instead. Hezekiah now applies this ruling to the whole nation and arranges for Passover to be observed in the second month of the year.

Great stress is placed on the invitation that Hezekiah sends throughout the land (v. 6). It includes all Israel, from Dan to Beersheba, north as well as south. This is the first real opportunity to unite the whole land since the division of the kingdom. Even the remnants of the far northern tribes, such as Asher (v. 11), Zebulun (v. 10) and Issachar (v. 18), are invited. The response is patchy. Many northerners refuse to come (v. 10), but there is some response (vv. 11, 18). Perhaps the Chronicler is indicating to his readers in the fourth century the need to adopt a conciliatory attitude to the northern population in their own day.

Passover

It was not just the date of this Passover which was irregular. Because of the difficult circumstances, it was not possible to carry out all the proper rituals. As a rule, those participating in the Passover celebration and its meal had to be in a proper state of ritual purity. These ritually clean laymen would kill the Passover lambs and bring them to the priests. However, on this occasion many of the northerners had not gone through the appropriate rituals (v. 17). Are they to be barred from the celebrations?

Two actions are taken to deal with the problem. First, the Levites act as intermediaries and perform the task of killing the lambs and bringing the blood to the priests at the altar (v. 17). Second, Hezekiah offers up a prayer asking for God's forgiveness on the people (vv. 18–19). The Chronicler is scrupulous about liturgical matters, but he is not rigid and inflexible. Given the choice between proper ritual observance according to the rule book or somewhat irregular worship from the heart, he opts for the latter. It is the spirit, not the letter of the law, that matters, as both Paul (2 Corinthians 3:6) and Jesus (John 4:23–24) affirm.

Seven more days

Another unusual feature of the festival is that it lasts twice as long as normal (v. 23). After the seven days of Unleavened Bread, another seven days of festivity follow. This is presented as evidence for the spontaneous religious fervour of the people. The festival held by Solomon for the dedication of the temple had also lasted two weeks (2 Chronicles 7:8–9). For the first time since the reign of Solomon, representatives of all Israel gather at Jerusalem. The number includes not only Jews but also the 'resident aliens' or 'sojourners'. These were non-Jews who lived in the land of Israel. They too are entitled to eat the Passover, according to Numbers 9:14.

The chapter ends with the statement that the king's prayer has been heard (v. 27). This echoes the sentiments of Solomon's prayer at the dedication of the temple (2 Chronicles 7) and especially the words of 7:14, 'If my people...'. For together the monarch and people have humbled themselves (v. 11), prayed (vv. 18–19), sought the Lord's face in Jerusalem (v. 13) and turned from their former wicked ways (v. 14). This remarkable Passover is a clear example of mercy shown by the compassionate God of heaven.

PRAYER

Lord, help us to learn the lessons of Hezekiah's Passover.
Show us when it is right to 'bend the rules' and 'lighten up'
for the sake of your kingdom.

CLERGY STIPENDS

Like ripples on a pond, the transformation moves outwards—first the temple itself, then the city of Jerusalem and finally the rest of the country. Hezekiah now turns his attention to making the religious gains secure. He does this by restoring the system of regular payments to the priests and Levites which had lapsed.

Contributions

Hezekiah first of all re-establishes the twenty-four divisions of the priests (1 Chronicles 24) and of the Levites (1 Chronicles 23) in order to secure the smooth running of temple affairs (v. 2).

In many ways, the temple and its sacrificial system were at the heart of the economic life of the nation. Providing for the needs of the temple and the many clergy was a large-scale enterprise. The royal family owned many estates in the land and from these came the animals that provided for the regular public sacrifices at the temple. These took place daily, morning and evening, with additional sacrifices each sabbath and at the pilgrim festivals (v. 3). The obligation on the ruler to provide for these occasions is outlined in Ezekiel 45:17. During the Persian period, when the Chronicler lived, this same responsibility was undertaken by the Persian rulers, according to Ezra 6:9 and 7:21–23. Thus the monarch provided for the temple's needs. However, it was the responsibility of the people to supply the needs of the priests and Levites who ministered at the sanctuary. Since the tribe of Levi owned no land, its members were dependent on the land-holding tribes to provide for them.

According to Numbers 18:8–24, the system worked in the following way. The priests received their share from three types of offering:

- the dedicated gifts (18:8).

- the 'wave offering' (18:11).

- the offering of first fruits (18:13), that is, the harvest offerings of the first of each crop or flock.

The Levites received their share from the system of tithes (Numbers 18:21), amounting to one tenth of all produce. Bear in mind that there were many more Levites than priests, so the amount needed to support them was greater. Originally this system operated in a literal way, with the bringing of produce. With the introduction of coinage in the Persian period, the monetary value could be substituted instead.

The people respond willingly to the orders of the king, just as those living in the times of Moses and of David had done. Produce is brought from the third month (the feast of Weeks/Pentecost), when the grain harvest is ready, until the seventh month (the feast of Tabernacles), when the fruit is ripe.

The chief priest at this time is named Azariah (v. 10). This is unlikely to be the same Azariah who lived forty years earlier, in the reign of Uzziah (26:20). Perhaps it is his grandson, as there was a custom of naming boys after their grandfather.

Storage and distribution

Arrangements need to be made for the proper storage of the produce, and special storerooms are set aside for the purpose (v. 11). Then the produce has to be distributed. Each individual priest over the age of three (that is, once he is weaned) is entitled to receive (v. 16). Likewise, each family of Levites with members over twenty years old receives a share (v. 17). Of the three categories of priestly portions mentioned in Numbers, the dedicated gifts could only be eaten by the male priests themselves (Numbers 18:9–10). The other two categories, the 'wave offering' and the first fruits, could be consumed by all women and children in the household (Numbers 18:11, 13). In verse 18, the Chronicler makes a special point of mentioning the faithfulness of the clergy.

It was relatively easy to distribute to the priests on duty or living in Jerusalem itself. However, a system was needed to distribute to those living in the rest of the country whose divisions were 'off duty'. Representatives are therefore appointed in each town to oversee the fair apportioning of the gifts (v. 19).

REFLECTION

How many paid clergy will the churches be able to sustain in the twenty-first century? Does the future lie with unpaid clergy earning their own living, like Paul the tent-maker? How much are the clergy worth, and how much are congregations prepared to pay?

ASSYRIAN MENACE

The picture drawn of Hezekiah in 2 Chronicles is in many respects similar to that in 2 Kings. However, the emphasis in Chronicles is significantly different, like a portrait taken from a different angle. Just as in the instances of David and Solomon, so too in the case of Hezekiah, it is the religious rather than the political programme that is the focus of the Chronicler's attention. Thus he has spent three chapters on Hezekiah's religious reforms at the start of the reign. Now he squeezes into just one chapter material that occupies three whole chapters in 2 Kings 18—20. He therefore abbreviates much of the material from Kings, while still retaining the basic picture. Perhaps he assumed that his readers would already be familiar with the story in the 2 Kings version. So, for instance, he mentions the miraculous sign in verse 24, but does not say what it was.

Sennacharib

Sennacharib ruled Assyria from 705 to 681BC and campaigned vigorously in his military expansion westwards. Judah and its king, Hezekiah, found themselves caught up in all this. In the past, the Chronicler has often construed invasion by foreign armies as a sign of God's displeasure, but not so in this case. Hezekiah has been a faithful king. The invasion is a result of Sennacharib's own ambitions, and therefore cannot and will not succeed.

Hezekiah's policy is the biblical equivalent of the famous advice to soldiers: 'Trust in God, my boys, and keep your powder dry!' In other words, while remaining faithful to the Lord, he also takes sensible precautions as the Assyrian army advances (vv. 3–6). In the Middle East, water is a vital commodity. Reliable access to water was essential, both for a city under siege and for the besieging soldiers outside the walls. Hezekiah has already taken care of the city's water supply (see v. 30). Now he prevents the enemy troops from getting access to springs and wells in the surrounding countryside.

In addition, the walls of Jerusalem are extended, and a second enclosing wall is built. Archaeologists have found the remains of a wall in the Old City of Jerusalem, which has been dated to the time of Hezekiah. Additional walls may also have been built as the city expanded. Having taken sensible precautions, Hezekiah encourages the people in verses 7–8. His words are similar to Joshua's speech before the campaign to capture the promised land (Joshua 1:9)—the king puts his whole trust in the Lord God.

Boasting and blasphemy

We know that the siege of Jerusalem took place in 701BC, because we have not only the biblical account, but also Sennacharib's version of events. Inscribed on a prism, now in the British Museum, is an account of the Assyrian king's campaigns. The tone reflects the boasting and bombast which we find in this chapter. Sennacharib claims to have captured forty-six cities of Judah and to have received tribute from the Judean king. As for Hezekiah himself, Sennacharib claims, 'He himself I shut up like a caged bird within Jerusalem, his royal city.' It is noteworthy, however, that for all his boasting he does not claim to have ever captured the city.

The Assyrian heralds are sent to try to undermine morale in the besieged capital (vv. 9–15). They seem very well informed about Hezekiah's reform programme and seek to make mischief by spreading alarm and despondency. For the Chronicler and his readers, however, the Assyrian envoys make one basic theological error. Not only do they compare Hezekiah to any other king, but they have the nerve to suggest that the Lord is no different from all the other gods of the nations. No less than three times, they infer that he is powerless to save (vv. 15, 17, 19). This is the ultimate insult and offence for the Chronicler. In reality, the Assyrians have arrayed themselves 'against the Lord and his anointed', as Psalm 2 so memorably affirms. The nations rage and plot in vain, and the Lord laughs them to scorn. He will protect his son, the anointed one, and the enemies will perish in the way. No wonder that the New Testament writers were quick to apply Psalm 2 to the story of Christ, the Anointed Son. The rest of this chapter in 2 Chronicles will show how the sentiments of the psalm can also be applied to the dramatic events of 701BC.

MEDITATION

Read Psalm 2 and imagine it applied first to Hezekiah and then to Jesus.

'CRISIS! WHAT CRISIS?'

The prophet Isaiah lived through the events of the Assyrian crisis, and many of the prophecies in his book come from this period. The book of Isaiah suggests that sometimes king and prophet did not see eye to eye. Nevertheless, as 2 Chronicles 32:20 asserts, when the chips were down, monarch and seer were united against Sennacharib.

Hezekiah's rescue

Initially Isaiah had spoken an oracle which portrayed Assyria as the rod of God's anger against his people (Isaiah 10:5). By his proud and boastful taunts, however, the Assyrian aggressor has overreached himself. In Isaiah 37:21–29, we can hear the prophet's rebuke to Sennacharib for his haughty arrogance. He will be humbled and will return without final victory to his own land. That is indeed what happened, and twenty years later, in 681, the powerful Assyrian monarch was murdered by two of his own sons (v. 21). He met his end in one of the temples of the Assyrian gods. So much for the ability of these deities to protect the sovereign!

Hezekiah's sickness and recovery

The Chronicler gives only the bare bones of this incident, which is described much more fully in 2 Kings 20. The sign, mentioned in passing in verse 24, is the miracle of the shadow moving backwards on the palace sundial. This is the only place in Chronicles where there is any hint of criticism against King Hezekiah. We are not told what Hezekiah's pride related to. Our first response might be to conclude that we have been here before. Previous kings, such as Asa and Uzziah, had fallen sick because of their pride. This time, however, the outcome is different. Hezekiah responds by showing true humbleness of heart and is consequently healed of his sickness. Once more, the Chronicler is contrasting the actions of this 'good' king with those of his predecessors. There is no doubt that, in the mind of the Chronicler, Hezekiah was an admirable king.

Hezekiah's tunnel

One of the regular ways in which the Chronicler signals the positive benefits of a good king's reign is by his building projects. Hezekiah is credited with significant building works throughout the country. At the same time, he grows rich and famous and receives visits from foreign envoys. All these features echo Solomon in all his glory.

Verse 30 highlights one particular construction feat. It is the provision of an adequate water supply for Jerusalem by redirecting the waters of the Gihon spring down to the Pool of Siloam. This provided for the expanding population of the city and offered a secure supply during times of siege. A long underground tunnel, which still exists today, is usually identified with the work of Hezekiah. It is about 530 metres long and shaped like a letter S. In 1888, an inscription was found near the Siloam Pool entrance to the tunnel. It is written in ancient Hebrew and describes the moment when the two teams of workmen, who had been working from either end of the tunnel, finally broke through in the middle. The tunnel is large enough for people to walk through. Having waded through it myself, I can certainly vouch for it as a major piece of engineering work. It is a credit to the tunnellers who produced it so long ago.

Babylonian envoys come to enquire about the miraculous sign from heaven (v. 31). The Babylonians had a keen interest in the observation of the heavens. Matthew 2 tells of astrologers who came in search of another king of the Jews, as a result of their observation of the heavens. 2 Kings 20 gives a somewhat different reason for the arrival of the envoys. They come to pay respects to Hezekiah on behalf of the Babylonian ruler, Merodach-baladan. This energetic prince was proving to be a thorn in the side of the Assyrian empire. We should note that this is the first reference to Babylon in Chronicles. Here the reference seems harmless enough, but one hundred years later Assyria will be no more, and mighty Babylon will have taken its place. Nebuchadnezzar of Babylon will succeed where Sennacharib of Assyria failed, and will seize the city of Jerusalem—temple, houses, tunnel and all.

PRAYER

Give thanks for those who provide us with access to clean water.
How easily we take such engineering miracles for granted!
Pray for places in the world without clean water.

The PRODIGAL KING

Between the reigns of the 'good kings' Hezekiah and Josiah, the people of Judah are condemned to endure the dismal reigns of Manasseh (697–642) and Amon (642–640).

Manasseh's evil reign

The Chronicler follows his source in Kings very closely in verses 1–9. The long reign of Manasseh represents the low point in the religious history of the kings of Judah. The list of the sins committed during this reign include everything that was corrupt and false in the eyes of the Chronicler. Worship was offered once more on the high places away from Jerusalem, the temple itself was defiled by pagan worship, mediums and wizards did a roaring trade! Worst of all, Manasseh 'made his son pass through fire in the valley of the son of Hinnom' (33:6). This may be a reference to the terrible practice of child sacrifice. Remember that in later times the valley of Hinnom became a rubbish dump, with fires burning day and night (see 28:1–4). In the New Testament, under the name Gehenna, it became a picture of hell itself.

The people of Israel had now acted even more corruptly than those nations God had driven out of the promised land in the book of Joshua. So God's people in turn will be driven away from the land. Exile and deportation beckon them.

Manasseh comes to his senses

Manasseh is a record-breaker. Despite being the worst king Jerusalem ever had, he reigned for longer than any other—fifty-five years in all (v. 1). How could this be, if God rewards goodness and punishes wickedness? The author of Kings saw the wickedness of Manasseh as the last straw. It finally tipped the scales and made the exile inevitable—but God in his mercy stayed his hand for the time being (2 Kings 21). The Chronicler deals differently with the theological problem. He tells of Manasseh's humiliation and repentance in verses 10–13. This material is not found in Kings. Through records from the palace of the Assyrian kings, we know that there was an internal rebellion around 652–648, during the reign of the Assyrian king,

Ashurbanipal. Perhaps Manasseh joined in the rebellion to try to free himself and his country from Assyrian overlordship, and paid the price.

Without doubt, the author of Chronicles depicts Manasseh as the 'prodigal king' of Judah. Like the good-for-nothing younger son in Jesus' parable of the prodigal son (Luke 15:11–32), so Manasseh too finally comes to his senses in a far-off country, a long way from home. He repents of his evil and is restored. Note that the place of his exile is none other than the city of Babylon (v. 11), rather than Nineveh, the capital of Assyria. He returns to his own land, a chastened man, and begins to rebuild the city walls and remove the offending practices from its religious life (v. 16). His own life mirrors the experience of the Israelite people in their exile and restoration, a theme close to the Chronicler's heart. Manasseh's prayer (v. 19) is unknown in the Bible itself but a version is given in the Apocrypha. The single chapter that makes up the prayer of Manasseh in the Apocrypha is a typical example of a prayer of confession. Though the Chronicler does not appear to have known it, he would probably have approved of its sentiments.

Amon's brief reign

The brief reign of Amon suggests that the reforms of his father Manasseh were superficial. We do not know whether Amon fell victim to political plotting or religious intrigue. For the Chronicler, it is a lack of humility that leads to Amon's downfall. Whereas Manasseh was repentant and contrite, Amon is stubbornly proud, and pays the price (v. 23). His death opened the way for the young king Josiah, and consequently for a new religious policy to emerge.

MEDITATION

What are the 'false gods' we have erected in our lives, as individuals and as a community? Do you really believe that God loves the 'prodigal', or that wicked people can fundamentally change? Try to think of some modern examples.

A BOY, a BOOK & a COVENANT

The Chronicler now introduces us to the last of his heroes, the young king Josiah. His reign lasted from 640 to 609, and was to see the final religious reforms during the period of the kings of Judah. After this interlude, it is downhill all the way for the nation and the monarchy.

The boy king

Josiah was only a boy of eight when he came to the throne in 640 following the assassination of his father. No doubt, for the first part of his reign real power would rest with a regent, as it did during the childhood of King Joash. Nevertheless, the Chronicler is keen to show that Josiah's heart was right with God, even from an early age. From the eighth year of his reign (v. 3), when he was still only sixteen years old, he began to seek the Lord. Four years later, he began to implement a thorough reform of religious practice in Jerusalem and the rest of the country.

The pace of religious reform in Judah perhaps went hand in hand with changes on the wider political scene. In 627, the powerful king of Assyria, named Ashurbanipal, died. Archaeologists excavated his palace in Nineveh in the nineteenth century. They found an extensive library of clay tablets which has helped historians to reconstruct the history of Mesopotamia. After Ashurbanipal's death, the great empire rapidly fell apart. Soon the Babylonians had regained their independence, and to the east, in modern-day Iran, the powerful forces of the Medes were ready to strike at the tottering empire.

Josiah's reform therefore coincided with a brief period of independence for Judah. Alongside a return to the proper worship of the Lord, there was a growing sense of national pride. Judah was no longer subject to Assyria or to its gods, so could reaffirm the covenant with the Lord God of Israel. The reform programme was thorough and complete. The burning of human bones on the altars made the altars ritually unclean so that they were permanently defiled and could never be used again (v. 5).

The book of the law

The temple in Jerusalem had suffered much neglect since the days of Hezekiah. In order to remedy this, Josiah begins a careful restoration programme. We should not be surprised by now to find Levites supervising the building works. We are not told what the carpenters and masons thought of having members of the temple guild of singers supervising their work (vv. 12–13)!

What was the book of the Law which the priest Hilkiah found (v. 14)? Was it the whole of the Pentateuch (the first five books of the Bible), or a portion of it? For the past two hundred years or so, the majority opinion has been to identify it with the book of Deuteronomy, or at least with the central chapters 12—26. The action Josiah takes is fully in line with the instructions of the law code, found only in Deuteronomy, that there should be a single legitimate place for sacrifice. In 2 Kings, Josiah is the first king to put this into practice by making the Jerusalem sanctuary the only shrine of worship and removing all the 'high places'. In Chronicles, reforming kings like David and Hezekiah have already followed this policy. Josiah receives full marks from the Chronicler, but his position is rather less prominent than in Kings, since his actions are not unique. So, for instance, Chronicles devotes four chapters to Hezekiah (29—32) but only two to Josiah (34—35).

Huldah the prophetess

Normally in the Old Testament, only males could rule over Israel or serve in the temple. However there was one sacred role that both women and men could play. That was the role of prophet, for the Spirit blows where it wills (as Jesus said in John 3:8), and is no respecter of person or gender. When he consults the prophetess, Josiah receives both bad news and good news. The bad news is that the downfall of Jerusalem is already decreed. The good news is that the king will not live to see it happen. It would not be appropriate for such a disaster to happen during the lifetime of a true servant of God like Josiah.

At the heart of the book of Deuteronomy stands the idea of a covenant between God and his people—a solemn binding treaty that unites Israel and the Lord (v. 31). It is entirely fitting, therefore, for this chapter to close with a description of just such a covenant ceremony. Once again the author stresses the concept of 'all Israel'. Just as in the time of Hezekiah one hundred years before, here too 'Israel' includes the remnant of the northern tribes as well as the south.

PRAYER

Give thanks for the wind of God's Spirit, blowing free in the world.

TRIUMPH & TRAGEDY

Two major events in the reign of Josiah are described in this chapter. First we have the impressive celebration of Passover in the spring of 622, and secondly the fateful battle at Megiddo in 609. They encapsulate both the triumph of Josiah's reign and the tragedy of his untimely and unnecessary death.

Passover time

Chapter 30 gave a description of a remarkable Passover celebration in the time of Hezekiah. Nearly one hundred years later, King Josiah oversees an equally impressive ceremony. There are some significant differences between the two festivals, nevertheless. The earlier one was in many ways irregular. It was held in the second month of the year, and various regulations were broken in order to allow people to participate. Josiah's Passover feast is celebrated correctly in the first month, and the Chronicler insists that all is done in strict conformity with the rules.

This is one of the chapters in Chronicles that emphasizes the teaching role of the Levites. Giving instruction was originally a priestly task, but by the Chronicler's own day the Levites were increasingly taking on this function. A good example of this is in Nehemiah 8, where the Levites instruct the people about the meaning of the Law. With the ark safely residing in the Holy of Holies, appropriate roles had to be found for the Levites (v. 3). They therefore took a major part in the preparation of the Passover. In earlier times, the layman at the head of each family would kill a Passover lamb, as described in Exodus 12. By the time of Josiah's Passover, the ceremony is much more organized. It centres on the temple at Jerusalem and the roles of the various clergy groups are carefully defined. Levites do the slaughtering and skinning of the sacrifices and they take the blood to the priests to be cast on the altar. Afterwards the Levites cook the meat and deliver it to the people (vv. 11–13). The Levites are the official and recognized go-betweens for the people and the priests. If we look for a modern equivalent to this description of Levites, we could compare it with the role of the deacon assisting at the celebration of the eucharist in some church traditions.

The death of Josiah

The scene moves on thirteen years to 609. By now, the Assyrian empire
is on its last legs. All its great cities, including Nineveh, have fallen to
the Babylonians and Medes, as portrayed in the vivid little prophecy
of Nahum. Its last king, Ashur-uballit, is struggling to survive. The
Egyptians appear very late on the scene to assist the hard-pressed
Assyrian remnant. There is a good political reason for the sudden
appearance of the Egyptians at this time. Egypt is worried by the ever-
growing power of Babylon under its king Nabopolassar and the energetic crown prince Nebuchadnezzar. The Egyptians would dearly love
to establish a power base in Mesopotamia by placing a garrison at
Carchemish on the River Euphrates. In order to do that, Pharaoh Neco
must march his troops through the Holy Land.

Josiah has no love at all for the Assyrians and endeavours to stop
Pharaoh's advance (v. 20). Neco tries to dissuade the king of Judah from
interfering (v. 21). This is not Josiah's fight, and in any case God has
commanded Neco to advance. The king takes no notice of this warning;
after all, it comes from the mouth of an Egyptian monarch, not a genuine prophet of the Lord God. Among the books of the Apocrypha is 1
Esdras, which retells these last two chapters of 2 Chronicles and the
book of Ezra. In that version, Josiah receives a warning not only from
Neco but also from the prophet Jeremiah (1 Esdras 1:28).

Josiah's action turns out to be not only a piece of political folly but
also an act of disobedience. He defies the warning, which is genuinely
a word from the Lord, and pays with his life. Megiddo was a notorious
place of battles in biblical times. In the book of Revelation, it gives its
name to the place of the final battle, Harmegedon (Hill of Megiddo).
The story of Josiah's fall echoes the stories of earlier kings. Hezekiah's
Passover was followed by the invasion of Sennacharib. This time, however, there will be no miraculous deliverance for the king. The trick of
disguising himself does not work for him, any more than it did for
Ahab. As usual, retribution follows swiftly in Chronicles. After a positive reign, Josiah meets a sad and undignified end. Standing in his
chariot, he receives a mortal wound. His death is reminiscent of that of
his ancestor Ahaziah.

MEDITATION

*'Why do bad things happen to good people?' If you have a cross or
crucifix, spend a few moments in silence before it.*

DECLINE & FALL

1 Chronicles 3:15–16 provided a family tree of Josiah's descendants. We must bear in mind that it was customary for a new king to assume a throne name on his accession.

Jehoahaz

Jehoahaz reigned for only three months in 609 (vv. 1–4). He was, in fact, one of the younger sons of Josiah. About Johanan, the eldest, we know nothing. Perhaps he was already dead, in which case Eliakim was next in line. Jehoahaz was placed on the throne by the popular will of the people, perhaps in order to continue Josiah's anti-Egyptian policy. Pharaoh Neco removed him and placed his older brother on the throne. According to 2 Kings 23:34, Jehoahaz died in Egypt, as prophesied in Jeremiah 22:11–12.

Jehoiakim

Eliakim took the throne name of Jehoiakim and ruled for eleven years from 609 to 598 (vv. 5–8). He was indebted to Egyptian power for his throne and no doubt pursued a pro-Egyptian policy, which the Chronicler saw as evil (v. 5). However, in 605 the Egyptians suffered a disastrous defeat at Carchemish at the hands of Nebuchadnezzar, now king of Babylon. It is possible that Jehoiakim was briefly taken to Babylon as a captive, as Manasseh had been. The opening verses of the book of Daniel certainly imply this. However, Chronicles seems to suggest that Jehoiakim was exiled at the end of the eleven years of his reign. 2 Kings, by contrast, speaks of his death and burial in Jerusalem (2 Kings 24:6). Jeremiah 22:18–19 shows what the prophet thought of him.

Jehoiachin

Comparison with 2 Kings 24:8 reveals that a slight error has occurred in the copying of Jehoiachin's age in verse 9. Kings says that he was eighteen years old and ruled for three months (598). Chronicles has him at eight years old and ruling three months and ten days. Perhaps the 'ten' was missed out and when the error was corrected was misunderstood to refer to days rather than years. He was deported to

Babylon, and in Jeremiah 22:24–30 the prophet laments for him. He spent the rest of his days as a prisoner, as a ration tablet from Babylon bearing his name confirms.

Zedekiah

Zedekiah is another king who ruled for eleven years (598–587). In verse 10, however, we hit a problem in the family tree. According to the Hebrew text of Chronicles, he was the elder brother of Jehoiachin. In 2 Kings, he is identified with Mattaniah, a son of Josiah, and was therefore the uncle of Jehoiachin. Kings is closer in time to the events, but some people think Chronicles has preserved the correct information—especially if he was only twenty-one at his accession.

His is the last of four dismal reigns (v. 12). Each of these kings did evil in the sight of God, according to Chronicles. Zedekiah is guilty of bringing 'pollution' into the temple, though the general public, leaders and priests are also held responsible. As always, God sends prophets to warn his wayward people. In particular, Jeremiah suffers ridicule and persecution at the hands of the authorities (Jeremiah 38). Finally, after a failed rebellion against Babylon, the city falls in 587 and the temple vessels, along with the people, are taken off to Babylon.

Cyrus of Persia

Jeremiah had spoken of a seventy-year period of exile (Jeremiah 25:11; 29:10). The Chronicler links this with the idea of sabbath rest for the land, as outlined in Leviticus 26:34–35. During the exile, the land lay fallow and was 'rested' and restored, ready for the exiles to return. In 539, Cyrus of Persia captured Babylon and in the following year he issued a proclamation enabling the Jews to return and rebuild the temple. 2 Chronicles ends with a quote from the edict, pointing forward to a new future (v. 23). The story goes on and will find a sequel in the books of Ezra and Nehemiah.

REFLECTION

2 Kings ends with Jehoiachin's release from prison in 561BC.
2 Chronicles ends with the events of 539BC.
What might the different endings of these two histories imply?

ROYAL PORTRAIT GALLERY

In summing up the presentation of David in 1 Chronicles, I likened the Chronicler to a portrait artist with a paintbrush, rather than a photographer with a camera. The same is true of the material in 2 Chronicles, which covers roughly the same four hundred years of history as the books of 1 and 2 Kings. Often the Chronicler is content to follow the outline of the royal portraits given in the earlier history work. Nevertheless, his work is not just a reproduction of an 'original'. The Chronicler has painted his own picture with its distinctive features, even though he often follows Kings word for word. In his portraits he distinguishes clearly between light and shade in order that readers may see the issues clearly and apply the lessons learned.

North and south

We have seen how the Chronicler omits all the details of the reigns of the northern kings ruling from their capital of Samaria. Nevertheless, he wastes no opportunity in describing times in their joint history when north and south interact—sometimes as friends and sometimes as enemies. He clearly considers the northern tribes to be at fault and to have been led astray by the sin of Jeroboam I. Nevertheless, there was always a remnant which allied itself with the Davidic rulers in Jerusalem. Sometimes he even shows the northerners in a positive light—as, for instance, their kindly treatment of the captured prisoners in chapter 28. When Samaria fell in 722, many refugees made their way south and Hezekiah sought to rule over a united kingdom once more. The Chronicler's vision of 'all Israel' includes north and south, Samaria and Jerusalem. Does this reflect the author's dream to see the growing rift between 'Jews' and 'Samaritans' healed?

Good and bad

Chronicles usually follows Kings in identifying 'good' monarchs. The heroes of both books are rulers such as Solomon, Jehoshaphat, Hezekiah and Josiah. Chronicles, however, raises the profiles of Jehoshaphat and Hezekiah at the expense of Josiah. Both works also have out-and-out villains like Jehoram, Ahaz and Zedekiah.

Despite these similarities, Chronicles can also provide important new insights into the character of some of the kings. In Chronicles, King Abijah slips out of the shadows to become a much more positive figure. Manasseh, by God's grace, is given opportunity to repent of his dreadful misdeeds, whereas in Kings his loathsome actions are the final straw. In Chronicles, each generation must answer for its own deeds.

Priests and Levites

At the time when Chronicles was written, around 350BC, there was no Jewish king. The Persian empire was dominant, though it would soon be conquered by the Greek army of Alexander the Great. Nor was the voice of prophecy heard—the age of the great prophets was now past history. The prophetic voices of the past survived through the written scriptures, which were increasingly studied and discussed. Priests, and especially the high priest, had a significant role not only in religious but in political affairs too. The Levites were developing an important role as teachers and this teaching role in Judaism would continue to grow and develop into the 'rabbi' of New Testament times.

So the Chronicler points to the part played in history by particular priests such as Zadok, Jehoiada, Zechariah the martyr, Azariah and Hilkiah. He also highlights the role played by Levites in the reforms of Hezekiah's and Josiah's reigns. Here he sees the continuity between his own time and the distant past, going back to David or even to Moses.

Past and future

The Chronicler believes that there are lessons to be learned from the past. It provides patterns for the present and hints for the future. Chronicles is perhaps not so future-oriented as some of the prophetic books. It does not speak directly about the coming Messiah or the future 'age to come'. Yet it is not closed to the future. 2 Chronicles ends with the words of Cyrus' decree, and these same words open the book of Ezra. The books of Ezra and Nehemiah will tell the next phase of the story. The author of Chronicles wants his readers not only to know the story of their past, but also to learn from it, to interpret it and to make sense of it.

PRAYER

Lord, give us wisdom to interpret the events of our own time,
as the writers of scripture did for theirs.

A HISTORY LESSON

The city of Jerusalem fell to the Babylonian invaders in 587BC. Many of the inhabitants of Judah were taken into exile. We should not assume, however, that the land was totally devoid of people. Many from the poorest classes were left behind and, no doubt, other nationalities migrated into the land to fill the vacuum. For nearly fifty years the exile continued. Some of the pain of that time is reflected in books such as Lamentations and Obadiah, and in some of the psalms such as 74, 89 and 137. Large portions of the prophetic books of Isaiah, Jeremiah and Ezekiel were probably edited during this time. It was a very significant moment in biblical history. However, the Bible itself has little to say about the situation in Judah during these fifty years.

The silence is finally broken by the account in the book of Ezra. The stories told in this book and the subsequent book of Nehemiah shed much-needed light on the events from 538 to 432. It is through these books that we catch a glimpse of the Jewish people during the first hundred years or so of Persian rule. They are no longer independent but are a small part of the mighty Persian empire. Their country is known simply as the province of Yehud (Judah).

The book of Ezra provides snapshots of the challenges and difficulties, the joys and sorrows of the restored community. In many ways, the history of this period in Judah is shrouded in mystery. Nevertheless, there are some Persian inscriptions and documents from the sixth to fourth centuries which fill in the background. In addition, the Greek historian Herodotus provides an account of the growing power struggle between the Persians and the Greeks.

The time-chart opposite depicts the events of the Persian period. It covers two hundred years of history, from the fall of Babylon in 539 to the Persians' eventual defeat by Alexander the Great in 331.

REFLECTION

Consider these words from a hymn:
'God is working his purpose out as year succeeds to year.'

Persian ruler	Events of the reign	Biblical refs
Cyrus (556–530)	539 Cyrus captures Babylon and it becomes part of his empire.	Isa. 44:28; 45:1; 47; Jer. 50
	538 Issue of decree allowing return home.	Ezra 1
	First group of exiles return.	Ezra 2
	Altar is rededicated.	Ezra 3
Cambyses (530–522)	525 Conquest of Egypt. It too becomes part of the Persian empire and the Persian kings are known as the 27th Dynasty of Egypt.	
Darius I (522–486)	520 Rebuilding of temple in Jerusalem recommences under Joshua and Zerubbabel.	Ezra 5 Hagg. 1 Zech. 6
	515 Temple rededicated.	Ezra 6; Zech. 8
	490 Battle of Marathon when Persia invades Greece.	
Xerxes I (486–465)	480 Battle of Salamis where Persians defeated by Greeks.	Story of Esther (Xerxes = Ahasuerus)
Artaxerxes I (465–424)	458 Mission of Ezra according to most likely date.	Ezra 7
	445 Mission of Nehemiah	Neh. 1
	432 Nehemiah's second term as governor.	Neh. 13
	428 Alternative date for Ezra's mission.	
Darius II (424–404)		
Artaxerxes II (404–359)	398 Latest possible date for Ezra's mission.	
Artaxerxes III (359–338)	Possible period for the work of the Chronicler.	
Arsas (338–336)		
Darius III (336–331)	331 Alexander the Great captures control of the whole Persian empire. He dies young and is succeeded by his generals, not his son.	Dan. 11:3–4 1 Macc. 1:1–7

TWO UNSOLVED MYSTERIES

The books of Ezra and Nehemiah both contain material written in the first person. These sections are usually referred to as the 'memoirs' of Ezra and Nehemiah. They are probably the oldest parts of the books, going back to the time of Ezra and Nehemiah themselves. They form the heart of the material that was subsequently worked over and expanded by the final editor of the books. This final edition was composed about one hundred years later, so the memoirs date from around 450 to 430BC, while the final form of the books as we have them dates from 350 to 330.

Despite being relatively short books, Ezra and Nehemiah have produced two intriguing puzzles for scholars. They are puzzles to which no completely satisfactory answer has been given, and they continue to divide the world of biblical scholarship. They are versions of those two imponderable questions—'Which came first?' and 'Whodunnit?'

Which came first?

Among riddles, one of the most difficult to answer is 'Which came first, the chicken or the egg?' In biblical scholarship, this translates into 'Who came first, Ezra or Nehemiah?' According to the witness of the books themselves, the answer is quite clear. Ezra came first, in the seventh year of Artaxerxes, followed in the twentieth year by Nehemiah. Assuming that the king in question was Artaxerxes I, then Ezra arrived in Jerusalem in 458 and Nehemiah followed on in 445. These are the dates I have given in the time-chart.

So what, you may ask, is the problem? Scholars argue that if this order is correct, then the only conclusion to be drawn is that Ezra's mission was a failure. This is because Nehemiah has to go over much of the same ground again, only a few years later. For example, Ezra 10 describes the enactment of laws against mixed marriages, but in Nehemiah 13:23–27 the situation appears no better, in fact it seems worse. That is problem number one. Problem number two is that neither of the two men ever mentions the other. Ezra's memoir contains no mention of Nehemiah, nor Nehemiah's of Ezra. The only time they appear together is in Nehemiah 8, which really seems to be a story about Ezra. Nehemiah is merely a spectator in the background. The story in Nehemiah 8 is a narrative in the third person, told about Ezra and Nehemiah, and not a first-hand account. Did the final editor make a chronological error in linking these two figures?

Therefore the 'early date' has been challenged, and two suggestions are offered which place Ezra after Nehemiah. The 'middle date' assumes that 'in the seventh year of Artaxerxes' (Ezra 7:7) is a scribal error and that the proper number should be thirty-seven. The thirty-seventh year of Artaxerxes I would be 428 and would place Ezra about five years after the last dated event in Nehemiah 13. However, there is no real evidence for this, and it is purely guesswork. The 'late date' assumes that the seventh year of Artaxerxes refers to the reign of Artaxerxes II. This would put Ezra's arrival in the year 398. If so, then the editor of the books was a poor historian who has telescoped events in a very unsatisfactory way. Could he have made such a clumsy error only fifty to sixty years after Ezra's time? Most commentators seem to be coming to the view that the traditional date of 458 is correct—but that the length of Ezra's ministry in Jerusalem may have been quite short.

Whodunnit?

The second mystery surrounds the identity of the author, or better still, editor, of Ezra-Nehemiah. In many respects, the style and vocabulary are similar to those of Chronicles. Yet in certain other respects, the outlook and theology are not the same at all. The attitude to northerners is more positive in Chronicles, much less so in Ezra-Nehemiah. The similarity in style may simply indicate that the Chronicler and the editor of Ezra-Nehemiah lived at about the same time but were not necessarily one and the same. The strongest evidence that the Chronicler was also the editor of these two books comes from the repetition of the last two verses of 2 Chronicles as the opening verses of Ezra 1. Whether this represents the text of the 'first edition' of these works or a later editing of them, we shall never know. Scholars are fairly evenly divided over whether or not the Chronicler is the author or editor of Ezra-Nehemiah—but it is no longer taken for granted as it used to be.

REFLECTION
Why do mysteries appeal so much to the human imagination?
Who is your favourite fictional detective from TV, films or books?
Why do they appeal to you?

A MEDLEY *of* MATERIAL

In many ways, the book of Ezra strikes modern readers as rather untidy. It jumps about over a long historical period from one incident to another. Furthermore, it seems to be made up of very diverse material. The reader of Ezra will probably identify at least four different types of writing.

Stories about Ezra: Although Ezra gives his name to the whole book, he appears as a character only in chapters 7—10. Sometimes stories are told about Ezra, using the third person, and at other times stories are told by Ezra, using the first person. It has often been supposed that there is a so-called 'Ezra memoir', written by Ezra himself, lying behind these chapters. This was then edited by a later author to give us the material we have today. Many scholars believe that Nehemiah chapters 8—9 were originally part of this memoir. In these chapters, it is Ezra who is the dominant character, with Nehemiah as a mere onlooker. A similar editing process may have happened to the memoirs of Nehemiah; however, they are rather more extensive than the scattered fragments of Ezra's recollections.

Other narratives: The first six chapters of Ezra contain historical information about the early Persian period. This includes the reigns of Cyrus in chapters 1 and 3, Artaxerxes in chapter 4, and Darius in chapters 5 and 6. The information is not very detailed, but it is supplemented by the third kind of material.

Official archives: The narratives in chapters 1—6 are largely carried along through the insertion of official documents from the Persian court relating to affairs in the province of Yehud. Such archive material is found in the following sections: 1:2–4; 4:8–22; 5:6–17; 6:1–12; 7:12–26. Whoever composed the book of Ezra was able to get hold of these official documents and incorporate them into the account.

Genealogies and other lists: The liking for genealogical lists which was a feature of Chronicles is also a marked feature of the books of Ezra and Nehemiah. They are found in chapter 2; 8:1–14; and 10:18–44. With their snippets of information, they provide a glimpse into the day-to-day events of the post-exilic Jewish community.

A common theme?

Is the book of Ezra, then, merely a hotch-potch of different material carelessly thrown together by a second-rate editor? That would be a very harsh judgment. There is, in fact, a common theme which runs through this book and the contemporary account of Nehemiah. Their aim is to demonstrate how the people of God were reborn and how they survived in the changed political circumstances of the Persian empire.

From a theological point of view, the editor emphasizes that God was at work in the rebirth of the people. However, that rebirth takes place in the difficult political circumstances of Persian power politics. Time and again, the efforts of the Jewish people are frustrated by their opponents, who accuse them of disloyalty to the Persian government. The editor of Ezra-Nehemiah is keen to show that the return to Jerusalem, the rebuilding of its temple, the repair of its walls and the institution of the Mosaic Law posed no threat to Persian sovereignty. From Cyrus the liberator onwards, the Persian kings show tolerance and approval of the Jewish hopes and aspirations.

Similar stories are told elsewhere in the Bible of Jewish heroes and heroines learning to live peaceably in a foreign court or land, despite the inevitable tensions. These stories include Joseph in the court of Pharaoh, Daniel among the rulers of Babylon and Queen Esther at the court of Ahasuerus (Xerxes). The Jewish people may have strange customs in the eyes of their masters, but they are not a political threat. They seek only to be obedient to the commands of God.

For this reason, the most likely setting for the final editing of Ezra and Nehemiah is towards the end of the Persian period, some time before the conquest by Alexander in 331. This is roughly the same period as the work of the Chronicler, though whether he was the editor of Ezra-Nehemiah too is still a much-debated point.

REFLECTION

Imagine you had to fill a small scrapbook with items relating to your life and times. What snippets might you include—photographs, letters, newspaper cuttings, mementos? What picture of you might emerge from all this?

An UNLIKELY SAVIOUR

Cyrus, a prince of the Achamenid family in southern Iran, came to power in his own small province in 556. In the space of less than twenty years, he united the Medes and Persians, and made conquests in Asia Minor (modern Turkey), coming within reach of the Greek islands. Finally, in October 539, he captured the great city of Babylon almost without a fight. The author of Ezra sees these dramatic events as the fulfilment of God's promises through the prophets. Jeremiah had twice spoken of a seventy-year period of Babylonian subjection (Jeremiah 25:11; 29:10), while chapter 51 of Jeremiah provides a graphic description of the fall of the tyrant city. Chapters 40—47 of the book of Isaiah make explicit mention of Cyrus. They even dare to call him the 'anointed one' or 'messiah' (Isaiah 45:1). The Jewish historian Josephus, writing at the end of the first century AD, says that the Persian king had read these prophecies. Earlier prophets saw God using foreign rulers to achieve his purposes. He raised up the Assyrian king to punish the northern kingdom, and chose Nebuchadnezzar of Babylon as his instrument against Jerusalem. In the same way, Cyrus is now seen as the instrument of salvation.

The king's edict

This is the first of the official documents quoted in the book of Ezra (vv. 2–4). Another version of the edict appears in Ezra 6:3–5. Some scholars think that the version in this chapter, which is given in Hebrew, was the original spoken announcement made by heralds to the Jewish populace. The version in chapter 6 is in Aramaic, and may represent the 'official' written document.

The Persian policy of returning exiled peoples to their homeland made good political sense. It helped to gain the favour of these conquered peoples and would therefore diffuse thoughts of rebellion. Cyrus treated not only the Jews but also other conquered peoples in this way. A famous inscription known as the 'Cyrus cylinder' has been discovered by archaeologists. It proclaims the king's decrees concerning the restoration of temples in Babylon. It says, 'I returned to (their) sacred cities on the other side of the Tigris, the sanctuaries of which have been in ruins for a long time, the images which used to live therein.'

Cyrus himself was probably a believer in the Zoroastrian religion which worshipped the 'god of light', Ahura Mazda. His policy of toleration stood in contrast to those of the previous Assyrian and Babylonian powers. Unlike these Mesopotamian kingdoms, or Egypt, the land of slavery, there is little animosity towards the Persians in the Bible. By contrast, Babylon was to become a byword for oppression, even in the New Testament (Revelation 18). For the author of our text, Persian rule is acceptable, so long as it does not interfere with the Jews' religious beliefs and practices. The Jewish people must remain distinct and not intermarry with foreigners, but it is possible for them to live in harmony under a tolerant foreign power.

Homeward bound

Verses 1 and 5 speak of God 'stirring up the spirit' of Cyrus and of the people. These words echo the prophecies in Isaiah 41:2 and Jeremiah 51:11. It is not clear whether the neighbours who give gifts in verses 4 and 6 are fellow Jews or Gentiles. If the latter, then there is an echo of the theme of the 'spoiling of the Egyptians' found in the Exodus story. In that story, the Egyptians gave gifts to the departing Israelites to speed them on their way (Exodus 12:35–36).

The temple vessels, which are carefully listed in the inventory, represent an important continuation between Solomon's first temple and the plans for the building of the second temple. Amid so much change, there is continuity as well.

The identity of Sheshbazzar, the 'prince of Judah' in verse 8, is something of a mystery. Josephus and some modern writers think that he is the same person as the later governor, Zerubbabel. It was common for people to have more than one name. However, chapter 5 would seem to rule out this identification, since there are quite separate references to Zerubbabel (5:2) and Sheshbazzar (5:14, 16). Others think that Sheshbazzar is the same as the royal prince Shenazzar mentioned in 1 Chronicles 3:18, the fourth son of the exiled king Jehoiachin. The most likely explanation, however, is that he was simply the first, perhaps short-lived, governor of Judah and not necessarily a descendant of David.

PRAYER

Pray for the people of modern-day Persia/Iran and their leaders.

PASSPORT CONTROL

In the West today, we live in a very individualistic society, part of the 'me' generation. It was not like this in the ancient world, nor is it in many non-Western societies even today. Your identity came from the clan or family, town or village to which you belonged. You were first of all part of a community, and only secondarily a distinct individual. That is why we need to escape from our individualistic Western ways of thinking in order to appreciate the significance of this chapter.

Yes, it is another long list of names similar to those we encountered in Chronicles. Yes, it may be one of the 'boring bits' according to our value system, but not for the author of Ezra-Nehemiah. He found it so stimulating and significant that he included it twice—once here in Ezra and again in Nehemiah 7. Clearly our outlooks are not the same! This list was so important to our author because it was about the establishment of identity. These people, as much as the temple vessels, represented the precious continuity between past and present, before the exile and after it. God's promises to Abraham, Isaac and Jacob concerning land and descendants still stood. God had not gone back on his word.

The list is divided into clear and distinct sections.

Leaders (v. 2): The equivalent list in Nehemiah 7 includes one extra name, Nahamani, that has been lost from here. When added, it gives the names of twelve leaders. This is the same number as the tribes of Israel, and no doubt is an echo of the twelve tribes who first took possession of the land under Joshua's leadership hundreds of years before.

Lay people (vv. 3–35): This list is divided between family names in verses 3–20 and place names in verses 21–35, beginning with Bethlehem. The numbers identified with the towns and villages of this second part are quite small, counted in hundreds or even tens. However, there are two exceptions. Verse 31 mentions 'the other Elam', but its figure of 1,254 is the same as the number of the family group called Elam in verse 7. That looks like too much of a coincidence. Secondly, the total of 3,630 for Senaah (v. 35) is very high. Some think it may not be a place name but may refer to some specific group or class of people.

Priests (vv. 36–39): Four priestly houses are mentioned, numbering 4,279 out of the total of 42,360 returners. So more than ten per cent of those returning were priests, eager to work again at the temple.

Levites, singers, gatekeepers (vv. 40–42): By contrast, the number of Levites, at 74, is very small and the number of singers and gatekeepers not much better. This contrasts with the emphasis on these groups found in the books of Chronicles.

Other temple personnel (vv. 43–58): Perhaps these groups owe their origin to those whose story is told in Joshua 9. In that account, the descendants of the Gibeonites became 'hewers of wood and drawers of water for the congregation and for the altar of the Lord' (Joshua 9:27). Some of the names are non-Israelite foreign names and many are, in fact, nicknames. Examples from the list include Hasupha (Quick), Lebanah (White), Nekoda (Spotted) and Hakupha (Stooped). Some, like the Meunim (2 Chronicles 20:1; 26:7) or Nephisim, may originally have been prisoners of war, since they are the names of ethnic groups.

Disputed lines (vv. 59–63): The entry qualifications were quite strict and not every family could prove its origins, though they were not prevented from returning to the land on account of this. For the priestly families, however, it was a particularly serious matter. If they could not prove their descent from the family of Aaron, then they could not act as priests or have a share in the 'most holy food' (v. 63) which was part of the priests' dues for temple service.

The Urim and Thummim (v. 63) were used for discerning the will of God. They were probably like dice with the equivalent of 'yes' and 'no' on them. In the first temple period, they were kept in the high priest's tunic. However, they disappeared in the destruction of 587 and were never recovered for use in the second temple. Later rabbinical teaching identified them as one of five things in Solomon's temple which were missing from the second temple. One of the others was the Holy Spirit—which we might consider even more crucial!

Those who return bring with them gifts for the rebuilding of the temple. Since there is no longer a king, the second temple will be much more of a community-funded project than the first temple.

PRAYER

Remember those families who in the present time leave one land in order to make their home in another.

MAKING *a* START

The opening verses of chapter 3 are set in the early years of the return. The altar was dedicated in September 538 and work began on the foundations of the temple in the following spring. If we compare this account with what is said in the prophetic books of Haggai and Zechariah, some difficult historical questions arise. When exactly did work start and who was responsible for it?

Community leaders

There are two prominent leaders connected with the rebuilding of the sanctuary. In verses 1–2 and in the books of Haggai and Zechariah, they are named as Zerubbabel the governor and Jeshua the high priest. In Haggai and Zechariah, the latter's name is spelled 'Joshua' and the Good News Bible uses 'Joshua' in Ezra too. Both men have family links back to the last days of the old city of Jerusalem.

Verse 2 identifies Jeshua as the son of Jozadak. The list of high priests in 1 Chronicles 6:15 mentions a Jehozadak as the high priest taken into captivity in Babylon.

Zerubbabel's royal pedigree is set out in 1 Chronicles 3:15–20:

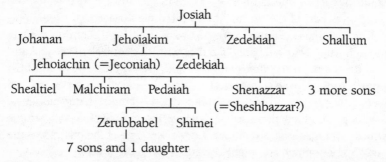

The question of where the elusive Sheshbazzar fits in has already been discussed in the section on Ezra 1. He could be Jehoiachin's fourth son, Shenazzar, or an alternative name for Zerubbabel. Most likely, however, he is neither of these and not even of the royal line. Almost all texts, including Ezra 3, count Zerubbabel as the son of Shealtiel. This may be a case of the application of the rules of Levirate marriage, as described in Deuteronomy 25:5–10, or of adoption. In either case, we must assume that Shealtiel had no son of his own and that Zerubbabel, though the natural son of Pedaiah, was counted as Shealtiel's heir. Haggai and Zechariah, who were his contemporaries, make much of Zerubbabel's royal messianic claims. The book of Ezra, however, makes no such claims. He is simply one of a number of governors who ruled the province for the Persians.

The altar of God

One of the first tasks of the returning group was to rebuild the altar (vv. 3–6). We do not know if sacrifices had continued after 587. If so, the returning group would consider them to be polluted and illegitimate, because the old altar had been made unclean. The rebuilding of the altar establishes a link in the chain of continuity between the first and second temples. The re-establishment of the regular times for sacrifice forges another link. These sacrifices include both the daily offerings and those for the appointed feasts. Calendars are an important part of national and religious identity. Think of the significance of Easter for Christians, Ramadan for Muslims, Divali for Hindus. It is not surprising that the rift between Jews and Christians in the century after Christ was significantly widened when Christians ceased to observe the Jewish calendar.

Clearing the ground

The preparations for the building work (vv. 7–9) may remind us of the activities of David and Solomon. The historical problem is whether these preparations are part of the first attempt to rebuild, in 537, or of the later successful venture in 520—515. Were Jeshua and Zerubbabel around in 537, or did they come on the scene later? According to Ezra 5:16, the foundations were laid by Sheshbazzar, but then the work broke off. Haggai and Zechariah, writing around the year 520, speak as if the temple is still in ruins and nothing has been done. Perhaps one way of reconciling these differences is to suppose that Sheshbazzar made a start in 537, but that nothing much came of it and that by 520 everything had to start virtually from scratch. It is clear that the real work of rebuilding did not take place in the 530s, in Cyrus' reign, but only after 520 in the reign of Darius.

PRAYER

Pray for those who have to start rebuilding their homes
after natural disasters or after the turmoil of war.

LAYING FOUNDATIONS

According to the book of Ezra, work began on the temple rebuilding and repairs in 537. Yet by 520 very little had been accomplished, as the prophet Haggai bitterly complains (Haggai 1:4). The first twenty years or so after the return present a very mixed picture, with reasons for rejoicing and for sorrow. In these early years, foundations are laid. These include both literal foundation stones and also fundamental attitudes which characterize post-exilic society for generations to come.

'A day of small things'

The brief description of the laying of the foundation stone (vv. 10–13) echoes the story of the laying of the foundation of the first temple. This second temple is both new and not new, a new beginning and also a continuation. Much of the fabric of the first temple was destroyed in the fire that engulfed Jerusalem in 587. Nevertheless, a good deal of the foundations may have remained. The ground plan was already there for the people of 537 to follow. Think of how many ancient churches have been built and rebuilt on one site. On one piece of sacred ground, succeeding generations build different architectural expressions of the same basic faith.

Once the altar is dedicated, the work on foundation-laying is the next most important item. The priests play upon their designated instruments, the trumpets, while the Levites accompany them with cymbals. The chorus they sing appears often, for example in Psalms 100:5 and 106:1, and especially as a regular refrain in Psalm 136.

Yet some people weep at what they see. It is fifty years since the 'old' temple went up in flames. Men in their sixties, seventies and eighties remember it well. For them, it will always be 'the temple'. No doubt, during the long period without a temple, its beauty had grown in their eyes. We find a similar response in Haggai 2:3, and the words of Zechariah 4:10 perhaps hold the clue. For all the brave endeavours, it seems to the old timers that they live in a 'day of small things'. They are convinced that they are not the people that their forebears were. However, such an attitude can become dispiriting to all concerned and can undermine morale. Religious communities afflicted by melancholy about 'the good old days' often become exceedingly dispirited and depressed, and consequently end up doing nothing. Fortunately in this instance the sound of weeping does not drown the positive sound of rejoicing.

Stirrings of opposition

A group appears on the horizon offering assistance to the builders (4:1–5). They are described as descendants of those settlers brought in to repopulate the devastated northern kingdom after the destruction of 722. In particular, they claim to have entered the land during the reign of King Esar-haddon (681–669). No doubt they married some of the survivors of the northern kingdom and adopted worship of the Lord, the God of that land. However, they would have also continued with religious observance and practice from their former pagan background.

The returned exiles refuse any help or hint of cooperation from these people. The group from Babylon are not willing to recognize them for three reasons:

- They do not have a proper pedigree: they are not true descendants of Abraham, but of mixed race.

- They do not have a proper liturgy: they have mixed true worship with their own native customs.

- They do not have a proper history: they are not part of the true remnant. Those returning from Babylon claimed that privilege for themselves alone. In the language of Jeremiah 24, they are the 'good figs' while those left in the land are the 'bad figs'.

How do individuals or communities decide whether it is right to compromise or not? When are accommodation and compromise right and a sign of strength and when are they wrong and a sign of weakness? Or we might ask, 'When do firmness and steadfastness become arrogance?' Do you think Zerubbabel was right to reject the offer of help, either from the religious point of view or from the community relations point of view?

REFLECTION

Ponder your own attitude to Christian groups different from your own. Which groups do you work with ecumenically? Which groups do you have no dealings with? What are your basic principles?

FAST FORWARD

Verse 5 described the frustrations experienced by the would-be builders of the temple from about 537 to 520. The material in verses 6–23 is, on a strictly chronological view, out of place. It deals with events in the reigns of later kings, Xerxes (486–465) and Artaxerxes (464–424). Furthermore, the subject matter is the building of the city wall, not the temple. Verse 24 then picks up the story again at the beginning of the reign of King Darius (522–486).

What we have here is a technique by the author which is similar in some ways to the 'fast forward' button on a video recorder. In verses 1–5, he tells of the beginnings of opposition to the rebuilding programme. This opposition comes from a group of supposed well-wishers. Verses 6–23 continue the theme of plotting and accusation against the community of returned Jews in Jerusalem. The pattern described in summary in verses 4–5 will continue for most of the next century. Each move forward by the community will be met with a countermove by their opponents. The power politics of the whole area will be played out like a deadly game of chess. Thus, while this section disrupts the time-line and is out of sequence, it fits the developing theme of our author. We need not suppose that he is an inept historian who has hopelessly muddled up his kings and dates.

Official correspondence

Three separate examples of diplomatic correspondence sent to the Persian court are mentioned, one each in verses 6, 7 and 8. In verse 6, we have a letter of accusation, dated around 485, at the start of Xerxes' reign. The names of the accusers are not mentioned. In verse 7, there is a letter from Mithredath, Tabeel and others to King Artaxerxes. Again, this may be from the early part of his reign, perhaps between 465 and 460, prior to Ezra's mission. Finally, in verse 8 we have the letter of Rehum and Shimshai, also in the reign of Artaxerxes. Perhaps it comes from the period between the arrival of Ezra in 458 and of Nehemiah in 445.

Although the author may have had copies of all this correspondence, he chooses to give full details only of the third. At this point, he quotes both the original complaint and the king's reply in full. The official diplomatic language of the time was Aramaic (v. 7) and at verse 8 the author switches from Hebrew to Aramaic in order to quote verbatim. This Aramaic section will continue until 6:18. Apart from Daniel 2:4—7:28, this is the longest section in Aramaic in the whole of the Old Testament.

The opposition seize upon the building of the city walls as a sign of disloyalty. When Xerxes came to the Persian throne in 486, the land of Egypt was already in revolt, and Babylon soon made a break for independence too. Both rebellions were crushed, but in 460 Egypt tried once more to regain independence. They were defeated by Megabyzus, the Persian governor of the province 'Beyond the River'. However, a couple of years later, this same governor led an internal revolt. At just this point in history, in the year 458, Ezra arrives in Jerusalem.

Perhaps the description which Nehemiah hears from his brother Hanani in 445 about the destruction of the walls and gates of the city of Jerusalem reflects the events of this turbulent period (Nehemiah 1). The cessation of building in verses 21–22 may indicate that the opponents were successful in preventing progress on the walls in the period 458–445. It is often the case that local issues get sucked into the intrigues of superpower politics. During the Cold War, many parts of Africa, the Middle East and elsewhere were caught up in the rivalries between the USA and USSR. Leaders, governments and dictators could (and did) get away with murder by aligning themselves with one of the 'big players' on the political scene. Jerusalem and Judah may only be a small area in a huge empire. Nevertheless, Ezra and Nehemiah are treading in a political minefield, quite apart from the religious dimension to their work.

PRAYER

Remember in your prayers:
the small countries of the world without power and influence;
people whose lives are affected by the decisions of larger nations or
of multi-national businesses.

STOP—GO

The comments in 4:24 have brought us back to the main story in the period around 520BC, the second year of King Darius. It is time to recommence the account of the building of the sanctuary.

Prophecy versus bureaucracy

At this point (5:1–5), we are introduced to the work of the prophets Haggai and Zechariah. We can compare the details in this chapter with information gleaned from the books of the two prophets. Darius came to the throne of Persia in 522, but he had to spend the first two years dealing with internal rebellions and a power struggle for the throne. For a short while, the great Persian empire looked shaky and appeared to be tottering. A hint of this may be found at the end of Haggai where the prophet speaks of kingdoms overthrown and civil war (Haggai 2:22–23).

Was this an auspicious time to relaunch a temple building project? The prophets thought it was—though others in the community may not have been so sure. Both Haggai and Zechariah had links with the priesthood and its ritual and would naturally support the rebuilding. Zechariah may well have been from a priestly family. Their words to Joshua and Zerubbabel had the desired effect, and work on the long-delayed project restarted.

Even in a time of some political confusion, there was still no getting away from the eagle-eye of Persian bureaucracy. The sprawling empire was divided into a number of large territorial units called a 'satrapy', and the chief administrator of each was called a 'satrap'. At the time of Haggai and Zechariah, the regions of 'Babylon' and 'Beyond the River' formed one satrapy. In other words, the region of Mesopotamia and the land west of the River Euphrates formed one administrative area. The satrap lived in Babylon and his deputy was located 'beyond the river (Euphrates)' in the city of Damascus. This deputy was Tattenai and he paid an official visit to Jerusalem with his secretary and other investigating officers. His enquiries are not particularly hostile and he does not forbid the work continuing. Nevertheless, as any good bureaucrat would, he wants to make sure that the work has proper approval. After all, a temple structure might easily be a fortress in disguise!

Tattenai's enquiry

Once more (vv. 6–17) we have a copy of an official document from the Persian administration, plus, in chapter 6, the reply received. Where did the author of the first six chapters of Ezra get this information? He seems to have been Jerusalem-based, rather than a resident in Babylon or Persia, so the most likely source of his information is from official archives preserved in Jerusalem itself. In these opening chapters covering the early Persian period, our author relies very heavily on such official records. His other possible source is the biblical material provided in prophetic books such as those of Haggai and Zechariah.

We learn a little about the actual structure of the second temple from Tattenai's description. In addition to blocks of stone, timber is laid in the walls (v. 8). Archaeology confirms that important structures were often built with several layers of stone followed by a layer of timber. This was probably a protection against earthquake damage. Tattenai includes in his report the response of the Jews to his initial investigations. Their words show that they have taken to heart the lessons of their history (v. 12). The theological outlook of success followed by failure and retribution, which was a prominent part of the theology of Chronicles, is repeated here too. The message is clear—the God of heaven and earth is in control of all history.

The individual satrapies covered very large areas of territory. They were therefore subdivided into smaller units called 'provinces'. The province of Judah (or Yehud) was thus a part of the wider satrapy. The shadowy figure of Sheshbazzar appears again briefly here in this résumé and he is credited with laying the foundations of the temple in the 530s. The elders' words in verse 16 might suggest that work went on continually from 537 to 520. However, the impression gained from Haggai and Zechariah themselves is that work had come to a standstill and that a fresh start had to be made in 520. The reason for this may have been not just external opposition but also an economic downturn, inflation, bad harvests and an erosion of confidence.

REFLECTION

Many ancient churches are now 'listed buildings'.
Think through the issues of heritage preservation,
on the one hand, and the desire of a congregation to change
its buildings in order to serve the present age.

The KING'S EDICT

King Darius responds to governor Tattenai and his colleagues. The language used is the lofty style of Persian royalty addressing and commanding their subjects. Many inscriptions from the Persian period confirm that the style of address in these pieces of correspondence is utterly typical of the time.

Checking the files

A search is made of the royal records and the appropriate document is found, not in Babylon but in Ecbatana. The city of Ecbatana was the capital of the land of the Medes. Cyrus had captured it in 550 and it was used as a summer residence, a place to escape from the burning summer heat. Perhaps the document was part of the treasury or finance department files. It confirms the building project that was commissioned in 538 after Cyrus had captured Babylon.

The decree of Cyrus cited in verses 3–5 repeats information from the beginning of the book of Ezra. However, comparison of Ezra 1:2–4 with 6:3–5 shows that they are not word-for-word copies. The material in chapter 1 reads more like a public proclamation. The material here is much closer to an official memorandum. Note, for instance, that it specifies the size of the building as well as the stone and wood construction materials. The fact that the document gives exact dimensions is significant. This might suggest that it was drawn up by the king's civil servants, in consultation with the leaders of the Jewish community. It is possible that the building was to be the same size as Solomon's temple, which was sixty cubits long, twenty cubits wide and thirty cubits high, according to 1 Kings 6:2. This converts into 27 metres long, 9 metres wide and 13.5 metres high. However, the Hebrew of Ezra 6:3 only has two dimensions, both of sixty cubits (27 metres). This looks like a case of a copying error by a later scribe.

Darius replies

The new king confirms the edict of his predecessor-but-one, Cyrus. The implication of the decree is that the money for the repairs should not come from the central 'ministry of finance' but rather from the tax revenues of the region 'Beyond the River' (v. 8). We are dealing here with a taxation issue rather than a straightforward grant from the royal treasuries. So it is not quite as generous as it seems. Nevertheless, it is impressive that a worshipper of the Persian deity Ahura Mazda should encourage the construction of the house of the Jewish God. The Lord of Hosts will receive sacrifices subsidized by Persian taxes!

This tolerant, liberal attitude is found elsewhere among the Persian kings. They did expect some pay-off for their endeavours, as the Cyrus cylinder inscription makes clear. It reads, 'May all the gods whom I have resettled in their sacred cities ask daily Bel and Nebo for a long life for me.' So there were benefits from a policy of restoration. Firstly, it kept the local populations happy and loyal if they felt their own deities were being respected. Secondly, prayers could be offered for the royal family as part of the local liturgies. It is worth noting that in Britain, synagogue services still include a prayer for the British royal family. People living as a minority need to be able to point to their loyalty to the existing institutions.

Here we see the other side of post-exilic relationships between Jews and foreigners. Earlier we saw how Joshua and Zerubbabel refused any help from, or contact with, the 'people of the land'. They will have nothing to do with their near neighbours. Yet they will accept money and protection from the Persians and will pray to God for their welfare. It is possible to translate this situation into a modern-day parallel. For instance, it could be applied to the present political situation of Israel, the Palestinians and the USA. Some groups in the United States, including Christian ones, have given substantial sums to organizations within the State of Israel. Others support the Palestinian cause. Or consider a different approach and reflect on the situation of Christian groups living as small minorities in predominantly Muslim lands. Think of the day-to-day issues that they have to face. How far can they accommodate to the local culture, and how far should they remain distinct?

PRAYER

Pray for minority groups living in your own community.
Remember the small Christian groups that exist in the midst of
other dominant religious cultures.

A NEW TEMPLE

At long last, the edicts of the kings of Persia take full effect and, between the years 520 and 515, work on the building scheme moves ahead rapidly. Finally, by the beginning of 515, the successor to Solomon's temple stands on the original site of its illustrious predecessor.

Completion

Governor Tattenai obeys the king's command and gives full cooperation to the enterprise (vv. 13–15). The comment of our author in verse 14 is significant. The building is finished by the command of God and by the decree of the Persian kings. The initiative lies with God, but it also needs the cooperation of human beings. The Lord may be over history but humans are not mere puppets whose every action is controlled by God, the great puppet-master. In order to complete the building project, all the human actors must play their part. The list of characters includes Cyrus, Darius, Tattenai, Sheshbazzar, Joshua, Zerubbabel, Haggai and Zechariah. It also includes a cast of unnamed characters—builders, carpenters, priests and Levites. Divine initiative and human effort combine here.

In Christian theology, the debate about divine grace and human responsibility came to a head in the fifth century. It centred upon the clash between the views of the North African bishop, Augustine, and the British monk, Pelagius. Augustine championed divine initiative, while Pelagius emphasized human responsibility. In the end, Augustine won the day and Pelagius was seen as a false teacher or heretic. Perhaps in the end both had an element of truth, and we need to find a way of expressing both/and rather than either/or. This verse in Ezra does just that.

Dedication

The ceremony following the completion of the sanctuary (vv. 16–18) is marked by the same joy that attended the end of Solomon's building project. Significantly, though, the numbers of beasts offered for sacrifice is far, far smaller. This may reflect the much more difficult economic situation in the early post-exilic period. The returning groups were made up only of descendants of the tribes of Judah,

Benjamin and Levi. Nevertheless, twelve goats are slaughtered as a sin offering, representing all the twelve tribes of Israel. The Judean community in the Persian province of Yehud sees itself as the successor to 'all Israel'. At this point, the theology of Ezra-Nehemiah is at one with that of Chronicles.

Celebration

The work is completed in the spring of the year 515 (v. 19). The first pilgrim feast to be celebrated is the festival of Passover, on 21 April 515. There are deliberate echoes here of two previous Passover celebrations linked to restoration programmes in first temple times. They are those of Hezekiah, described in 2 Chronicles 30, and of Josiah, outlined in 2 Chronicles 35.

Some additional individuals have attached themselves to the Judean community (v. 21). We cannot know for sure whether these were 'lapsed Jews' returning to the fold or converts to Judaism from the surrounding Gentile population. The post-exilic community of those who returned is not a totally closed one—it is possible to gain access to it, but only on that community's own terms.

The final verse describes Cyrus as 'king of Assyria' rather than Persia. This is probably deliberate rather than a slip of the pen. The Persians saw themselves as the inheritors of both the Babylonian and Assyrian empires. They ruled all of the lands of Mesopotamia, including Assyria. Two centuries previously, the Lord had raised up Assyria to be 'the rod of my anger' (Isaiah 10:5). Now the same Lord has stirred up Cyrus to be the vehicle of salvation (Isaiah 45:1). Both exile and restoration are part of the web of history, within the remit of the Lord of heaven and earth.

REFLECTION

Recall moments when you have celebrated the completion
of a project. How did you feel then? What emotions were stirred
within you?

EZRA'S MISSION

Between the end of chapter 6 and the start of chapter 7, we must make a leap of fifty-seven years from 515 to 458. We have passed from the reign of Darius, ignored the reign of Xerxes, and arrived in the seventh year of Artaxerxes. This assumes that the king is Arta-xerxes I (nicknamed Long Hand) who came to the throne in 465, rather than Artaxerxes II (nicknamed Memory Man) who began his reign in 405. In my introduction to Ezra, I gave reasons for accepting the biblical evidence for the earlier date rather than the later.

Ezra the priest

At this point in the story, Ezra is still spoken of in the third person (v. 1). This implies that it is the work of a later editor who is introduc-ing the character. Ezra's own 'memoirs' will begin in verse 27. Right at the beginning, Ezra's credentials are established, including his priestly credentials. Like all priests, he is a descendant of Aaron (v. 5), but he has a very high pedigree indeed. He is of the high priestly line, no less, and so has David's high priest Zadok as an ancestor (v. 2). Verses 1–5 include a list of sixteen generations from Aaron to Ezra. However, it is not a complete list of every generation. The names of many high priests from the time of the monarchy are missing. The list can be compared with the fuller version in 1 Chronicles 6 which con-tains twenty-three generations between Aaron and the post-exilic period. So this is a partial list of Ezra's ancestors. Nevertheless, it ties him in very firmly to the significant high priestly family of pre-exilic times. In this case, having a good pedigree will help his cause no end! The name of his 'father' is given as Seraiah. This may be the name of his natural father, or it may be a reference to a more distant 'father/ ancestor'. Seraiah was the name of the last but one high priest before the fall of the kingdom (1 Chronicles 6:14). If Ezra was descended from one of the younger sons of this Seraiah, it might explain why his branch of the family was no longer in the running to be high priest. The name Ezra itself is a shortened form of the name Azariah (meaning 'the Lord helps'). At least three of the high priests of the monarchy period bore this name.

Ezra the scribe

One of the major roles of the priests was, of course, to offer sacrifice and to ensure that it was done properly. In addition to this, they had a general responsibility for interpreting the Torah (Law of Moses) and settling difficult cases. Gradually, as more and more of the Torah was written down, the need for literate 'experts' in interpretation became apparent. So the position of scribe or teacher of the law emerged into the daylight of history. Ezra is one of the first people in the Bible described as a 'Torah expert' or 'scribe' (v. 6). By New Testament times, the role of rabbi was much more fully developed—and you no longer needed to be a descendant of Aaron to fill that teaching role. To this day, you can be a Rabbi (Teacher) without being a Cohen (Priest). So Ezra, as priest and scribe, is both a link with the ancient Israelite past and the first of a new kind of figure in Judaism. His links with the interpretation of the Law led him to be seen as a kind of second Moses in some later Jewish works. In performing both these ministries, as priest and scribe, the hand of God will rest upon him (vv. 6, 9).

Ezra's group make their 'exodus' from Babylon in the spring of 458. They actually leave on the 12th day of the first month (Nisan) according to his own memoir in 8:31. It takes three and a half months to make the journey, so that they arrive on the first day of the fifth month (Ab). The journey itself would be more than eight hundred miles by slow caravan routes. Like Abraham centuries before, they would travel up the Euphrates to Haran, then down to Damascus and across to Galilee. Then they would follow either the Way of the Sea down the coast to Joppa, or the Jordan valley route to Jericho, before making their way up into the hills and finally reaching Jerusalem.

Recollections of a much earlier 'going up' from the land of Egypt, also in the month of Nisan, were no doubt impressed upon their hearts and minds. Seasons and dates can carry sacred significance as much as places and events.

PRAYER

Ezra is both a priestly figure and an interpreter of tradition.
Pray for those who offer a sacramental ministry, and those who
offer a ministry of preaching and teaching.

PERMISSION GRANTED

This section provides us with the last trawl through the Persian royal archives. Therefore, verses 12–26 switch back again to the language of Aramaic in order to quote exactly the details of the king's decree.

The king's order

There are many features of the decree in verses 12–20 which can be compared with what we know of Persian court correspondence. The title 'king of kings' was one particularly favoured by the Persian monarchs, presiding over a far greater empire than any Egyptian pharaoh or Assyrian king had ever known. Not until the coming of Alexander the Great would a bigger empire be established in the ancient Near East. The mention of seven counsellors close to the king can also be confirmed from non-biblical sources. The Greek historian Herodotus, writing from this period, makes similar mention of the seven counsellors who advised the Persian king.

Ezra's task can be summarized as follows:

- He is to make general enquiries regarding the religious situation in Judah.

- He has permission to take silver and gold from the royal treasuries to finance his measures.

- In addition, he is allowed to seek freewill gifts from both Jews and non-Jews.

- He is to purchase animals for sacrifice and other offerings needed for temple rituals.

- He is to take vessels, possibly new ones, for use in the temple services.

His brief is mostly concerned with overseeing the proper operation of the ritual side of the Law of Moses.

Note to treasurers

Included in the decree is a special section addressed to the provincial leaders and administrators of 'Beyond the River' (vv. 21–24). As in

the previous order issued by Darius in chapter 6, the local governments are to cooperate in implementing the imperial decree.
Nevertheless, limits are set on what can be provided. The assistance
to the Jerusalem temple is none the less considerable, and, in addition, all the temple staff are to be exempt from taxes.

Note to Ezra

The decree ends in verses 25–26 with a special note addressed to
Ezra. In addressing him, the Persian king refers to 'the wisdom of your
God which is in your hand' (RSV). Is 'wisdom' another way of speaking of the Law? If so, then the reference is to a literal 'book of the
Law' that Ezra brings with him—perhaps the full Pentateuch. Certainly by the time of Jesus, 'wisdom' and 'Torah/law' were identified
as one and the same. More likely, however, the phrase is more general
and refers to Ezra's God-given expertise in interpreting Jewish law.

Ezra is charged with appointing judges and magistrates not only in
Judah but in the whole region of 'Beyond the River'. This does not
mean that, for instance, every citizen of Damascus would be subject
to the Law, whether Jew or Gentile. Rather, the Law code that Ezra
enforces is to apply to Jews in every part of the satrapy, not just in
Judah. This indicates that by the fifth century Judaism was becoming
established as an identifiable religious community with a common
core of teaching and practice. The heart of Judaism will be found
increasingly in the study of the Law as observed in the synagogues,
wherever they are in the world. What Ezra is instructed to do here is
remarkably similar to King Jehoshaphat's actions in 2 Chronicles 19.

Ezra's benediction

For the first time (vv. 27–28), Ezra speaks in the first person in his
memoir, though this blessing can hardly have been the original start
of the document. Later we will find similar kinds of prayer on the lips
of Nehemiah.

REFLECTION

Consider the place of Bible study and reading in your own
devotional life. Why is it important to you?

A LIST *without* LEVITES

Included in the memoirs of Ezra is a list of the heads of families who
made the journey with him. The group totals about 1500 males plus
women and children. As such, it is a much smaller group than the
42,000 who made the first return eighty years earlier. In 538, it had
proved difficult to recruit Levites, and things are no better for Ezra in
458. The start of the expedition is delayed while suitable volunteers are
sought.

Family lists

The list in verses 1–4 is well structured and carefully presented. It
begins with the names of two families of priests and goes on to
mention one family head, Hattush, who is of the line of David. This
same man is mentioned in 1 Chronicles 3:22 among David's descendants. Here in Ezra, his royal blood is mentioned but nothing much is
made of it. By the time Ezra, Nehemiah and Chronicles were written,
descendants of David's line no longer aroused any real messianic hope.
The grand declaration in the last verse of Haggai, that David's descendant Zerubbabel would be like 'a signet ring' chosen by God, had
seemingly come to nothing. These hopes had been dashed, and the
dreams of a speedy restoration of the monarchy began to fade. Such
dreams would not do Jewish-Persian relations any good. The Jewish
people were having to learn to make the best of a bad job by using the
Persian system rather than trying to break free from it.

Next come twelve key family groups, each introduced in the same
way. First we have the name of the ancestor from the past from whom
the family takes its name. (The technical term for this is 'eponymous
ancestor', but it is perhaps easier to think of it in terms of a modern
surname.) Then comes the name of the current head of the family,
together with his father's name. Finally we are given the number of
males in that extended family. The twelve groupings are the same
eponymous groups as those listed in Ezra 2:3–14. What this means is
that, in 538, family groups in Babylon were divided between those
members who went home in the first return and those who stayed
behind. No doubt communications continued to flow back and forth
between Jerusalem and Babylon. Now, in 458, Ezra manages to per-

suade some of the grandchildren or great-grandchildren of those who remained behind to finally take courage and go home. Of course, Ezra himself was probably a descendant of someone who had chosen to stay in Babylon in 538. Uprooting yourself in order to go back to a so-called 'homeland' which you have never seen is a difficult step. The heart is tugged two ways—between a desire to return 'home' and a wish to remain in a place that is relatively secure. Dare one exchange the known for the unknown? No wonder families were divided about what to do. After the household of Adonikam comes the comment, 'the last' (v. 13). Does this mean that they were late turning up? Probably not, but rather that with the departure of Eliphelet, Jeuel and Shemaiah, the last of Adonikam's family group left Babylon to return to Palestine. From such notes, little personal family stories emerge out of history. These 'boring' lists suddenly throw a brief shaft of light on an ordinary family from nearly two and a half thousand years ago.

A lack of Levites

The numbers returning with Ezra are relatively modest—just two priestly family groups, one Davidic and twelve other lay families. There are no levitical families at all. Perhaps one reason for this is that the situation in Jerusalem was not very promising. This is indicated by the book of Malachi, which comes from the period 500–450. It depicts a rather depressed and dispirited community that has grown tired and lax in its observance of worship and of the Torah. Ezra is determined to have a full and proper representation of 'all Israel' in his caravan train. This means including Levites in his entourage as well as priests and laity. After some delay, two family heads agree, at short notice, to pack up and join themselves and their dependants to the emigrants. Together, the families of Sherebiah and Hashabiah number thirty-eight males. Just as the group that left Mount Sinai was carefully lined up in order by Moses, so Ezra, a second Moses figure, can now arrange his caravan across the desert.

PRAYER

Pray for third and fourth generation immigrants who feel the ties between the 'old country' and their new homeland slipping away. Remember those who sometimes choose to return to the land of their birth for their retirement—only to find that things have changed.

TOWARDS *the* SUNSET

After a slow start, the Ezra memoir begins to pick up pace. In this section, we hear of his boasts and his apprehension, his plans and his precautions, and of one hundred days of arduous travel towards the setting sun.

By the waters of Babylon

The exact location of the Ahava waterway (v. 15) is not known. Presumably it was one of the many canals that formed a network around the city of Babylon. The delay in finding Levites to accompany them has cost time. They will leave the caravan park or caravanserai on the twelfth rather than the first day of the month.

Psalm 137 begins with the famous, plaintive words, 'By the rivers of Babylon—there we sat down and there we wept when we remembered Zion.' In this scene, we view a group of Jews engaged in prayer and fasting by the Ahava canal. Fasting was practised with increased regularity after the exile. It could accompany rites of mourning or, as here, it could be undertaken before embarking on a difficult venture. What role do you see for either individual or community fasting today? Should we take it more seriously than simply as a token during the season of Lent?

Ezra makes a personal confession to us, his readers. He says he was ashamed to ask the king for an armed escort to protect the caravan. After all, had he not boasted to the king that they were all under the protection of God (v. 22)? As the psalmist says, 'Some trust in chariots and some in horses, but we trust in the name of the Lord our God' (Psalm 20:7, NIV). Ezra was beginning to realize the potential folly of his words. Now he had responsibility not only for gold, silver and other precious commodities, but also for the lives of women, children and men.

Nehemiah, on his journey to Jerusalem, was perfectly happy to accept the king's armed escort (Nehemiah 2:9). Who was right, do you think? Was it the idealist Ezra, or the realist Nehemiah? The pious scribe or the down-to-earth administrator? When is an act of faith really an act of folly? Sometimes it is necessary to hold in tension the truth of both these two sentences—'Faith can move mountains' and 'God helps those who help themselves'.

Verse 24 suggests that Ezra chose twelve priests and twelve Levites (Sherebiah, Hashabiah and ten others) to have charge of the gold, silver and temple vessels. Now it becomes clear exactly why Ezra was so keen to recruit Levites. According to Numbers 3 and 4, it was both priests and Levites who were responsible for carrying the precious ark and all its accompanying vessels during the desert wanderings. This is a second journey towards the promised land and it is modelled on the first. Ezra is very keen to stress how scrupulous he was with regard to all the treasures, and he accounts for every item separately as he hands them over for safe transport by the clergy.

Westward ho!

The group leaves the caravanserai on 12 Nisan 458 and heads west (v. 31). After about one hundred days, the weary group arrives in Jerusalem having covered eight or nine miles per day. It is now the first day of the month of Ab (7:8–9), mid-summer, hot and sultry. A few days later, a much-relieved Ezra hands over the goods to the temple treasurers, two priests and two Levites. The procedure of having four men in charge of the temple banking system seems to have been a feature of this time. Twenty years later, Nehemiah will appoint four new people to these posts (Nehemiah 13:12–13). Once more, Ezra insists that he has acted correctly throughout and fulfilled all his responsibilities. Perhaps the memoirs of Ezra and Nehemiah were originally composed as official reports back to Persia, or even as a defence against accusations of wrongdoing.

We are given a final summary of the sacrifices offered by the new residents of Jerusalem (v. 35), along with reports to the local Persian administration (v. 36). This would include the head of the satrapy and also the local governors and administrators, primarily, of course, the local governor of Jerusalem itself.

REFLECTION

Would you have been inclined to act more like Ezra (the idealist) or Nehemiah (the realist)? In what ways does this show itself in your behaviour and attitudes?

MARRIAGE MATTERS

The last two chapters of Ezra are concerned with the issue of mixed marriages in the community. For those who live in relatively tolerant and liberal, even permissive, Western societies, these chapters make uncomfortable reading.

There are two opposite and extreme ways of reading texts like this. The first is to accept uncritically our own culture and standards at the dawn of the third millennium. If we do that, we will sit in judgment on these texts and reject them outright. We will see them as hopelessly antiquated, racist and dangerous. We will close our eyes to what they might have to say to us.

The second option is to accept uncritically the texts themselves and to seek to apply them to our society today. If we do that, we let these texts sit in judgment on us and on our values. However, to implement such laws in today's 'global village' would be impossible and undesirable. We close our eyes to what we have learnt in more recent times if we revert to the attitudes of the fifth century BC.

These are emotive, powerful texts. Perhaps we need to listen to the story itself first, and to reserve judgment until later.

A community problem

One of the issues that confronted the people of Israel when they first entered the promised land was what to do about the nations who already lived there. The Pentateuch, and especially the book of Deuteronomy, forbade intermarriage with the seven nations occupying the land of Canaan.

Ezra has arrived with a mandate to enforce the Torah—including the instructions from Deuteronomy. He finds that the groups of settlers who have returned since 538 have met with an even more thorny set of problems. Intermarriage has taken place between leaders of the community (both lay and clergy) and non-Jews. As an expert on the Torah, Ezra seeks to apply the old laws in the new situation by extending the list of forbidden nations. He interprets the prohibition to include not only Canaanite groups but also other foreigners from outside Canaan, such as Ammonites, Moabites and Egyptians (v. 2), which were not named in the old laws. So Ezra seeks to reinterpret the ancient laws in the new context after the exile. Groups such as the Jebusites and Perizzites no longer existed in Ezra's day, but this did not mean that the laws were redundant.

The Torah was very strict on the definition of what constituted 'proper' and 'improper' mixing of all kinds of things. This included seemingly trivial things like not mixing dairy and meat products (the kosher food laws), and not mixing fabrics of different kinds in a garment. However, it also included fundamental things like sexual relations, which go to the very heart of both private and community life.

Ezra's protest and prayer

Having been officially informed of the situation, Ezra takes swift and very public action (vv. 3–15). Like some of the prophets of old, he engages in a piece of 'street theatre'. He positions himself in the courts of the temple and stages a silent protest until the time of the evening sacrifice at about 3 p.m. He performs other ritual actions of mourning and then begins his prayer to God. Usually prayers were said standing up—like the Pharisee in the synagogue in Jesus' parable (Luke 18:9–14). It was right to stand straight before God, not to cower or grovel before him. However, for his prayer of contrition and confession (vv. 6–15), Ezra kneels in the dust with pleading, out-stretched hands in order to implore God's mercy.

Psychologically the prayer is brilliant. Ezra begins by identifying himself with the sinful people—he does not stand aloof from them. This is a community sin, not just a private matter, and he cannot exempt himself from it. Gradually he catalogues the past failings of the people. He quotes from the Law of God and ends with an open question. Will God destroy his people, as he is entitled to do? Or will the remnant survive? The future of the post-exilic community in Judah hangs in the balance.

REFLECTION

Try to get into the mind of Ezra in order to appreciate what was the real problem of the mixed marriages. Reflect on how hard it can be to see things from the perspective of a different culture, time and place.

'THOSE *who* TREMBLE'

Ezra's public prayer and protest achieve their aim. A sizeable crowd gathers in the temple courtyard. Paradoxically it contains a large number of women and children, as well as the men. Decisions taken on this day will profoundly affect the family and community life of those present, and also future generations within Judaism.

A new covenant

Support for Ezra comes from a certain Shecaniah (v. 2). He is a descendant of the Elam family group. This family had representatives among those who returned in 538, and more have just returned with Ezra. Presumably Shecaniah represents one of the well-established families in Judah. Ezra has ended his prayer on a deliberately sombre note, but Shecaniah is more positive. He sees hope for forgiveness, but only if the whole people will make a new start. They must acknowledge their wrongdoing and make a new covenant with their God (v. 3).

Ezra's support is now growing. In 9:4 we were introduced to a group called 'shakers' or 'quakers', who allied themselves with Ezra's cause. They represent pious and devout Jews who hold to a firm and rigorous policy. Perhaps they are later representatives of a group called those 'who tremble at his word' in Isaiah 66:5. That text probably comes from about 520–500BC, and the term 'shakers' may have been used as a nickname for them. In the same way, the term 'Quaker' was used as a nickname for the followers of George Fox, and 'Methodist' for the supporters of John Wesley.

Shecaniah is convinced that the way forward is to act according to the Torah (vv. 3–4). Unfortunately there are virtually no specific rules about divorce in the Pentateuch. There is plenty about not marrying foreign wives, but not about what to do if you have! However, Deuteronomy 24:1 speaks of the right of a man to divorce his wife if he finds 'something objectionable' in her. Note that the woman does not have the right to get rid of an objectionable husband! The way forward adopted by these hard-liners is to show that foreign wives are 'objectionable' or inappropriate, because of their foreign attitudes and beliefs.

Standing in the rain

Along the sides and back of Solomon's temple stood three-storied chambers used for storage and administration (1 Kings 6:5–6). Similar structures were present in the second temple. Ezra spends the night in a vigil of prayer and fasting in one of these chambers belonging to a priest, Jehohanan (v. 6). Then a proclamation is issued, summoning all people in Yehud province to come to the temple courts. Since Judah was only about thirty-five miles by twenty-five miles in size, everyone could be expected to attend within three days.

The assembly takes place on the twentieth of the ninth month, Kislev (v. 9), which falls in midwinter. Jerusalem is high in the Judean hills and the weather in December can be quite cold and wet. Not only heavy rain, but even hail and snow are possible. In view of the complexity of the issue and because of the bad weather, the assembly agrees that no quick decision about marriage separations ought to be made. Instead they set up a commission. Sometimes, forming a committee is merely a way of avoiding an issue, but it can also be the only sensible way of tackling a thorny problem.

A minority of four men opposes the majority opinion (v. 15). What are they opposing? Is it the idea of separations or the plan for the commission? If they oppose the divorce suggestion, they represent the 'lax' party, perhaps having foreign wives themselves. If, however, they are opposing the idea of the commission, then they may represent instead the 'rigorous' or 'severe' party that wants a quick decision. One of them is called Meshullam, and a man of that name is mentioned as a supporter of Ezra in 8:16. In any case, their objections are overruled by the majority and the commission is set up. The commissioners take their time. After all, how many generations do you need to go back to decide whether a person is of 'foreign blood'? The commission sits from the end of December 458 until the end of March 457. It judges on many cases and delivers a verdict of guilty on one hundred and ten individuals.

PRAYER

This time, try to put yourself into the shoes of one of the foreign wives, or imagine yourself as one of the husbands being asked to put away your wife. What is going on inside you?

GUILTY PARTIES

The book of Ezra ends in a very strange way. It concludes with a list of more than one hundred names of men who were found 'guilty' and who went on to send away their wives and children. This number is actually quite small. Does it mean that others refused to be part of this scheme of ethnic cleansing? We are left with many more unanswered questions. What happened to Ezra after the spring of 457? Did these measures stir up opposition from some leading priests or laymen? Was Ezra removed by the Persians for being too zealous and stirring up trouble in Jerusalem? What, if any, provision was made for the now homeless women and children? All these are legitimate questions, but this is an instance in which the Bible simply does not tell us.

It is time, therefore, to return to the question we set aside at the beginning of chapter 9. Which of the two stances should we take with these painful chapters? Do we accept them or reject them? Do we say 'yes' to Ezra's policy, and affirm scripture, or do we say 'no' to his policy so as to stand against scripture?

'Yes' to Ezra

If we are to say 'yes' to Ezra, then we need to understand the situation in which he found himself. Today, we tend to see everything in individual terms. As we read this long list of names, we are inclined to feel the personal tragedies of Nethanel, Shimei, Elijah, Joseph or Joel, not to mention their loving wives and dependent children.

However, the issue for Ezra and his supporters was not the individual happiness or otherwise of these particular families. His concern was with the well-being of the community as a whole. Intermarriage threatened the very existence of the community and its religious basis. Today, those groups of Christians who live as small minorities would understand this well. To marry someone of a different faith community is, in effect, to 'marry out'. Many Jewish communities in Britain and the USA face the same issue. It has been said that the biggest threat to Judaism in the West is not violent anti-Jewish attitudes—horrible though they are. Rather it is the danger of assimilation to the host culture—and the most obvious way is through intermarriage. The faith will be diluted and its distinctiveness lost. The salt will have lost its flavour. For these reasons we may say 'yes' to Ezra, even if we do not like it. We should accept that if religious structures are to survive intact they may, inevitably, end up hurting individuals. It is a price to be paid.

'No' to Ezra

Exponents of the 'no' position would argue that it is utterly inappropriate to take the programme of Ezra and apply it to today. That was the error of the old apartheid regime in South Africa. To use the language of 'holy seed' or 'holy race' from Ezra 9:2 today is both dangerous and unacceptable. Paradoxically the Nazis in the 1930s used exactly the language of 'blood' and 'soil' to discriminate against Jews in pursuit of the myth of 'pure Aryan blood'.

In the end, Ezra's solutions are cruel and harsh by the standards of our time—and, indeed, by those of the New Testament. It is not the policy advocated by Paul in 1 Corinthians 7 when he is asked to rule on what a Christian married to a non-Christian should do. Instead he advocates staying together so as to try to win the partner for Christ. Similarly, Jesus opposes divorce on any grounds (Mark 10:9). Would he endorse this policy of Ezra?

These two opposite ways of approaching Ezra are not just arguments about technicalities. We may conclude that Ezra's solution was right for his own day but wrong for ours. Couples of 'mixed marriages' are an increasing feature of today's mobile society. Furthermore, intermarriage does not take only place between partners from different ethnic groups. There are also particular issues to be faced in interfaith marriages, where one partner is Christian and the other is Jewish, Muslim, Hindu or Sikh, or has no religious faith. How will the children be brought up? What festivals should be observed—both faiths' traditions, only one, or none at all? The same concerns arise between partners of different Christian traditions, especially between Roman Catholic and non-Catholic partners. When such couples are unable to share communion, some of the pain of Ezra 10 rises to the surface once more. Individuals still bear the brunt of the pain today, just as in 457BC.

PRAYER

Pray for those who belong to 'mixed marriages' of culture or religion and for their children.

NEHEMIAH *the* BOOK

From the account of the scribe Ezra, we move to the story of the governor Nehemiah. In these two books we see the related but distinctive work of two men—one a priest, the other a layman. In terms of biblical chronology, the one story follows directly on from the other. Indeed, the Hebrew Bible counts the two books as one single book of Ezra-Nehemiah, without any break between them.

No one doubts that the person responsible for editing Ezra was similarly responsible for the editing of Nehemiah. We can never know for sure whether this was the author of Chronicles, or an acquaintance of his, or someone quite different. As we have seen, there are many similarities between Chronicles and Ezra-Nehemiah. There are enough differences, though, to raise doubts about joint authorship. Of course, it could be that the same editor was responsible for all the books, and that the differences arise from the different type of material that he was editing. After all, an autobiography is a different kind of literature than a history book.

The collected material in Nehemiah can be broken down into three distinct kinds—personal memoirs, other stories, and lists.

Nehemiah's memoirs

This material constitutes the largest amount and can be found in Nehemiah 1:1—7:5 (minus chapter 3), and 12:31—13:31. Covering about sixty per cent of the book, the Nehemiah memoirs are far more extensive than those of Ezra. They are also much more vivid, detailed and racy in style than Ezra. You really do get the feel of Nehemiah's raw emotions, and come to know him as a character.

There are several suggestions as to why Nehemiah wrote down his life story. I think we can dismiss the modern idea of a diary or autobiography. Ancient Hebrew writers almost certainly did not think in this way. There are two other main possibilities:

- **To 'remind' the king.** Perhaps this work, especially in chapters 1—7, is part of an official report which Nehemiah sent back to the Persian court. He may have done so as a matter of course, in order to show that he had fulfilled his mission. Alternatively he may have had to answer charges brought by his opponents, and so the memoir may be his defence to the king.

- **To 'remind' God.** An interesting feature of the work is the frequent calls upon God to 'remember me'. This is especially true in chapter 13, appearing in verses 14, 22 and 31. It makes the memoir read more like an appeal to God than to the earthly king, Artaxerxes.

Of course, it is possible that the original report to the king in chapters 1—7 was adapted a dozen years later by Nehemiah when the events of chapter 13 took place.

Other narratives

These stories are found in chapters 8—9 and 10:28—11:2. They are told in the third person, not the first person. It is noticeable that Nehemiah is only a spectator in the events of chapters 8—9. Ezra is the leader and spokesman. Some people think that these chapters were originally part of Ezra's memoir, but that the editor has rearranged them to fit here. We will study this in more detail at the appropriate point. Clearly, these chapters derive from the editor and not from Nehemiah himself.

Lists

Quite long lists are found in chapters 3; 7:6–73; 10:1–27 and 11:3—12:30. It is quite possible that the editor copied them from archives preserved in Jerusalem. During this period, it was important to be able to prove who you were, who your ancestors were and which land you owned or from which village you came. This was all part of the establishment of identity and the building up of community solidarity in the period after the exile.

So the book of Nehemiah contains varied material, from 'vivid' first-hand accounts, through 'solid' narrative, to 'tedious' lists. Through it all, we get a glimpse of provincial life around the mid-fifth century BC. It is like a snapshot of a particular year or two, or a searchlight cutting through an otherwise dark and obscure scene.

REFLECTION

Give thanks for the personal insights that can be derived
from autobiographies.

NEHEMIAH *the* MAN

The action of the story takes place following Nehemiah's request to visit Jerusalem in 445. Most of the events described in chapters 1—7 take place within a period of less than a year following his arrival. The final chapter of the book is set twelve or more years later, some time after 433. Whereas there has been controversy over the specific dates of Ezra's mission, there is almost complete agreement that the book of Nehemiah covers the period from 445 to around 430.

From the book, we learn that Nehemiah was in a privileged position in the court of King Artaxerxes, who reigned from 465 to 424. Clearly Jews, as well as other foreigners, could rise to positions of considerable influence in the Persian court. Many Jewish families were doing quite well in exile in the east. This may explain why many were reluctant to make the dangerous and financially very risky decision to leave Persia and start all over again in Judah. For all that, there was clearly regular contact between the Judean community and the Jews of the dispersion, even in faraway Susa. News and information flowed backwards and forwards, along with a steady trickle of returners and some financial support for the 'old country'.

The perils of autobiography

The memoirs of Ezra and Nehemiah are practically unique in the Old Testament. Apart from some of the poems of Jeremiah, they provide the closest insight into the lives and thinking of any Old Testament characters—and this is especially true of Nehemiah. We see things through Nehemiah's own eyes. Most of what we learn about him and his time, we learn from his own first-hand account. This makes for an exciting story, full of twists and turns, hopes and fears, successes and disappointments.

However, we do need to bear in mind that what we hear is Nehemiah's own story. It is his account of events, and we see things only through his eyes. We need to remember that all writing is to some degree biased—and that includes the book you are now reading! All writing comes from a specific point of view. It is not neutral. However, this is particularly true of autobiography.

This does not mean that Nehemiah is wilfully deceitful or a brazen liar. It simply means that he tells us those bits of information that he considers important. He also gives what in these days would be called his own 'spin' on the story, as do the authors of Chronicles and Ezra. The writers of autobiography usually want to show themselves in the best possible light, and this is certainly true of Nehemiah.

Consequently we do not have the other side of the story. We do not hear the version of events from the viewpoint of Nehemiah's opponents, just as we do not hear the views of the locals rejected in Ezra 4. We do not have the autobiography of characters such as Sanballat the governor of Samaria, or Tobiah from Ammon, or Geshem the Arab. The motives of the priest Eliashib in chapter 13 remain hidden from us. It really is too much to expect that one day archaeologists will dig up the autobiography of one of these men so that we can compare accounts!

So in one sense we are at a disadvantage, because we only hear one side of the story. On the other hand, there are advantages in autobiography too. We get to meet Nehemiah at first hand. We hear the tone of his voice, share his frustrations and rejoice in his achievements against all the odds. Nehemiah is not the most attractive or sympathetic character in scripture. Yet he comes across as a human, flawed individual who does what he considers right in difficult circumstances. Nehemiah is no plaster saint; he is flesh and blood, and we have the immense privilege of listening to his thoughts and entering into his world.

PRAYER

Thank you, Lord, for the preservation of the memoirs
of Nehemiah. As I read them, may I enter sympathetically
into his world.

The MAN *for the* MOMENT

Artaxerxes 1 came to the throne of Persia in 465, so the twentieth year of his reign would be 446/445. Nearly 150 years before, in 587, the Babylonians had destroyed Jerusalem and deported many of its people to Mesopotamia. Nehemiah must have been a descendant of one of those exiled families. Since the edict of King Cyrus in 538, some families had returned to try to rebuild the city and its life, but many others stayed in exile in foreign lands. Some, like Nehemiah, had done well for themselves. As fourth or fifth generation immigrants, they were relatively settled and secure. Yet they still had a fond attachment to 'the old country'.

Disturbing news

We cannot be sure whether Hanani (v. 2) was the literal brother of Nehemiah (though it is quite likely), or whether the phrase means 'brother in the faith' or 'fellow Jew'. He and his compatriots bring news of Jerusalem which is discouraging and depressing. The walls of the city are broken down and burnt, either from way back in 587 or perhaps as a result of the more recent Persian decree blocking rebuilding (Ezra 4). The phrase in verse 2, 'those who had escaped the captivity', could mean either people who had returned from exile or, alternatively, those families who had never been taken away. The prospects look bleak.

Nehemiah's prayer

Nehemiah's prayer in verses 5–11 is typical of the kind of prayers we find in the biblical books of the post-exilic period (for example, Ezra 9; Nehemiah 9; Daniel 9). It uses traditional language, perhaps the language of the liturgy of the time, as well as borrowing from parts of the Old Testament. These biblical texts were increasingly available in written form by the fifth century. The prayer speaks of the covenant mercy of God and of the sinfulness of humanity. It remembers the grace and forgiveness of God in times past, and looks with poignant longing to a better future. The language may be traditional, even stereotyped, but it rings with hope that the place of God's sacred Name may be re-established.

Yet, paradoxically, so much seems to depend on the whim of one man, the king of Persia. Nehemiah speaks of him, rather unceremoniously, as 'this man' (v. 11). As the tension mounts in the story, and the prayer reaches its crescendo, we finally learn that Nehemiah is cupbearer to the king. To us, this may sound an unimportant post, but in the world of ancient Persia it was a significant one. Some writers have suggested that, as one of the palace officials, Nehemiah may have been a eunuch. However, there is no evidence for this in the biblical text. It seems unlikely that a Jewish eunuch could instigate reforms like those of Nehemiah. Whereas in the oriental royal courts the practice of using castrated male servants was the norm, the Law of Moses explicitly forbids such men to participate in the assembly of the Lord (Deuteronomy 23:1). This was another distinguishing feature that set the Jewish people apart from their neighbours.

It is clear that Nehemiah is the right man in the right place—but is the time yet right?

PRAYER

Pray for those who work alongside today's political rulers—
for civil servants, advisers and lobby groups who, at the right
moment, can influence decisions and policies.

PERFECT TIMING

There is 'a time to keep silence, and a time to speak,' says the author of Ecclesiastes 3:7. This story of Nehemiah demonstrates the wisdom of that statement. Nehemiah waits for more than three months before he grasps the opportunity. He has heard the report from Hanani around December 446, but he bides his time until late March 445. He is waiting for just the right moment. In the Greek New Testament, there is a special word which is used for such a time. It is the word *kairos* and it is found in Mark 1:15. It is a moment that has to be seized, for it may not come again. In the 1980s, at the end of the apartheid era, the South African churches published an influential statement called 'The Kairos Document'. It spelled out their understanding of the urgency of the times and the need for action. Nehemiah now faces just such a moment in his life.

'’Twixt cup and lip’

There is an old proverb, 'There's many a slip 'twixt cup and lip'. Nehemiah, as chief butler or cupbearer to the king, would know that from experience! He was responsible for tasting the king's wine—to ensure it was not poisoned. He had to serve the wine in the appropriate way and observe all the etiquette of the royal court. In addition, he had to be a good companion for the king, jovial in his presence. He was not supposed to show his own personal feelings.

For months, Nehemiah has waited and has bided his time, and now the *kairos* moment comes. According to the contemporary Greek historian, Herodotus, it was quite common for Persian kings to grant special requests at important banquets. The month Nisan was the first month of the year in the Persian calendar, so it was an appropriate time for 'new year requests'. Nehemiah chooses his words carefully. He does not refer to the city of Jerusalem by name. After all, this same King Artaxerxes has issued an order forbidding building work to go on there, according to Ezra 4:21. Instead Nehemiah tugs at the king's heartstrings by asking permission to repair the ravages to his ancestors' tombs. This is guaranteed to win the king's sympathy—for it was a duty in the ancient world to tend the graves of your ancestors. Nevertheless, the Jewish cupbearer still trembles before he dares to speak. Like the Jewish heroine Esther, he knows he is taking a big risk. Therefore he sends up a quick 'arrow prayer' to God (v. 4) before he begins his speech.

'If it pleases the king...'

Nehemiah now proceeds with his carefully prepared speech in verses 5–8. At last he can ask for specific permission to rebuild the city (v. 5). Next to the king sits the queen consort (v. 6). The Hebrew term used is not the usual word for 'queen' and so may not refer to Artaxerxes' legitimate queen, Damaspia. Rather, it may have been one of the favourite concubines of the harem. Did she influence the decision in any way? If not, why does Nehemiah bother mentioning her at all? It is one of those little biblical mysteries that we can never solve.

Nehemiah has planned carefully. He asks for official letters granting him safe passage through the territory of 'Beyond the River'—letters for the satrap of the territory and also for the local provincial governors. He already knows the name of the keeper of the king's forest, Asaph. Furthermore, he knows exactly what he wants:

- Firstly, to repair the citadel or fortress just to the north of the temple.

- Then to repair the damage to the city walls and gates.

- Lastly, to repair his own ancestral home—a home, incidentally, that he has never seen.

The timing is perfect. In God's good time and with his own forward planning, Nehemiah is able to achieve his goal.

Help and hindrance

Unlike Ezra, Nehemiah is quite content to take a detachment of armed soldiers for an escort (v. 9). He is a practical man and he is on official state business. Not everyone is going to be friendly towards him, and we are now introduced to two of the principal 'villains' in the memoir, Sanballat and Tobiah (v. 10). It is not the last we will hear of them.

MEDITATION

Try to remember a 'kairos' moment in your own life. If you are facing such significant moments of decision, offer them now to God in a short 'arrow prayer'.

TOUR *of* INSPECTION

If we use our imaginations, it is not difficult to picture the scene described here. Quietly and stealthily by night, Nehemiah rides out to inspect the damage to the city walls. He takes a few friends, perhaps including some locals who know the terrain well. In some places it is easy to travel, sometimes the way is blocked by fallen rubble. Eventually, having completed half a circuit, Nehemiah has to turn back (v. 14). The debris makes the route impassable along the eastern slope running parallel with the Kidron Valley.

Nehemiah's inspection

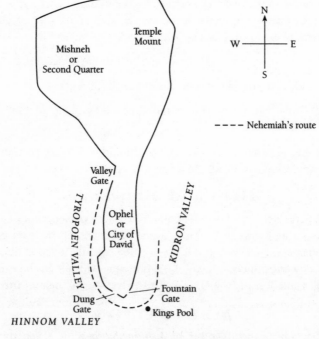

Three against one

Nehemiah now confers with the leaders of the community and discloses his plans and the favour he has with King Artaxerxes (vv.

17–18). It is not all plain sailing, however, and soon he finds himself in opposition to three powerful local leaders (v. 19). These three are not just ordinary citizens but well-known and influential figures. By coming to Jerusalem to be, in effect, governor of Yehud, Nehemiah has upset the balance of power. The neighbours of the province of Judah have a vested interest in keeping Jerusalem weak. They will therefore oppose any attempt to rebuild the shattered city, or to enhance its reputation. It would be easy to raise suspicions of disloyalty to the Persian monarch. Nehemiah will have to watch his back if he is to survive in the jungle of Middle Eastern politics.

Sanballat is governor of the northern territory of Samaria. Perhaps, before Nehemiah came, he had extended his influence southwards as far as Jerusalem. Remarkably we have surviving letters from the Egyptian town of Elephantine written around 408, which mention Sanballat as governor of Samaria. They also mention his two sons, Delaiah and Shemaiah. These two names ending in '…iah' suggest that the family were worshippers of Yahweh (the name of God in the Old Testament). They certainly would not regard themselves as enemies of the cause of Yahweh. This family continued to be important, and one hundred years later, around 340, another Sanballat married his daughter into the high priestly family.

Tobiah: His name means 'the Lord is good', so he too has a good Hebrew-sounding name. He seems to have been powerful in the territory of Ammon across the Jordan, perhaps as a servant or assistant to Sanballat. Two hundred years later, around 250, the family was still in control of the territory of Ammon.

Geshem or Gashmu was a powerful Arab chieftain. His territory included North Arabia and the southern part of Israel as far as the Egyptian border. A silver vessel dedicated by his son Qainu was discovered at Tell el-Maskhuta in Lower Egypt.

So Nehemiah finds himself surrounded on three sides by powerful foes—Sanballat to the north, Tobiah to the east and Geshem to the south. He is going to need both God's providential care and his own powerful survival instincts if he is to bring his dream to fulfilment.

MEDITATION

Try to find a picture of the present-day walls of Old Jerusalem.
Form a picture in your mind of Nehemiah and his donkey
clambering the slopes by night.

BUILDING *the* WALLS

We now have an account of the building of the walls. I will comment on particular features in the text. In the following section, you will find a diagram and a key to help you follow the biblical account. The description begins at the Sheep Gate (point a) in the north-east corner and goes round anti-clockwise.

The north

The first section is along the northern wall (vv. 1–5) and it was the responsibility of the high priest, Eliashib, and his family. Eliashib was the grandson of Jeshua, the high priest at the time of Haggai and Zechariah. Later the family would fall out with Nehemiah (13:28), but at this point they seem to work in harmony. We need not suppose that the high priest himself did very much of the physical labour but that he took upon himself responsibility for ensuring the work was done. Only the nobles of Tekoa hold back (v. 5), although the men of the area do a double stint of work (vv. 5 and 27). Perhaps Tekoa's leaders in the south felt threatened by pressure from Geshem the Arab.

Jerusalem was vulnerable to attack along its northern wall. Mention of rebuilding, not just repairs, suggests that this area was extensively damaged. The Tower of the Hundred and the Tower of Hananel may have been part of the citadel or fortress north of the temple itself. John 5 mentions the Sheep Gate as the place where Jesus healed the lame man by the pool of Bethesda. Today the Crusader church of St Anne stands on the site.

The west

The Mishneh, or Second Quarter, had extended the old city considerably to the west. The original wall was presumably built during King Hezekiah's reign at the end of the eighth century (2 Chronicles 32:5). However, we do not know for certain whether Nehemiah's wall followed the same line 250 years later. Jerusalem may have been considerably reduced in size again by this time, due to the disasters that had befallen it. Verses 6–13 give the details of the rebuilding on the western side.

The south

The details in verses 14–15 are rather sketchy. The Dung Gate was opposite the slope leading down the Valley of Hinnom (or Gehenna in the New Testament). This was the traditional site of Jerusalem's rubbish dump. The Fountain Gate at the south-eastern corner may have led to the spring of En-rogel or Fuller's Spring in the Kidron Valley. It is possible that this southern section of the wall was in better repair than the northern section.

The east

The list now goes on to detail the work on the eastern slope (vv. 16–32). It seems likely that the terraces of the eastern area of the city, on the steep slope down towards the Kidron Valley, had largely collapsed on top of one another. This is the point where Nehemiah had to turn back because of the rubble. Consequently the decision seems to have been taken to abandon the old line of the pre-exilic city wall and rebuild higher up the slope. This eastern side therefore required a much greater amount of labour than those sides that merely needed repairing. Since a new wall had to be built, the references now tend to be to places opposite or in the vicinity of the new wall, rather than to names of previous gates.

We have to confess that the exact location of many of these features along the eastern side is unknown. However, as the wall which protected the temple, it was a very significant section indeed.

Combined effort

At last the roll-call of contributors to the wall building is completed as the list finally returns to the north-eastern corner by the Sheep Gate (v. 32). We do not know whether Nehemiah himself compiled this list as a record of the valiant effort of the builders, or whether it comes from another hand.

PRAYER

Lord, we remember those who today are employed in the building trade. Thank you for the skills that provide us with homes and the material comforts and security that accompany them.

MAPPING *the* CITY

This chapter appears to be a very boring list, yet it represents a significant community enterprise. The work of repair and rebuilding helped to bring together the fragmented community around Jerusalem. It involved priests and Levites, inhabitants of outlying villages, guilds of craftsmen, along with a group of women who worked on part of the wall section (v. 12). The list may seem long and tedious, but the work done by these men and women deserves recognition. So often, the constructive work of the kingdom of God is, likewise, done by very ordinary people. Down the ages, churches have been not only built upon the foundation of 'apostles and prophets' (Ephesians 2:20) but maintained and preserved by faithful souls whose names are scarcely known—except to God. In God's sight, the contribution of Shallum, Rehum and Meremoth is not forgotten. Nor, for that matter, is our unremarkable and yet significant labour for the kingdom. We too place our 'stones, wood, brick or straw' as co-builders with Paul, Peter, Apollos and the rest (1 Corinthians 3).

a = Sheep Gate (v. 1)
b = Tower of the Hundred (v. 1)
c = Tower of Hananel (v. 1)
d = Fish Gate (v. 3)
e = Old or Jeshanah Gate (v. 6)
f = Broad Wall (v. 8)
g = Tower of the Ovens (v. 11)
h = Valley Gate (v. 13)
i = Dung Gate (v. 14)
j = Fountain Gate (v. 15)
k = Pool of Shelah or Siloam (v. 15)
l = Stairs (v. 15)
m = Tombs of David (v. 16)
n = Artificial Pool (v. 16)
o = House of Warriors, or barracks (v. 16)
p = Armoury (v. 19)
q = House of Eliashib (v. 20)
r = Court of the Guard (v. 25)
s = Water Gate (v. 26)
t = Horse Gate (v. 28)
u = House of Temple Servants (v. 31)
v = Muster or Inspection Gate (v. 31)

PRAYER

Lord, help me to realize that I have a part to play in the work of the kingdom. Make me a builder and not a demolisher. Amen.

Nehemiah's Jerusalem

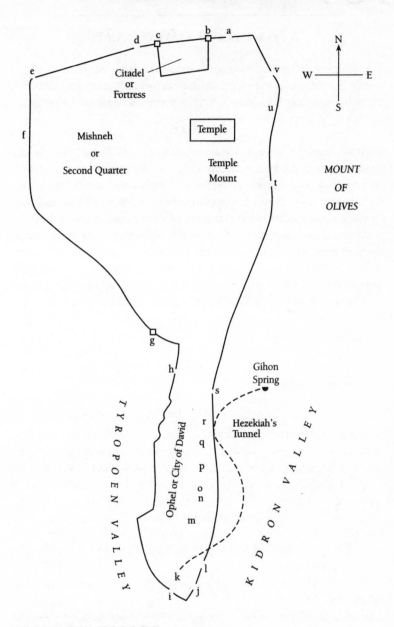

'ONLY HALF WAY UP'

The story of the wall-building now resumes with an account of the events surrounding the work. In this section, we meet four different kinds of vocal expression—a taunt, a prayer, a threat and a song.

A taunt

Sanballat and his yes-man Tobiah resort to the old ploy of ridicule and sarcasm (vv. 1–3). I am not sure that the old proverb is true, 'Sticks and stones may break my bones but words can never harm me'. Words may not break bones, but they can sap morale and self-confidence, and this is the intention of the opposition here.

Perhaps Sanballat and company are beginning to be anxious that Nehemiah's crazy venture may succeed after all. Taunting and name-calling may be rather childish, but let us never forget that winning the propaganda war has been a vital part of the strategy in many modern conflicts. It was true in World War II, and resurfaces at almost every election time!

After King Hezekiah built the wall around the Second Quarter, he had to endure the taunts of the king of Assyria's propaganda chief, as recorded in 2 Chronicles 32. Now, with the walls going up again, history is repeating itself.

A prayer

Once more we overhear Nehemiah at prayer (vv. 4–6), and this time it does not make for pleasant listening. Nehemiah's prayers are generally brief and to the point. Ezra, on the other hand, was a rather long-winded cleric, as we see from Ezra 9 and Nehemiah 9. In this instance, Nehemiah calls down wrath and judgment on his opponents and asks God never to forget what they have done. It is not pretty, and modern-day believers can hardly use it as a model prayer. It plainly goes against the words of the Lord's Prayer, '…as we forgive those who sin against us'.

Nevertheless, this type of aggressive prayer is not unique to Nehemiah. Indeed, in verse 5 he is quoting words originally found in the mouth of the prophet Jeremiah. These words from Jeremiah 18:23 are part of an even more explicit prayer of rage and anger and an outpouring of resentment against opponents. Similarly a number of psalms are of this same type, such as Psalms 35 and 59. Christians rarely use this material, and are sometimes inclined to feel rather superior that they do not pray like this. We should remember, however, Jesus' parable about the self-righteous prayer of the Pharisee (Luke 18:9–14). At least Nehemiah's prayer is honest, and there is no doubting the intensity of his feelings. Perhaps some uptight Christians need to learn to express their true feelings to God in the same way—even if some of the angry words are none too elegant. I think God is big enough to take it.

A threat

To the list of three regular opposition parties, a fourth is added. The people of the province of Ashdod in the west join the fray (v. 7). Now the citizens of Judah and Jerusalem are surrounded on all sides:

SAMARIA

ASHDOD   • Jerusalem   AMMON

ARABIA

The reasons for their opposition may well have been political and economic rather than religious. Nehemiah, as governor of a revived Judah, alarmed the neighbouring provincial governors, who could see a threat to their own positions and status.

A song

Finally the toll of constant taunts and threats begins to tell on the builders. A sad refrain is heard coming from some of the workers (v. 10), expressing their fear that the whole enterprise may prove too much. It is a song of lament in 3/2 time, the metre favoured for such songs. Fears within threaten to undermine—so now is the time for Nehemiah to show his true mettle as a leader.

REFLECTION

How do you express your anger and frustration in prayer to God?
Does the thought of doing so make you feel uncomfortable?

RESTORING MORALE

Faced with a serious threat of internal dissent and falling morale, Nehemiah takes decisive and effective action. He knows that it is necessary to combine faith and common sense in order to succeed. This is Nehemiah's strategy for the building not only of walls but also of morale. Here we see him acting not just as governor but also as commander-in-chief of the local militia.

Deeds and words

Nehemiah takes immediate action to remedy the deteriorating situation. He must reverse the loss of confidence among the workers by taking both practical and psychological steps (vv. 13–14). He assembles the whole company in full sight of any 'spies' watching from outside, and addresses the assembly. Everyone has brought some kind of weapon with them, even if it is only a crude staff or a spear. The people are ill-equipped; nevertheless, it shows that they mean business and will not surrender lightly to their enemies. Nehemiah then makes a speech which is similar to the kind of stirring stuff found on the lips of Joshua when addressing his men before a battle. This is a clever psychological move on the part of Nehemiah. He is reawakening the collective memory. In comparison to the heady days of Joshua and the capture of the promised land, the events of 445 may seem small. Yet, says Nehemiah, you too are descendants of Joshua's generation, you too must fight for the future welfare of your homes and families. A good military tactician knows how to use words effectively in order to motivate people. Nehemiah has this gift.

Tools and weapons

The enemy's tactics have come unstuck and they call off their intimidation. Did they really intend to fight, or was it just bluff? Certainly Sanballat and company would have been in serious trouble with the Persian overlords if they had attacked Jerusalem. For the time being, the danger is past. Nehemiah does not relax his guard but puts into place a long-term strategy to ensure security, so that the rest of the building work can go on unhindered. He makes four tactical moves in verses 15–20:

- Some of his own hand-picked servants become a permanent armed police force. Perhaps they were the bodyguards who came from Persia, or were local men assigned to the governor.

- In addition to these 'professionals', all those carrying loads are equipped with some kind of weapon, even if it is just a stone. They will always be in a state of readiness for conflict.

- The actual builders need both hands free to do the work. However, they are each to wear a short sword, just in case.

- Arrangements are made for a muster at the sound of the trumpet. Once more there are echoes of the 'glory days' of long ago, when the armies of ancient Israel gathered for battle at the blast of the trumpet. Once more the old battle cry is heard, 'Our God will fight for us.'

Day and night

When Nehemiah arrived, he found Jerusalem lacking not only walls but also population (see 7:4). Many of the workers on the building project come from outlying villages. Time is being lost in travelling and there is the risk of absenteeism. Nehemiah reorganizes the building rota by introducing a more professional system. Everyone is to stay within the city, both to work and to sleep. Presumably a rota of those on night patrol is also arranged in order to protect the holy city.

Nehemiah takes no chances. He blends together his faith and his actions. In New Testament terms, he unites the 'faith' of Paul and the 'deeds' of James in an effective combination. In the figure of Nehemiah, we see how Paul's theology of trust in God combines with the practical concerns of the letter of James. Nehemiah has both the vision and the practical strategy to turn the dream into reality.

PRAYER

Give thanks for imaginative people, those with vision and ideas.
Give thanks for practical, down-to-earth people who get things
done. Praise God when these two aspects of character are found
in one individual.

ECONOMIC MATTERS

From the external dangers posed to the community, the story moves to another set of dangers. Internal economic pressures were just as threatening to the welfare of the Jewish people. It was no use building a protecting wall to keep enemies out if, within that wall, the situation was rotten through and through, and 'brother' was set against 'brother'. So, for a time, Nehemiah has to leave off dealing with building matters in order to concentrate on economic concerns.

Burden of debt

It is possible that Nehemiah's solution to the building work in the last chapter added to the already difficult economic situation in the province. We know from 6:15 that building the wall took a total of fifty-two days, from the end of July to mid-September. By the end of this period, the harvesting of the summer fruits, such as olives, figs and dates, would be necessary. If men were staying put in Jerusalem, then they could not work in the olive groves and orchards. Therefore, the women add their voices to the call for change.

Three classes of people are getting into debt:

• the poor, landless day-labourers who always were vulnerable in difficult economic conditions (v. 2).

• those who had land but were having to mortgage it. They were in danger of losing it and becoming day-labourers instead (v. 3).

• those who owned land but were feeling the burden of the Persian tax system, which was certainly a heavy drain on Judah in the fifth century (v. 4).

Jubilee

Leviticus 25 gives instructions regarding debt slavery. People who got into debt could 'sell' themselves and their labour, or that of their families. However, once in debt it was difficult to get out again—as both individuals and whole countries know only too well today. Those who have been lending and taking pledges have not, technically, been breaking the Law. However, it clearly goes against the spirit of God's will, as given in the Torah in Leviticus 25. Back in 458, Ezra had called an assembly to deal with the issue of mixed marriages. Now Nehemiah calls an assembly to tackle the issue of debt.

Nehemiah acknowledges that he and his entourage share some responsibility in this matter (v. 10), for they too have been lending and taking pledges. He leads from the front and sets an example for others to follow. In effect, Nehemiah proclaims a special, one-off 'year of jubilee'. The law of the jubilee year is given in Leviticus 25:8–17. It involves the cancelling of debt and the return of land and property to those who were caught in the debt trap.

It is often claimed that the biblical law of jubilee was a 'dead letter', never put into practice. Nehemiah's action shows that in certain circumstances it can be put into effect and it can work. Nehemiah symbolically shakes out the fold of his garments (v. 13). He empties his pockets and calls on the rich to do the same.

Perks of the job

Nehemiah's first term as governor lasted from 445 to 433, and we now learn something of how his administration worked. Taxes had to be paid to the Persian central treasury as a matter of course. In addition, the governor was entitled to levy a charge for expenses incurred by himself and his household. Nehemiah claims that, while former governors had enjoyed this privilege, he has chosen to waive his right and pay the expenses out of his own pocket (v. 15). Clearly Nehemiah is a man of some considerable wealth if he is able to do this. For the first time, in verse 19 we find a plea from Nehemiah asking God to remember him. This prayer will be repeated three times in the last chapter of the book. The account here in verses 14–19 may well have been composed at the same time, perhaps at the end of his term of office, or even close to the end of his life.

REFLECTION

Pray for families who are burdened by debts, and for those organizations who seek to tackle the issues surrounding the unpayable debts of poor countries.

CONSPIRACY THEORIES

In this chapter, we learn that not all the opposition to Nehemiah's actions came from outside the Jewish community. He faced internal hostility which threatened to undermine his position and credibility.

An offer of talks

Sensing that their influence in Jerusalem's affairs is weakening, Nehemiah's opponents offer the chance to meet and talk (vv. 1–4). What could possibly be wrong with diplomacy and a round-table conference? Nehemiah, however, does not see it that way.

For one thing, the venue looks suspicious. The plain of Ono is some distance to the north-west of Jerusalem. It is not too far from the coast, on the way to the port of Joppa. It could be regarded as 'neutral territory' near the borders of the provinces of Judah, Samaria and Ashdod. It could also, potentially, leave Nehemiah quite exposed and vulnerable to physical attack. Time after time he therefore refuses to meet his adversaries. Is Nehemiah being too suspicious, assuming that his opponents have the worst possible motives? Or is he being properly cautious in the face of real danger?

An open letter

Sanballat now resorts to a form of blackmail by sending an 'open' letter to Governor Nehemiah (vv. 5–9). The fact that it was an open letter and not sealed meant that it could be read by anyone. It is a mischievous device, intended to fan the rumour that Governor Nehemiah has plans to become King Nehemiah.

If such a report should ever reach the Persian monarch, then Nehemiah would be in serious trouble—especially if, as some commentators think, he was of the line of David. Around 520 messianic hopes had been associated with Zerubbabel, a descendant of David's line. The Persians may have got wind of this, which could explain his sudden disappearance from history. The Persians would not think twice about removing Nehemiah if hints of his 'kingly' standing were brought to their attention. It is precisely this that Sanballat threatens to do. If some so-called prophets have been speaking out of turn (v. 7) in the streets of Jerusalem, then Nehemiah is even more vulnerable.

An untrue prophecy

A prophet named Shemaiah now appears on the scene (vv. 10–14). Our knowledge of prophecy of this time is really quite limited, though Zechariah 13:2–6 shows that respect for it had been lost. If prophets like Shemaiah could be hired to speak falsely, it is little wonder that the ancient institution of prophecy was becoming devalued.

The meaning of the phrase 'shut in' or 'confined' in verse 10 is not clear. Perhaps Shemaiah is ritually unclean for some reason, or perhaps he has shut himself indoors in one of those 'acted parables' that prophets performed to draw attention to their message. He wants Nehemiah to shut himself in the temple to avoid assassination. He argues that Nehemiah should seek sanctuary there—not just in the open courts by the altar, but actually within the sacred temple building itself. This is, of course, completely 'off limits' to a layman like Nehemiah. Witness what happened to King Uzziah when he transgressed the holy place (2 Chronicles 26). Nehemiah will not run, and will not hide. Neither would Jesus when he was told that Herod Antipas planned to kill him (Luke 13:32). Shemaiah was not the only prophet to trouble Nehemiah. This is evident from the reference to a prophetess, Noadiah, and other unnamed individuals in verse 14.

An exchange of information

The wall is finally finished after fifty-two days of hard work (v. 15). It is late September or early October in the year 445. The achievement is considerable. It boosts Jewish morale and leaves the opponents downcast. Nevertheless, Jerusalem is a far from united city. Many of the nobles retain contacts with one of Nehemiah's main enemies. Tobiah has links with the Jerusalem aristocracy through his own marriage and that of his son. It is probable that he has trading links with the city, and the nobles are anxious not to disrupt the lucrative trade arrangements. Perhaps this will explain the background to the events in the last chapter of the book.

REFLECTION

The noble institution of prophecy had become debased in Nehemiah's time. Why is it that religious institutions can sometimes 'lose their soul'?

SECURITY MEASURES

This long chapter is made up of two unequal parts. First comes a brief description of the final arrangements made by Nehemiah to secure the city. Then, as part of that process, we have the census list of the original group of returners which is also found in Ezra 2.

Wide-open spaces

Jerusalem, like most cities, would have had within its walls a strong fortress or citadel that could be defended even if the city walls were breached. Some medieval cities in Europe provide a later Western equivalent.

A military governor is appointed to be in charge of this citadel and of the fortifications in Jerusalem. Who exactly was this? Verse 2 mentions two names, Hanani and Hananiah, which are of course very similar. The name Hanani is in fact just a shorter form of the longer name Hananiah—like Mike and Michael. It is possible that Nehemiah chose two people, who happened to have similar names, to be joint commanders-in-chief in Jerusalem. His brother Hanani has already been mentioned, whereas Hananiah has not, and so his good character is commended. Alternatively, the two names could refer to just one man. We could read it as 'Hanani (that is, Hananiah)', in which case it is Nehemiah's brother alone who is put in charge.

Furthermore, the instructions about guarding the gates are not entirely clear. The text in the New Revised Standard Version and several other versions suggests that the gates are not to be opened at sunrise. Instead, the guards are to wait until the sun is hot. This is rather strange, and the interpretation of the New English Bible is perhaps better. The gates are to be shut when the sun is hot—in other words, during the midday siesta. A city might be vulnerable then. After all, in the year AD410 the great city of Rome fell to the Vandals when some of the guards at one of the gates were literally caught napping.

That list again!

Nehemiah's memoir in the first person now breaks off and will be resumed only towards the end of the book. What we have next, in verses 6–73, is a lengthy repeat of the material we read earlier in Ezra 2. By means of this repetition, a link is made between the first group of returners in 538 and their descendants nearly one hundred years later.

Although this method of doubling up material may seem strange and wasteful to us, it is quite common in the Bible. We find many instances of such 'doublets' throughout the scriptures. In the Old Testament, the prophetic promise of 'swords into ploughshares' is found twice, once in Isaiah 2:2–5 and again in Micah 4:1–4. Similarly, the words of Psalm 60:5–12 are repeated word for word in Psalm 108:6–13. In the New Testament, Luke tells the story of Paul's conversion on the road to Damascus no less than three times, in Acts chapters 9, 22 and 26. So the Bible often has us 'seeing double', or sometimes even treble. What is the implication of this?

It is possible to approach this question in two quite different ways. We need to ask questions about origins and sources. Who wrote the original and who did the copying? We could engage in a fascinating but rather fruitless exercise, asking which came first. Did the editor copy it from the Nehemiah memoir into Ezra 2, or vice versa?

The way of the ancient rabbis was rather different. They worked with the assumption that there was no unnecessary repetition, deviation nor anything redundant in the scriptures. If there were two versions of something, then it was for a reason. They would go to great imaginative lengths to explain such things: for example, finding deep theological meanings in different spellings of the same word. Though we may smile at such practices and think them rather fanciful, they nevertheless grew out of a deep and abiding conviction about the sacredness of the text. This is something that modern commentators, with their historical and rational preoccupations, can sometimes overlook.

PRAYER

Lord, teach me the value of sometimes 'seeing double'.
Save me from the temptation of always trying
to order things too neatly.

WATER GATE

For the time being, we leave the memoirs of Nehemiah, though we shall return to them at the end of the book. For the next few chapters, Nehemiah virtually disappears from the scene, while Ezra once more steps into the spotlight. Ezra and Nehemiah are presented here as contemporaries. Ezra the priest is up on the platform and Nehemiah the governor is down in the crowd before the Water Gate. This is fitting, since a reading of the Law was a matter for a priest and scribe, not for a layman, not even a governor.

The correct interpretation of this chapter lies at the heart of the whole chronological debate about these books. If the information in the chapter is correct, then Ezra and Nehemiah worked together as contemporaries. Yet there is a real problem with this interpretation. Why do their respective memoirs never so much as mention the other? Why isn't Ezra supporting Nehemiah in his struggles, or helping to build the wall along with the other priests? If Ezra arrived in 458, what has he been doing for the last thirteen years?

Many modern commentators conclude that this chapter was originally part of the Ezra memoir and that it was moved to its present position by the final editor of the two documents. The reading of the Law would then be dated to the autumn of 458. This would place it during Ezra's first year in Jerusalem, rather than the present setting in the autumn of 445, which is Nehemiah's first year. If the books were finally edited a century or more later, then the editor may have assumed that the work of these two men overlapped in time as well as complementing each other. As a writer and editor, he may have felt that it made more sense for such a ceremony to take place only after the walls of Jerusalem were secure.

Reading and interpretation

The public gathering on the first day of Tishri, the seventh month, takes place in an open square (vv. 1–8). This was a space where all could attend, women and children as well as men. It is an important date in the calendar, the beginning of the Jewish New Year (called in Hebrew *Rosh Hashanah*). Ezra stands on a specially built platform, and thirteen of his supporters are with him. Meanwhile, down below, another thirteen Levites help to make sense of what is being read. Are they chanting it in unison, or are they moving about individually among the people? Furthermore, are they acting as 'interpreters' or as 'translators'? If the first, then they will be explaining the meaning of certain sections of the Law. If the second, they will be translating the Law from Hebrew into Aramaic. One way or another, Ezra ensures that the people not only hear but also understand the Law.

By the fifth century, Aramaic had begun to replace Hebrew as a spoken language for the Jewish people. By the time of Jesus, it was the custom to have the reading of the scripture first in Hebrew, and then in the Aramaic language. The technical term for this Aramaic version was a Targum. At first they were oral and spontaneous, but eventually versions of the Law and of the Prophets were written down. These written Targums still survive and are an important witness alongside the other translations of the Old Testament into languages such as Greek, Latin, Syriac or the Coptic dialects of Egypt.

Weeping and rejoicing

Verse 9 briefly mentions Nehemiah standing in the crowd, but he plays no part in the ceremony. If the event originally took place in 458 rather than 445, then it must have been an unnamed governor who was present. If these ceremonies did take place in 445, then Nehemiah would certainly have given them his full support.

The description of these events is rather similar to the occasion of Josiah's impressive Passover portrayed in 2 Chronicles 35. This time, however, it is autumn rather than springtime. According to Deuteronomy 31:10–13, the book of the Law should have been read at this time of year once every seven years. Deuteronomy also stresses the importance of children hearing it, and this is just what happens before the Water Gate. It is a new year, hence a new beginning and a time to put away sadness and regret. Furthermore, it is a time to share the joy with others who are too poor to provide portions of food for themselves. Ezra and Nehemiah, like Chronicles, are books that affirm parties and celebrations. The weeping of the people for past failures (v. 9) is transformed into joy.

REFLECTION

Which of the two men, Ezra or Nehemiah, do you think was the more significant? Which one do you like better?

MIRTH & MOURNING

These two sections (8:13–18 and 9:1–5) depict two contrasting public assemblies. The end of chapter 8 recounts the joyous worship of the community at the feast of Booths, or Tabernacles, from the 15th to the 22nd of the seventh month (Tishri). Chapter 9 recalls the solemn day of fasting held on the 24th of the month.

The Feast of Booths

After the events of New Year's Day, the majority of the people return to their homes. Some of the leaders of the community stay on in Jerusalem for a further seminar, which takes place on the second day of the month. In particular, they study texts from the Law which concern the proper observance of the approaching festival of Booths.

There are a number of places in the Law of Moses which give regulations concerning the observance of the feast of Booths. The most important ones are Exodus 23:16, Leviticus 23:33–43, Numbers 29:12–38 and Deuteronomy 16:13–15. According to Leviticus, this festival was to remind the Israelites of the time that their ancestors lived in temporary shelters during the wilderness wanderings. Once the people of Israel had occupied the land, then the festival took on new meaning linked to the agricultural cycle. The seventh month was the month for harvesting the summer fruits and people would often sleep out in the fields in temporary shelters.

By the time of Ezra, some of the original meaning of the festival may have been forgotten. He is keen to emphasize the historical connection with the desert wanderings in order that the Jews of his day might reclaim their spiritual inheritance. In particular, attention is drawn to the events in Joshua 24. At the end of his life, Joshua held a special ceremony at the town of Shechem. There the people pledged themselves to live in covenant with the Lord their God. The current festival in the time of Ezra recalls that event. This must be the meaning of 8:17, rather than that Booths has not been celebrated at all since Joshua's time. After all, the temple of Solomon was dedicated at Booths (2 Chronicles 5), and those who returned with Joshua and Zerubbabel observed the feast (Ezra 3:1–4). Yet it had never been celebrated quite like this, says our author. The old festival really lived again in the hearts of the people. They understood its meaning, now that the Law had been properly explained to them. Perhaps, in a similar vein, you can remember a time when a particular Christmas, Easter or Pentecost suddenly came alive for you, and the real meaning shone through the trappings of the feast.

A day of fasting

The normal sequence of events for the seventh month is given in the clear description in Numbers 29:

- 1 Tishri: feast of Trumpets/New Year's Day (*Rosh Hashanah*).

- 10 Tishri: Day of Atonement (*Yom Kippur*).

- 15–22 Tishri: feast of Booths (*Succoth*).

The account in Nehemiah 8—9 makes no mention of the Day of Atonement on 10 Tishri. There are several possible reasons for this. Perhaps the day was not observed at all that year. Alternatively it may have been observed in the normal way but the text makes no special mention of it. Or perhaps, for our author, the events of day 24 took the place of Yom Kippur in that year.

The people are called to separate themselves from all foreigners, not just foreign wives. The reason for this demand is that they are being called aside to confess their corporate sins as a community. For it is Israel, the covenant people, who are responsible for the breach of covenant. They cannot blame foreigners for the mess they are in.

Here we see a people taking responsibility for their own failures. They are not seeking to blame others or to find an excuse by pointing to 'them'. If communities would do the same today, and stop making 'scapegoats' (see Leviticus 16) of other people, much of the conflict in local society and world politics might be eased.

REFLECTION

The feast of Booths is held in September or October each year. Jewish homes and synagogues have a special booth or 'Sukkah' built. If you have a local synagogue, see if you can pay a visit. Contact the local Council of Christians and Jews if you are unsure.

'HEAR OUR PRAYER'

Following the blessing of God's holy name in verse 5, we find this long prayer made up of confession (vv. 6–31) and petition (vv. 32–37). The Hebrew text does not name the speaker of the prayer. Perhaps that implies that the speaker was one of the Levites who appear so prominently in chapters 8 and 9. According to the text of the Greek translation, however, the speaker is Ezra himself, and this view is accepted by many of the English Bibles.

Genesis to 2 Kings

There are a number of places in the Bible in which the 'mighty deeds' of God are rehearsed. In particular, there is a class of psalms which catalogue the dealings of God with his chosen people. The most prominent of these are Psalms 78, 105, 135 and 136. All of these psalms concentrate on naming the great things which God has done, but there is one which provides a closer parallel to our present passage. This is Psalm 106, which is a kind of 'mirror image' to the preceding Psalm 105. Whereas Psalm 105 recounts the glorious things God has done, Psalm 106 emphasizes the failures and backsliding of the people of Israel. Like our present prayer, it may have been composed for a ceremony of national confession and lamentation. There is an equivalent passage in the New Testament too. In Acts 7, Stephen gives a long speech detailing the sinful history of God's people.

So while the prayer in Nehemiah 9 fits into the structure of the book reasonably well, it is quite possible that it was originally composed for some other occasion. Certainly its language and phraseology have left their mark on synagogue services down to the present day. Although not strictly poetry, it is written in the kind of style associated with public liturgies.

The prayer catalogues the dealings of God with his people. The further it goes on, the more it emphasizes the nation's need for God's grace and forgiveness.

Creation (v. 6): God is unique, above and beyond all things.

Abraham (vv. 7–8): Abraham's call, change of name and the covenant promises are all stressed.

Moses (vv. 9–22): From this point onwards, the fickleness of the people receives more emphasis. The descriptions of God's mercy and generosity in verses 9–15 and 19–22 surround the portrait of Israel's disobedience and lack of gratitude in verses 16–18.

Joshua (vv. 23–25): The period of the conquest of Canaan is described. Verse 25 hints at the people 'growing fat' and therefore beginning to forget who was the true provider.

Judges to Kings (vv. 26–31): The period of the Judges and the monarchy is characterized here by the pattern:

disobedience — punishment — appeal to God — salvation

This same pattern is found constantly throughout the books of Judges to Kings. It is like the beating of the waves on the seashore, but the tide is ebbing and, in the end, disaster will strike.

Slaves in our own land

First there was the tragedy of the fall of the northern kingdom to the Assyrians in 722 (v. 32). Hard on its heels came the decline and destruction of the southern kingdom, with the eventual capture of Jerusalem by the Babylonians in 587. The people who hear and recite this prayer are still living with the consequences of these disasters.

The Persians may, in some respects, be kinder than the Assyrians or Babylonians. Elsewhere, the books of Ezra and Nehemiah acknowledge help received from Persian monarchs and the state. Nevertheless, the Persians are still in control of the Holy Land. They are the masters and we are the slaves, says the prayer. The demands of taxation are heavy (v. 37). The land of milk and honey yields its good gifts chiefly for the benefit of foreigners far away. We may be living peaceably but we are not at peace, not experiencing God's true *shalom*. We are, in effect, slaves in our own land. Thus the voice of distress and subjection cries out for relief. The only basis for hope is the recognition that God is good, merciful and forgiving, and that his ancient loving-kindness does not fail. There is a gospel of grace here, as surely as in the comments of Paul in a passage such as Romans 5.

ACTIVITY

Are there examples of such prayers of public confession in Christian liturgy? Try to find one and use it as a prayer, or try writing one yourself.

A BINDING PLEDGE

The previous section has recounted the public prayer of confession and the appeal for God's mercy and forgiveness. The community now takes specific action, by entering into a firm covenant oath to change its way of life. These chapters therefore keep the right balance between reliance on God's loving nature and the need for practical steps for amendment of life.

The Book of Common Prayer sums this up well in words addressed to those coming to take Holy Communion. The prayer begins, 'Ye that do truly and earnestly repent you of your sins, and are in love and charity with your neighbours...'. We should not presume to call on the mercy of God if we are at odds with one another and unwilling to live as a covenant people.

The specific issues that are mentioned in the pledge are almost identical to those reported at the very end of Nehemiah's own memoir in chapter 13. These were clearly the matters that concerned the community at this time and which they recognized as needing reform.

The covenanters

At the head of the list of those who signed or, more correctly, sealed the covenant stands Nehemiah's name. He is followed by an otherwise unknown Zedekiah. It is possible that this was the scribe who drew up the covenant document. There then follows a list made up of twenty-one priests, seventeen Levites and forty-four laymen (10:1–27). By now, we have met most of these names before in the genealogical lists in the books of Ezra and Nehemiah. It reminds us that a covenant community is made up of committed individuals. Without that commitment, the covenant will soon fall apart on the human side.

We do not know if any other symbolic acts accompanied the making of this particular covenant. The language of covenant has deeply influenced New Testament and subsequent Christian theology. The Covenant Service of the Methodist Church, usually held at New Year, is one example of the use of such theology and liturgy. It is a service that is often valued and used by those of other Christian traditions.

The covenant pledges

The actions to be taken are very specific and relate to the ordering of the life of the community centred on Jerusalem (vv. 28–39).

Marriages (v. 30): No more mixed marriages are to be approved. Unlike the situation in Ezra 10, however, this covenant does not require existing marriages to be annulled. In one respect, however, the rules are tightened up. The Law of Moses only forbade intermarriage with certain groups, such as those nations occupying the land of Canaan. Now all marriage with foreigners is forbidden.

Sabbath trading (v. 31): The last chapter of Nehemiah describes some of the problems created by foreigners trading in the Jerusalem markets on the sabbath. Again the law is extended so as to forbid not just selling but also buying on the sabbath day.

Sabbath year (v. 31): The people promise to observe the statutes in the Law of Moses. In the seventh year, they will let the land lie fallow and cancel debts.

Temple tax (vv. 32–33): In order to build the tabernacle in the wilderness, Moses had imposed a half-shekel tax (Exodus 30:11-16). After the exile, the Persian government pledged itself to assist with the building and upkeep of the temple. However, in addition to this state sponsorship, a tax of one-third of a shekel is levied on all. Remember that it was payment or non-payment of this tax that threatened to get Jesus into trouble in the story told in Matthew 17:24–27.

Wood offering (v. 34): If the fire of the altar was to be kept burning, then provision needed to be made for a proper supply of wood.

Temple produce (vv. 35–39): Gifts of first fruits, choice fruits and tithes were expected according to the laws in the Pentateuch. The amount required was quite demanding and people did not always pay up! Once more, a proper system of regulation is required.

Lying behind this chapter is the realization that grand schemes and hopes need practical measures of organization to make them work.

PRAYER

To each the covenant blood apply,
Which takes our sins away;
And register our names on high,
And keep us to that day.

Charles Wesley (1707–88),
from a hymn used at Methodist Covenant Services

POPULATION SURVEY

In chapter 11, we encounter yet another long list of names—and there is more to come in chapter 12. As modern readers, we may sigh and think to ourselves, 'How tedious this is!' Our two options seem to be:

- to skip it altogether and breathe a sigh of relief.

- to grit our teeth and plod our way through the whole boring business.

With a little imagination, there is perhaps another option. As you read, remember that each of these names represents a family made up of real people living in real places. Each one has a story to tell, though mostly only their names survive. They share many experiences similar to ours. They have their hopes and fears, successes and failures, triumphs and disappointments. Human life is here, if we will pierce behind the dryness of the lists.

Moving house is said to be one of the most stressful things we can do. We should not underestimate the human cost involved in relocating to Jerusalem, as these families did.

The lists that we have in this chapter may well come from a variety of times and situations. They have been placed here by the final editor, rather than being part of Nehemiah's personal memoirs.

Decimating the population

Verses 1–2 most naturally follow on from 7:4–5, where we learned that the population of Jerusalem was inadequate and that Nehemiah sought to do something about it. It was at that point that Nehemiah's memoirs broke off. These two verses cannot be the exact continuation of the story, however. For one thing, they are told in the third person, not in Nehemiah's first-person journal style. Nor do they even mention him, but see the initiative coming from the people themselves. The decision is taken literally to 'decimate' the population. That is, one in ten of the families from outlying areas will be brought to fill up the wide-open spaces within the walls of the city. Although it seems that many of the leaders lived in the capital, relatively few of the ordinary working people did so. All the hype about 'Jerusalem the golden', 'the holy city' and 'the place the Lord your God has chosen' had failed to draw enough people to its streets and houses. Recovering from the devastation caused by the Babylonians back in 587 was never going to be easy, but it was proving harder than anyone had imagined.

Dwellers in Jerusalem

A list is supplied (vv. 3–19) of those who made the move to Jerusalem. Their names are given according to their groups—Judah (vv. 4–6), Benjamin (vv. 7–9), priests (vv. 10–14), Levites including singers (vv. 15–18), gatekeepers (v. 19). The section about Levites, in particular, gives some interesting snippets of information that fill out the otherwise bare list of names.

Other lists

The final editor of the book has added a selection of other lists, including a brief mention of the temple servants in verse 21. This is followed by a genealogy of Uzzi, the overseer of the Levites. He is the great-grandson of Mattaniah of the line of Asaph. This Mattaniah is mentioned in verse 17 as being responsible for leading the prayers. Therefore, this additional list naming his great-grandson must come from fifty to seventy years later than the time of Nehemiah, perhaps from about 375, towards the end of the Persian period. It must be one of the latest bits of Chronicles, Ezra and Nehemiah.

We are then given a brief glimpse of a man called Pethahiah (v. 24). He has to report to the Persian king about what was going on in the province. This is another small reminder that the people of Judah were not free, they remained a subject nation.

Finally we are presented with a list of places rather than people. These were places where Jews were settled. In many respects, they follow the pattern of the tribal settlement that we find in the second half of the book of Joshua. This dry list of names therefore has echoes of a more glorious past for the people of God.

MEDITATION

'I will make your pinnacles of rubies, your gates of jewels, and all your walls of precious stones' (Isaiah 54:12).
Prophetic speech was extravagant, poetic, imaginative. People like Nehemiah were needed to turn vision into reality. How might this apply to issues of social justice today?

FAMILY RECORDS

In this section, a compact list provides the names of priestly and levitical families in the post-exilic period. It also includes a list of high priests from the end of the exile in the 530s to perhaps as late as the time of Alexander the Great in the 330s.

Clergy lists

Verses 1–7 give the names of twenty-two priestly families who were considered to be among those who returned in the 530s. There are similar lists in Ezra 2 and Nehemiah 7, where the number of people in each family is also given. However, in those chapters, only four priestly families are named. It is possible that these four groups later subdivided as the families grew larger, and that these subdivisions are represented here. In the final, definitive list given in 1 Chronicles 24, the number of priestly groups has grown to twenty-four.

Verses 8–9 give a similar list of Levite families. Verse 9 may suggest a form of antiphonal singing, first by one group, then by the other standing opposite. In some cathedrals and churches, the psalms are still chanted antiphonally even today.

Verses 10–11 contain the names of six high priests from the period after the exile. 1 Chronicles 6 gave a list of high priests from the time of the monarchy. It ended with the destruction of Jerusalem in 587 when Jehozadak (Jozadak) was high priest (1 Chronicles 6:15). These two verses extend that list for another six generations at least. However, we should bear in mind that neither the Chronicles list nor the one here is necessarily complete. The names of some high priests may have been omitted altogether.

With that note of caution, it is possible to draw up a tentative line of high priests, with their approximate dates:

Jeshua, 538–515. Son of Jozadak (v. 26). The high priest of the return (538) and of the dedication of the temple in 515. How long he lived beyond 515, we do not know.

Joiakim, 480–450. Priest when Ezra arrived in 458 (v. 26).

Eliashib, 450–430. Active in 445, at the beginning of Nehemiah's time in Judah (3:1), and also in 432, during his second term (13:28).

Joiada, 430–420? Eliashib's son and Sanballat's son-in-law (13:28).

Jonathan/Johanan, 420–390. It is not clear whether the Jonathan of verse 11 and the Johanan of verse 22 are the same. They could be two separate high priests, Jonathan sometime between 420 and 410, and Johanan after 410. We know there was a high priest Johanan, because he is mentioned in a letter dated 408 which was found at the town of Elephantine in Egypt. The historian Josephus, who wrote at the end of the first century AD, also alludes to him. Josephus says that he killed his brother Jeshua in the temple because his brother was trying to claim the high priesthood.

Jaddua, 390–370/330. Again according to Josephus, he was the high priest during the victories of Alexander the Great in the 330s. However, if he was the son of Johanan, he must have been an extremely old man. Some people think there were two Jadduas and that Josephus' Jaddua was the grandson of the first one. It was quite common for boys to be named after their grandfather, so this suggestion is quite likely. Alternatively, of course, it is possible that the list does go down to 330 but that the names of some high priests are missing. It is hard to imagine only six high priests covering a period of two hundred years, from the 530s to the 330s.

A generation later

The next list (vv. 12–21) gives the names of the heads of priestly houses during Joiakim's time in the early fifth century. It takes the names from verses 1–7 and gives the individuals at the head of these families in around 475. Note, however, that only twenty-one of the twenty-two families are named. The family of Hattush (v. 2) has been omitted—probably by a careless scribe. The name of the family head of Miniamin (v. 17) has also been lost.

Concluding lists

The 'Book of the Annals' or official records (v. 23) is not our book of Chronicles but some archive from Jerusalem now lost to us.

REFLECTION

Some ancient parish churches have lists of clergy going back to the Middle Ages. In the same way, some church vestries have photographs of previous ministers. What might be the significance of such lists or photographs for worshippers?

AROUND *the* WALLS

In this section, we finally return to the Nehemiah memoirs that were broken off at 7:5. However, not all of this section comes from the hand of Nehemiah himself. His memoir has been reworked, with comments by the final editor in verses 27–30 and 44–47.

Preparations

The theme of music and celebrations features strongly in the festivities. The presence of plenty of musicians is therefore vital. When the levitical musicians were not on duty at the temple, they lived in outlying villages within a day's journey of the temple. Some of these were in the region of Netophah, south of Jerusalem, and others like Bethgilgal, Geba and Azmaveth, were a few miles north of the city.

Before the act of dedication, it was necessary to purify both the people and the city (v. 30). Proper preparation would involve sexual abstinence, clean garments and the offering of sacrifice. Perhaps ceremonies to cleanse Jerusalem itself would be observed.

Processions

Nehemiah's own account of events now resumes (vv. 31–43) with a description of the two processions, each going round half of the city walls. Religious processions were an important part of Hebrew worship. Psalm 48:12–13 envisages just such a procession, with the worshippers invited to go around the city, counting its towers, ramparts and citadels. Another vivid description of an ancient Israelite procession is found in Psalm 68:24–27 with the order:

singers — girls with tambourines — musicians — lay leaders

The two processions around the rebuilt city walls now follow the same formula. The six sections of each group are:

a choir — seven priests with trumpets — a named leader of music — eight musicians — a named lay leader — half of the lay leaders

On a previous occasion (2:11–20), Nehemiah had gone around half the city walls. Then it was secretly by night. Now it is all in the open, with praise and thanksgiving. On that night inspection, described in

Nehemiah 2, he started out from the Valley Gate on the western side of the city. We should imagine the two groups doing the same, with one group going anti-clockwise from the Valley Gate, and Nehemiah's group going clockwise. You can follow their progress by using the map in section 104. The first group goes right—that is, to the south—while Nehemiah's group goes left, that is, to the north. The southern group finally enters the city at the Water Gate (point **s**) and makes its way up to the temple area. The northern group goes round as far as the Sheep Gate (point **a**) and then enters the temple area through the Gate of the Guard (possibly point **v**, called the Muster Gate in 3:31). Thus, both groups arrive in the temple area.

Verse 36 is the only place in the Nehemiah memoirs where Ezra the scribe is mentioned. However, his name is rather loosely attached to the list and breaks up the symmetry of the two groups. It is possible that he should be identified with the priest Ezra who is named among the first group of trumpeters (v. 33). This would be one very firm piece of evidence that Ezra and Nehemiah's work did overlap. Although Ezra's main work was more than a dozen years before Nehemiah's, he may have come out of retirement to enjoy this moment of rejoicing. There is certainly an appropriateness about the two figures of Ezra and Nehemiah each completing their half-circle of the walls. Together these two, one clergy and one lay, had achieved their dream of 'building up' Jerusalem.

Procedures

The editor of the book gives a concluding summary of the achievements of the post-exilic period (vv. 44–47). Special mention is made, as so often, of the role of Levites, gatekeepers and singers. Verse 47 gives the chance for the editor of Ezra-Nehemiah to stand back and take the long view. He surveys the one hundred years from the 530s to the 430s, from Zerubbabel to Nehemiah. Despite the disappointments and shortcomings, the assessment is a positive one. The overall purpose of these books is to witness to the development and progress that were made. Out of the physical and spiritual ruins of Jerusalem, a renewed city and a renewed religious identity have been built.

MEDITATION

Read Psalm 68:24.
Imagine the scene and consider the value of religious processions.

A SECOND TERM

In this chapter, we leap forward from the year 445 to the end of the 430s and to the final years of Nehemiah's governorship. The editor has given us the long-term view in the final paragraph of chapter 12. Writing perhaps one hundred years after Nehemiah, he has been able to gloss over some of the difficulties. Nehemiah's journal, on the other hand, was written at the time of the events themselves. In it he has to confront the irritating day-to-day issues and points of detail. It presents a very human picture of Nehemiah under pressure. For that reason, I find the last chapter of Nehemiah a blessed relief—not at all an anti-climax, as some have described it.

Foreign influences

The issue of relationships with non-Jews again raises its head. In these verses, it is not so much the matter of mixed marriages. Here it is the more general question of everyday contact between Jews and Gentiles, and especially the issue of the place of Gentiles in the 'assembly' or 'congregation' of Israel.

The portion of scripture quoted here is Deuteronomy 23:3–6, which deals with the position of Ammonites and Moabites. The full story of how these peoples refused to help the Israelites as they journeyed towards the promised land is told in Numbers 21—24. The hiring of the prophet Baalam to curse Israel is recalled in verse 2. Of course, there are echoes here of what happened in Nehemiah's time. Sanballat and the Ammonite Tobiah had hired their own 'false prophet' Shemaiah to confront Governor Nehemiah (6:10–14).

The Law in Deuteronomy says that, as a result of their hostility, Ammonites and Moabites are to be excluded 'even until the tenth generation'. In this case, the people interpret the Law more strictly than a literal reading would imply. They take 'to the tenth generation' as meaning, in effect, 'for ever'. Also, they apply the rules to all foreign nations, not just those two traditional enemy peoples.

'While the cat's away'

After twelve years in post, from 445 to 433, Nehemiah either returns voluntarily, or is recalled, to Persia. During his absence of up to a year, things take a decided turn for the worse. The old saying 'While the cat's away, the mice will play' neatly sums up the situation.

The chief culprit is Eliashib the priest (v. 4), probably not to be confused with his namesake who was high priest (v. 28). The Eliashib here in question was an administrator of the various rooms attached to the temple, rooms used for storage purposes. With Nehemiah out of the way, his old enemies take advantage. Tobiah has trading links with the city and is 'near to', possibly related to, Eliashib. He uses his position of influence with the priest to secure one of the rooms for his own purposes, perhaps for business use.

Such use of the sacred premises, and by a Gentile too, was bound to raise Nehemiah's blood pressure. He throws out the Ammonite's belongings and has the whole place fumigated to remove the contamination. If such action seems severe, we should remember the similar actions of another Jew nearly five hundred years later. Jesus put paid to the business practices going on in Herod's temple and drove people out with a whip of cords (see John 2:13–22).

Reorganization

Things had gone from bad to worse in Nehemiah's absence (vv. 10–14). The tithes for the Levites were not being collected, forcing many of them to abandon their duties in the temple and go back to their settlements to earn a living. The lack of tithes hit the Levites particularly hard—the priests, after all, still had their share from the sacrifices. Proper collection of tithes was evidently an ongoing problem. We see this in Malachi 3:10, a text from just before the time of Ezra-Nehemiah. There, too, the people have to be chivvied into giving the right tithes. To set things right, Nehemiah appoints a 'gang of four' to oversee the process. They comprise one priest, one Levite, one musician, and one layman, Zadok, who may have been Nehemiah's own secretary. Even now, Nehemiah has not lost his ability to get things done.

MEDITATION

As you consider what Nehemiah did, compare these two Old Testament texts quoted by Jesus:
'Zeal for your house has consumed me.' (Psalm 69:9)
'My house shall be called a house of prayer for all peoples.'
(Isaiah 56:7)

'REMEMBER ME, O MY GOD'

As we draw to the end of Nehemiah's memoirs, we find that the sections are repeatedly punctuated with the phrase, 'Remember me, O my God' (vv. 14, 22, 29, 31). Right to the end of his life, Nehemiah finds himself fighting some of the same old battles which Ezra had fought a quarter of a century before. Conflicts continue to swirl around Nehemiah, and he does not necessarily receive much support from those sections of the community he thought he could trust.

Sabbath observance

Proper observance of the sabbath laws became increasingly important in the post-exilic period. It was one of the distinguishing features that set Jews apart from other races. There had always been a tendency for sabbath laws to be broken, however. Amos complains about those who cannot wait for the sabbath to finish so that they can get on with their trading schemes (Amos 8:5). The prophet Jeremiah stands by one of the city gates and denounces the breaking of sabbath laws concerning the carrying of burdens (Jeremiah 17:19–27). So Nehemiah is not alone in his views but is in good company.

The Law had forbidden manual labour on the sabbath and the selling of goods by Jews. Did that mean that they could not buy anything either, especially from a Gentile trader? Predictably, Nehemiah takes a severe line of interpretation.

In particular, he notices some Phoenician merchants from the city of Tyre selling fish (v. 16). Their stalls were probably set up near the Fish Gate in the northern wall of the city (point **d** on the map in section 104). Nehemiah takes immediate action—he is not the sort of man to wait around when something needs doing. As a temporary measure, he places some of his own trusted servants to guard the gates. They are to keep the main gates closed throughout the sabbath so that wagons and merchandise cannot enter. The traders are persistent, however, and simply set up their stalls outside the city walls. Let the Jews who want to trade come to them, they say: why hinder the activity of the free market?

Nehemiah is unimpressed, and not averse to using a little threat and intimidation himself. The merchants and their stalls are cleared away and do not return. As a more permanent solution, Levites are appointed to watch the gates of the city on the sabbath. The gatekeepers already had responsibilities for guarding the entrances to the temple. This is now extended to include the city as well. The 'holiness' of the sanctuary is spreading out to include the whole city of Jerusalem. In later times, the rabbis would claim that the holiness of Jerusalem surpassed any other city in the world. Even today, Jerusalem is known to the Arab world as *Al Quds*, 'the Holy'.

Mixed marriages yet again

The city of Ashdod (v. 23) was one of the chief cities of the Philistines, near the Mediterranean coast. Sharing a common border with the province of Judah, it is perhaps not surprising that there was intermarriage between young people from the border areas. It had happened before, as in the case of the young man Samson seeking a wife from the Philistines in Judges 14.

Nehemiah discovered that some children, having been taught to speak by their mothers, knew only the language of Ashdod. For a faith which was becoming so centred on the written word of God, recorded in the Hebrew language, this was disastrous. We can understand the pain still caused to Jewish parents when their son 'marries out'. Nehemiah quotes the example of King Solomon and his foreign wives—an episode the Chronicler chose to ignore. If this led to disaster for such a wise man as Solomon, how much more will it do so for us, argues Nehemiah.

Even the grandson of Eliashib, the high priest, has contracted a foreign marriage. To add insult to injury, it is with none other than the daughter of Nehemiah's arch-enemy Sanballat. This was contrary to the Law which said that priests could only marry virgin brides from their own kin (Leviticus 21:13–15). The man is expelled from the community—no doubt putting a further strain on relations with Samaria.

So the book closes on a rather downbeat note, as does Ezra. At least it ends on a note of prayer. I am tempted to ask whether Nehemiah, in some of his lowest moments, ever wondered if his life's work had been in vain. When we feel like that, there is only one prayer—the one that Nehemiah used again and again in this chapter.

PRAYER

Make this your closing prayer: 'Remember me, O my God, for good.'

WARTS & ALL

At the beginning of this study of Nehemiah, we looked at 'Nehemiah the book' and 'Nehemiah the man'. Now, at the end of our journey, we should perhaps take stock of both.

Nehemiah the man

It would not be difficult to form quite a negative impression of Nehemiah. He does not go out of his way to win friends. Through the distinctive style of his memoir, we gain an insight into some of his raw emotions.

Here are some of the negative opinions that could be put into the mouths of his detractors:

- 'An impatient man in a hurry to succeed.'

- 'An intolerant religious bigot.'

- 'A bad-tempered individual, prone to violence, who wants all his own way.'

- 'Cunning and devious in the extreme.'

On the other hand, we could replace those negative views with a positive set of qualities:

- 'A determined man at an hour of crisis.'

- 'A man of faith and prayer, totally committed.'

- 'A zealous defender of the Law of God who helped to rescue a struggling people from oblivion.'

- 'A man who was politically astute and needed to be.'

Which of these presentations do you recognize in the character of the man Nehemiah?

Nehemiah the book

A similar set of contradictory statements could be made about the book that bears Nehemiah's name. Here are some quotes from imaginary book reviews:

- 'One of the most biased presentations of history I have ever read.'

- 'Needs better editing; is full of tedious lists that slow the action down.'

- 'A piece of ancient writing of no relevance to us today.'

These bad reviews could be balanced by more positive opinions:

- 'A fascinating insight into one of the most obscure centuries.'

- 'A strange mixture of styles that somehow still works as a piece of literature.'

- 'As I read it, I kept making connections with the world we live in today. It opened my eyes to present-day realities as well as to ancient history.'

If you had to write a short review of the book, what would it be?

And finally...

Certainly neither Nehemiah the man nor Nehemiah the book is free from faults. Yet, in the end, I find them both valuable. Through the work, we catch a glimpse of both an individual man and a religious community. Nehemiah, like Ezra, played a significant part in the process of forming the religion we know as Judaism. It was into this community of second-temple Judaism that Jesus was born. Without the likes of Nehemiah or Ezra, the history of the Jewish people would be very different, and that of Christians too.

So I end this commentary on a positive note. It is true that neither the book nor the man is perfect—and for that I am most grateful. For, as Paul knew well, God chooses poor earthen vessels (2 Corinthians 4:7) rather than fine bone china! Yes, for all its faults, I think the story is worth reading. In the final analysis, I would have loved to have met Nehemiah. Mind you, I would have been very careful to keep in his good books!

PRAYER

For your servant Nehemiah and for the book that tells his story, we thank you, O God. Make us thankful too for those 'difficult' servants in our own generation. May we learn to appreciate them more. Amen.

FURTHER READING

Chronicles

Commentaries

Myers, J.M., *1 & 2 Chronicles*, Anchor Bible, Doubleday, 1965
Williamson, H.G.M., *1 & 2 Chronicles*, New Century Bible,
Sheffield Academic Press, 1982
Braun, R., *1 Chronicles*, Word Commentary Vol. 14, Word Books,
1986
Dillard, R.B., *2 Chronicles*, Word Commentary Vol. 15, Word Books,
1987
Japhet, S., *1 & 2 Chronicles*, Old Testament Library, SCM Press, 1993
Johnstone, W., *1 & 2 Chronicles* (two vols.), Sheffield Academic Press,
1998

Studies

Jones, G.H., *1 & 2 Chronicles*, OT Guides, Sheffield Academic Press,
1993
Williamson, H.G.M., *Israel in the Book of Chronicles*, Cambridge
University Press, 1977 (out of print)
Duke, R.K., *The Persuasive Appeal of the Chronicler: A Rhetorical
Analysis*, Sheffield Academic Press, 1990

Ezra-Nehemiah

Commentaries

Fensham, F.C., *Ezra & Nehemiah*, NICOT, Eerdmans, 1982
Clines, D.J.A., *Ezra, Nehemiah, Esther*, New Century Bible,
Sheffield Academic Press, 1984
Williamson, H.G.M., *Ezra, Nehemiah*, Word Commentary Vol. 16,
Word Books, 1985
Holmgren, F.G., *Ezra, Nehemiah*, Int. Theol. Comm., Handsel Press,
1987
Blenkinsopp, J., *Ezra, Nehemiah*, Old Testament Library, SCM Press,
1993
Grabbe, L.L., *Ezra, Nehemiah*, Old Testament Readings, Routledge,
1998

Studies

Williamson, H.G.M., *Ezra, Nehemiah*, OT Guides, Sheffield
Academic Press, 1987

Clines, D.J.A., 'Nehemiah and the Perils of Autobiography',
pp. 124–164 in *What Does Eve Do to Help*, Sheffield Academic Press,
1990

Bax, J. *Time to Rebuild: A Study in the Book of Nehemiah for Today's
Church*, Darton Longman & Todd, 1996

NOTES

NOTES

NOTES

NOTES

NOTES

NOTES

NOTES

NOTES

NOTES

NOTES

NOTES

THE PEOPLE'S BIBLE COMMENTARY

VOUCHER SCHEME

The People's Bible Commentary (PBC) provides a range of readable, accessible commentaries that will grow into a library covering the whole Bible.

To help you build your PBC library, we have a voucher scheme that works as follows: a voucher is printed on the last page of each People's Bible Commentary volume (as above). These vouchers count towards free copies of other books in the series.

For every four purchases of PBC volumes you are entitled to a further volume FREE.

Please find the coupon for the PBC voucher scheme overleaf.

All you need do:

- Cut out the vouchers from the last page of the PBCs you have purchased and attach them to the coupon.

- Complete your name and address details, and indicate your choice of free book from the list on the coupon.

- Take the coupon to your local Christian bookshop who will exchange it for your free PBC book; or send the coupon straight to BRF who will send you your free book direct. Please allow 28 days for delivery.

Please note that PBC volumes provided under the voucher scheme are subject to availability. If your first choice is not available, you may be sent your second choice of book.

THE PEOPLE'S BIBLE COMMENTARY

VOUCHER SCHEME COUPON

<table>
<tr><td>⌐ ¬
└ ┘</td><td>⌐ ¬
└ ┘</td></tr>
<tr><td>⌐ ¬
└ ┘</td><td>⌐ ¬
└ ┘</td></tr>
</table>

TO BE COMPLETED BY THE CUSTOMER

My choice of free PBC volume is:
(Please indicate a first and second choice; all volumes are supplied subject to availability.)

❏ 1 and 2 Samuel
❏ Chronicles—Nehemiah
❏ Psalms 1—72
❏ Psalms 73—150
❏ Proverbs
❏ Nahum—Malachi
❏ Mark
❏ Luke
❏ John
❏ 1 Corinthians
❏ Galatians and Thessalonians
❏ James—Jude
❏ Revelation

Name: . . . .

Address: . . . .

. . . .

Postcode: . . . .

TO BE COMPLETED BY THE BOOKSELLER

(Please complete the following. Coupons redeemed will be credited to your account for the value of the book(s) supplied as indicated above. Please note that only coupons correctly completed with original vouchers will be accepted for credit.):

Name: . . . .

Address: . . . .

. . . .

Postcode: . . . .

Account Number: . . . .

Completed coupons should be sent to: BRF, PBC Voucher Scheme, Peter's Way, Sandy Lane West, OXFORD OX4 5HG

Tel 01865 748227; Fax 01865 773150; e-mail enquiries@brf.org.uk
Registered Charity No. 233280

THIS OFFER IS AVAILABLE IN THE UK ONLY
PLEASE NOTE: ALL VOUCHERS ATTACHED TO THIS COUPON MUST BE ORIGINAL COPIES.